James E. Boswell

Rice Gold:
James Hamilton Couper and
Plantation Life on the Georgia Coast

By James E. Bagwell

Mercer University Press
2000

ISBN 0-86554-651-7
MUP/H485

First Edition.

∞The paper used in this publication meets the minimum requirements
of American National Standard for Information Sciences—Permanence
of Paper for Printed Library Materials, ANSI Z39.48-1984.

Library of Congress Cataloging-in-Publication Data

Bagwell, James E., 1941-
    Rice gold: James Hamilton Couper and plantation life on the
Georgia coast/by James E. Bagwell.–1st ed.
        p. cm.
        Includes biblioigraphical references (p.) and index.
        ISBN 0-86554-651-7 (alk. paper)
        1. Couper, J. Hamilton (James Hamilton), 1794-1866.
2. Plantation owners—Georgia–Glynn County–Biography. 3. Rice
farmers–Georgia–Glynn County–Biography. 4. Plantation life–Georgia
–Glynn County–History–19th century. 5. Agriculture–Georgia–Glynn
County–History–19th century. 6. Glynn County (Ga.)–Biography. 7.
Plantation life–Georgia–Atlantic Coast–History–19th century.
I. Title.

F292.G5 B34 1999
975.8'03'092–dc21
[B]   99-054193

Acknowledgments

Someone told me that historians worked best alone ferreting out the facts to put them into a meaningful whole. But, I have found this to be only partially true. Certainly in the compilation of this study, my debt to individuals is endless.

To my colleagues at Georgia Southwestern State University, I am especially obligated. To my first president, William Browning King, I owe immeasurable gratitude. From my first association with Georgia Southwestern, he gave me the leadership, support, and counsel that made this work possible. To my department chair of history and political science, Dr. Richard Baringer, I owe much for he gave me encouragement, friendship, and many "little pushes" just when I needed them to keep me working on this endeavor.

There are many librarians and interested friends to whom I owe much. The library staffs of Georgia Southwestern, University of Georgia, University of North Carolina, Duke University, University of Southern Mississippi, Georgia Historical Society, and the Georgia Department of Archives and History were particularly helpful. To Mrs. R. J. Thiesen of Atlanta, the great granddaughter of James Hamilton Couper, goes an especial thank you, for without her generosity the work would have been almost impossible. This gracious lady allowed me unlimited access to her extensive private collection of Couper papers and family memorabilia, which formed the early nucleus of my research.

I am primarily indebted to Dr. William Kauffman Scarborough, chair of the department of history, University of Southern Mississippi, who first introduced me to this fascinating subject while I was a graduate student there. His aid was inestimable. He encouraged me when my faith faltered and without his unswerving support I could not have completed my task. In addition, I would like to thank attorney William J. Murray of Americus and Mills B. Lane IV of Savannah for giving helpful insights and valuable criticism of the work. Also, to Dr. Julia Floyd Smith of Savannah, I am appreciative. She read the entire manuscript, giving valuable comments and suggestions. I am also indebted to my friends Gail Hooks and Bobbie Bagley for their generous support in Americus and St. Simons Island.

Rice Gold

To my family, I owe much indeed. To my mother, Floy Howell Bagwell, I owe more than words can express. She stood by me in those early and difficult days of the book's inception and without her help, it would have been difficult to have finished. I also received generous support from my sister, Anne, and my brother-in-law, Millard Simmons. To other family members, my nephew, Mill Simmons and his gracious wife, Gloria, whose support was continuous, I am grateful. Then, to my wife and children, I am principally indebted. They gave me the close comfort that all people need if they accomplish anything. This was certainly true in this case. It is with much love that I dedicate this book to them.

Dedicated to
My wife, Cindy
and my children,
Brad and Victoria

Table of Contents

Prologue

Along the rice coast of South Carolina and Georgia, where the Atlantic waves slap and meander through the sea islands, there developed a powerful aristocracy based on talent and spirit as well as wealth. These low country planters had power far greater than their numbers. In many ways, it could be said that they controlled their states. In Georgia they included such families as the Spaldings, Greenes, Armstrongs, Wyllys, Butlers, Kings, Coupers, and Floyds.

One of the most enlightened, benevolent and versatile representatives of this class was James Hamilton Couper, a rice planter in Glynn County, Georgia. Couper was a foremost scientific agriculturist, pioneering in the extraction of oil from cotton seed and the refining of sugar from ribbon cane. A horticulturist of note, he planted in his gardens virtually every tree and shrub indigenous to his region. His pronouncements on the production of rice became guidelines for the planters of the coast. He was a microscopist in the days when microscopes were rare. He was a member of the Academy of Natural Sciences in Philadelphia and was an acknowledged geologist, conchologist, archaeologist, ornithologist, paleontologist and herpetologist. He was recognized as an architect of note, and Christ Church, Savannah, survives as a monument to the quality of his work. He also designed racing boats and plantation houses. In addition, he was active in education in the South and was one of the founders of the University of the South in Sewanee, Tennessee. Keenly interested in the history of his state, he collaborated in the writing of George White's *Historical Collection of Georgia* and William Steven's *History of Georgia*. In his library of more than 5000 volumes, works on every discipline could be found. Some of his books were extremely rare and were sold by his heirs for large sums.[1]

James Hamilton Couper was one of the largest land and slave owners on the Georgia coast. The plantations under his care included Hopeton, Barrett's Island, Cannon's Point and Hamilton. Hopeton, which included nearby Carr's Island, was located on the southern side of the Altamaha at the point where the river's mouth begins to widen. The plantation contained 4500 acres and worked 600 slaves. Barrett's Island, situated adjacent to Carr's Island, was one of the many islands cluttering the mouth of the Altamaha River. This plantation employed a work force of about 195 slaves. Hamilton Plantation, located on Gascoigne Bluff on the southwestern end of St. Simons Island, contained 1500 acres and a slave force of about 130. The extensive Cannon's Point property comprised the two plantations of Cannon's Point and Lawrence with a slave force of ninety Negroes. Hopeton and Barrett's Island plantations were principally rice plantations; Cannon's Point and Hamilton were devoted almost exclusively to the cultivation of sea island cotton.[2]

When Dr. James Troup died in 1850, his will named Couper the guardian of his property and minor heirs. James Hamilton Couper thus controlled another plantation consisting of 1100 acres of rice lands and a slave force of 300 Negroes. By the early 1850s he was directing the labor of 1142 slaves on 2600 acres of rice lands. This did not include the slaves or lands on the cotton plantations of Cannon's Point and Hamilton. Thus, James Hamilton Couper had at one time the supervision of close to 1500 slaves and the management of extensive properties owned by others in addition to his own important plantations.[3] Couper's philosophy of life came from Cicero. "There is nothing superior, nothing more fruitful, nothing more worthy of a liberal mind than the pursuits of agriculture."[4]

Still, one might well raise the question of why should anyone wish to read a treatise on James Hamilton Couper. He was not a great military, political, literary, or scientific figure. He was certainly not individually famous by the world's standards. Yet, he possessed elements of greatness and, in examining his life, one can easily understand that greatness. He was in the same league with two of his neighbors on the Georgia coast—Thomas Butler King of Retreat Plantation, a planter politician, and Thomas Spalding, a scientific agriculturist much like Couper. James Hamilton Couper was a representative member of the planter aristocracy, with all the importance of their economic position and social aspirations. The qualities of honor, integrity, morality and noblesse oblige so characteristic of gentle classes everywhere were concentrated in James Hamilton Couper. In fact, he was more the ideal than typical. His family and friends realized and accepted this fact, but visitors were so struck by his innate gentility that they hastened to record it in their travel accounts. The only remark this writer has ever read that was not completely complimentary of the man was written the day of his wedding when teenager Mary Houston wrote that he was so entirely proper that impropriety gained a charm in his presence. He was well educated, an honor graduate of Yale, and a world traveler. He had a reading knowledge of five languages, several of which he spoke fluently. But more importantly, he was naturally elegant and personified the term "gentleman."

The significance of his life is mirrored in his accomplishments. At the early age of twenty his managerial qualities were so apparent that he was given charge of Hopeton Plantation by its owners, his father and James Hamilton. So competent was he in this position that in a few years he was able to acquire three plantations of his own as well as purchase a half interest in Hopeton.

In his planting career he first began growing sea island cotton, but, after a succession of years with low prices, he shifted his interest to sugar cane and concerned himself with making sugar. By 1830, he owned one of the finest sugar establishments in the country at Hopeton. But he soon realized that his climate and lands were not completely suitable for cane, and, by the middle 1830s he was committed to the culture of rice, although cane and cotton were still grown as secondary crops. By 1860, he was one of the largest planters in Georgia. According to a Brunswick newspaper, he had 800 acres of rice lands ditched and banked on the Hopeton mainland plus Wright's Island and Carr's Island just off the mainland, each of which supported 300 acres of rice lands. Hence, 1400 acres could be devoted to rice in any given year. However, it was Couper's practice to plant 800 acres each year in rice and devote the remainder of the acreage to cotton, sugar cane, corn, peas and sweet potatoes. But it was with rice that he was most successful. He used the system of water control which he had studied first hand in Holland and his diking and flood-gate system was regarded by engineers at the time as unexcelled. It was so effective that, after being instituted at Hopeton, no part of the plantation was ever damaged by a freshet. His system of water control became the model not only for Glynn County but for planters throughout the coastal South, who visited his home for the purpose of studying and understanding his system with the view of putting it in operation for themselves.

Not only did Couper experiment with the chief staples of cotton, sugar cane, and rice, but he was one of the leading scientific farmers of the Georgia coast. As a champion of crop diversification, he introduced new and valuable plants into his region and found new uses for old one. His signal success with the olive culture enhanced his reputation with agricultural experimentalists, and his advice on the cultivation of the tree and the manufacture of its oil was sought on the Gulf coast as well as the Atlantic. He was one of the few planters in the rice kingdom to practice crop rotation systematically. The result was that soils retained their fertility and better crops were made. He also analyzed his soils and matched certain rotations with fields that could most benefit from them. He utilized the agricultural principle of deep plowing effectively and matched the ingredients of his fertilizers to the composition of his soils.

But no planter, scientific agriculturist or otherwise, could achieve success in his agricultural pursuits without a more than adequate knowledge of slave management, and in this area James Hamilton Couper also excelled. He was considered to be one of the most benevolent slaveholders in the South. His slaves were taught to read and write and were given religious instruction regularly. They had leisure time, for most could finish their assigned daily tasks in five or six hours. They also were given Saturday afternoon off in addition to seasonal holidays. They received adequate food, shelter, clothing and medical care. Furthermore, certain prerogatives were afforded them, such as planting their own crops for sale, buying their freedom and appealing directly to the master for redress of grievances. The proprietor of Hopeton had real affection for his black slaves and tried to make life as rewarding as possible for them within the bondage system.

Yet, there was more to Couper's life than agriculture and slave management, and his interests and acquaintances carried him far from the peaceful fields of Hopeton. In 1826, he was appointed chairman of Georgia's first Board of Public Works. This was the era of the canal boom and he persuaded the board, the governor and a doubtful legislature that railroads and not canals were the best mode of transportation for Georgia's future. On the heels of this service, he and Major Joel Crawford were commissioned in 1831, by Governor John Gilmer of Georgia to ascertain the exact boundary between Georgia and Florida. By the end of the year the line was drawn and a long-standing dispute was resolved. Then in 1833, his ventures took him to the states of Alabama and Mississippi. At Mobile and Natchez he established the first mills designed to extract oil from cotton seed. Couper had always felt that cotton seed oil could be put to innumerable uses, and history has proved him correct.

He was also an acknowledged expert in the field of geology, conchology and paleontology. While supervising the digging of the Brunswick

Canal in 1834, he discovered the skeletal remains of the prehistoric Megatherium, or giant sloth. Relics of the animal had been found in other parts of the world, but this was the first evidence of the animal in the Western Hemisphere. In 1838, he was involved in the disastrous wreck of the steamship *Pulaski* as it sailed from Savannah to Baltimore and New York. By a succession of heroic acts he helped to save the lives of about a dozen people. In 1850, he was selected to represent his district at the Georgia Convention, which was called as a result of the passage of the Compromise of 1850. Feeling that the compromise encroached on the rights of the South, the states of that region decided to hold separate conventions to decide whether or not secession from the Union was necessary. Georgia held hers first and by the state's moderate action helped to prevent a secession movement from gaining momentum at the time. Couper as a moderate member of the steering committee, helped to guide the convention away from disunion.

In summary, James Hamilton Couper was one of the most advanced thinkers and one of the most scholarly men of any age in Georgia. He lived a life of usefulness, and his influence was both far-reaching and beneficial. Indifferent to the temporary power of office, its allurements and applause and without display or ostentation, he followed the life of thought and action that he had planned for himself, and in that life illustrated in the highest degree the best type of antebellum Southern society.

Notes

[1] Burnette Lightle Vanstory, *Georgia's Land of the Golden Isles* (Athens: University of Georgia Press, 1956) 93; see also Margaret Davis Cate, *Altama Plantation* (Brunswick GA: n.p., n.d.) 2; *Atlanta* (GA) *Constitution*, 13 April 1923, 7; Mary Traylor Thiesen (great granddaughter of James Hamilton Couper), interview with author, Atlanta GA, 6 May 1972.

[2] MS Census Returns, 1850 (Microfilm copy in Southern Historical Collection, University of North Carolina, Chapel Hill), Glynn County, Georgia; Hopeton Plantation Journal, 26 June 1850; 15 January 1852; 10 December 1853; 22 December 1854, vol. 2 of James Hamilton Couper Plantation Records, Southern Historical Collection, University of North Carolina, Chapel Hill; Caroline Couper Lovell, *The Golden Isles of Georgia* (Atlanta GA: Cherokee Publishing Company, 1970) 214.

[3] Typescript concerning Couper's rice lands and slaves, Mackay Stiles Papers, 1775-1912, Southern Historical Collection, University of North Carolina, Chapel Hill (microfilm, Southern Historical Collection, University of North Carolina, Chapel Hill), XLIII; Allen Johnson and Dumas Malone, eds.,

Dictionary of American Biography 20 vols. (New York NY: Charles Scribner Sons',
1930) 4:468.
[4]Vanstory, *Georgia's Land of the Golden Isles.*

James Hamilton Couper

Hopeton, the Winter Home of the Hamiltons and Coupers

Caroline Wylly Couper on her wedding day, Christmas, 1827. Wife of James Hamilton Couper. By permission of Mrs. R. J. Thresen, Atlanta, great granddaughter of James Hamilton Couper.

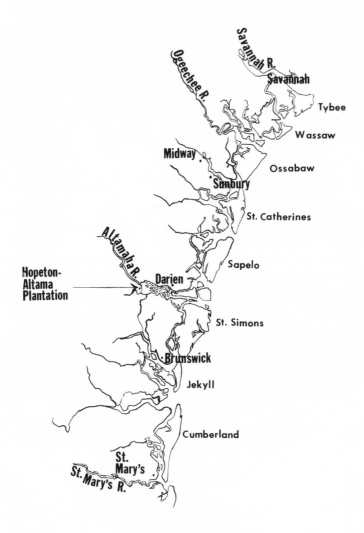

Coastal Georgia

Drawing done by artist Alan Anderson, Americus, Georgia, for the author.

CHAPTER I

Coastal Georgia—The Golden Isles

Nestled between the Savannah River to the north and the St. Marys to the south lies the Georgia coast, 150 miles of irregular shore dotted with islands. The Georgia tidewater is a fascinating region. It is a land of great black-water swamps, wide, sluggish rivers, and gray moss. The sea islands were dubbed "Golden Isles" by Spanish explorers searching for gold in the sixteenth century and the name remains today. Serene, lush and verdant, the area has appealed to Indians, priests, pirate adventurers and carpetbaggers. It was a region of great sea island cotton, rice and indigo plantations in colonial and ante-bellum times. The climate was delightful, mild in winter and moderated in summer by the gentle sea breezes from the ocean. The soil was fertile and the islands densely wooded, abounding in live oak, bay, myrtle, magnolia, jessamine, longleaf pine, palm and palmetto.

In the early days "rice was gold" on the Savannah River and plantations cluttered its banks. By 1750, planters were scrambling for the great river swamplands and tidal marshes in this, newest and youngest, of England's American colonies. This influx affected the city of Savannah, and the vicinity took on an urbane and cosmopolitan culture.[1] From her seaport wharves, ships laden with rice and sea island cotton departed for Liverpool and other European ports.[2]

The tidewater mainland has much in common with the islands. The climate, soils and vegetation are the same, and in some places the two areas are connected by long fingers of sea marsh. It was in this area along the Georgia coast that great rice plantations flourished during the early nineteenth century. They were generally situated in the deltas of the numerous rivers which water the area, especially the Savannah, Ogeechee, Altamaha, and St. Marys.

But other towns along the Georgia coast competed with Savannah for the plantation trade. To the south, just west of St. Catherines Island, near the banks of the Ogeechee River on the mainland, are found the sites of the former towns of Midway and Sunbury. Midway, a bustling Puritan settlement, and Sunbury, the capital of Liberty County, were thriving coastal towns in the late eighteenth and early nineteenth centuries. A quiet, peaceful little town today, Darien lies south of Sapelo

Island on the mainland at the mouth of the Altamaha River and was once a bustling river port and leading commercial center of Georgia.[3]

West and south of Darien lay the great river plantations of the Altamaha. During the early nineteenth centuries, a group of South Carolina rice planters came to coastal Georgia from the area of the Cooper and Ashley Rivers where they had earlier operated successful rice plantations. However, since little was known of fertilizers and crop rotation, land wore out quickly and planters were obliged to seek more new territory to cultivate. These men were prominent, wealthy and influential and established great estates on the banks of the Altamaha.[4]

During the generation after the revolution, major plantations were established along the mouth of the river. South of Darien, where the mouth of the Altamaha widens into a network of rivers interspersed with small islands, lay Butler's Island, the famous rice plantation of Major Pierce Butler. Major Butler's wife was a Middleton of South Carolina, and Butler himself had the blood of Irish earls in his veins. On the south side of the river to the west of Darien lay Hopeton, a great plantation owned by John Couper and James Hamilton, the only planters in the area who had not come from South Carolina. Adjacent to Hopeton were the plantations of Elizafield, Grantly and Evelyn, property of Dr. Robert Grant of Sand Pitt, South Carolina. Next to the Grant property were the plantations of Broadfield and New Hope, owned by William Brailsford of Charleston. Later, Hofwyl plantation was carved from this property and fashioned into a handsome estate. There were other plantations on the Altamaha, but the properties of Butler, Couper-Hamilton, Grant and Brailsford were the most outstanding.[5]

The fertile Altamaha delta was well adapted to the cultivation of rice. It was far enough from the sea so that the salt water would not damage the crops, yet close enough that the tides could be used in flooding the rice fields. The planters had been quite successful in South Carolina with the crop and now brought in hundreds of Carolina slaves who were experienced in rice culture to provide the labor. Great areas of marshland were drained, and canals, ditches and dikes were constructed along with sluice-gates and locks. Vast embankments had to be built along the sides of the plantation which fronted the river to prevent flooding during a hurricane. The plantations had an abundance of poultry, cattle, sheep and hogs. Mules were used for plowing and oxen for heavy work like pulling up stumps and turning cane and rice mills.[6]

The large plantations were developed into nearly self-sufficient units which supported hundreds of people. There were the cotton and saw mills, and rice and cane mills, and often small farmers would bring their crops to the great plantations for processing instead of taking the produce to faraway Darien, Sunbury or Savannah. Blacksmiths were equipped to shoe the horses and keep the vehicles in repair. Farm implements and crude furniture were made on the place. Coopers made kegs, barrels and casks, and tanners processed leather goods. There were cotton, sugar, and rice houses, cattle barns and dairies. Besides these, the planters kept smokehouses for curing meat, chicken houses, and stables for the saddle horses and carriages. Many plantations had slave hospitals and a general commissary for the issuing of supplies. Sometimes ice houses were used to store the ice brought from the North in the winter.[7]

These rice planters of the Altamaha migrated with the seasons. Nearly all had cotton plantations which were safer during the malaria season. In addition, most had two or more secondary residences. Some had vacation homes on the "salts" near Brunswick or at the mineral springs in Wayne County or in the Sand Hills near Tebeauville (now called Waycross). They had town houses in Savannah or Charleston. During the summer months, many would travel to the North or England, oftentimes accompanied by their families and several servants.[8]

The Altamaha planters, following English custom, had lawn parties and picnics, as well as ever-popular barbecues. At such events slave musicians would sometimes perform, and gymnasts would demonstrate their skills. Shakespeare clubs were formed, and members would don improvised costumes and read plays aloud, each acting a part. Just as the English enjoyed water parties on the Thames, the Georgians along the Altamaha had their boating parties at night, rowing and singing over the moonlit waters. In the daytime there were fishing, shrimping and crabbing expeditions. Another favorite pastime was hunting for the "Ogeechee limes" that hung from trees that grew close to the water.[9]

On the plantation, the day began at 6:00 A.M., when members of the household were awakened by their servants. Breakfast was served at 9:00 A.M. There was a light lunch at noon, and the main meal of the day was placed on the table at 4:00 P.M. Then at about 10:00 P.M., a late informal supper was served. The plantation houses were rarely without visitors, with people coming to stay weeks, months or even years. Dinner Parties were given with invitations reading "from four to ten," with guests arriving from all points on the river and sometimes from as far away as Savannah. When late evenings approached, there was a scrambling to get to the boats and through Cut's Passage before ebb tide. If the boats were caught in the passage at ebb tide, they could not pass because the water was too shallow. This storybook life on the Altamaha plantations lasted until the Civil War.[10]

St. Simons, the large island on which the Altamaha rice planters had long staple cotton plantations, is located just south of the river's mouth, continuing the chain of islands along Georgia's coast. About twelve miles long and two miles wide, it was on St. Simons that General Oglethorpe, soon after settling Savannah, built a strong fortress to protect the colony of Georgia from Spanish attack. Later, in 1742, the island was the scene of the Battle of Bloody Marsh in which the Georgians, led by Oglethorpe, defeated the Spanish, thereby ending years of dispute between England and Spain as to which country owned the land of Georgia.[11]

Eboe's Landing is located on the west side of the island. It was a favorite spot for slave ships to dock and hold their human cargoes in camps until they could be sold. On one occasion, a group of Africans from the Eboe tribe was encamped here. Refusing to submit to servitude and led by a chief of the tribe, they marched into the sea and were all drowned. To this day, many fishermen will not sink a hook off the bluff at Eboe's Landing.[12]

The most important element in St. Simons past, however, has not been her towns or her battles with the Spanish, but her plantations and their colorful and talented owners. The island was ideally suited for the cultivation of sea island cotton for it possessed that saline atmosphere so necessary in the crop's production. The island's fourteen cotton plantations, located in a circle around the island, utilized every inch of shoreline.[13] In addition to the Couper plantations and adjoining Cannon's Point was Hampton plantation, located on Butler's Point and the property of Major Pierce Butler. It was said that 1000 slaves worked the rice fields of his Butler Island plantation on the Altamaha and the cotton fields of Hampton plantation on St. Simons. Then there was Retreat plantation on the southern tip, which was the property of Major William Page. The latter was a friend of Major Pierce Butler and had moved to St. Simons from Page's Point, South Carolina. Also near Cannon's Point was Lawrence plantation, originally owned by John

Lawrence, but sold to John Couper in 1801 and considered a separate plantation from Cannon's Point. John Couper's son-in-law, Captain John Fraser, and his family lived there. South of Lawrence was Oatlands plantation, which belonged to Dr. Robert Grant, who subsequently sold it to the Coupers. Finally, there was the Village, located on the east side of the island and owned by Alexander Campbell Wylly, formerly of the Bahamas. The Village Plantation comprised more than 1000 acres and included the old Salzburger settlement known as "The Village"—hence the name of the plantation. Surely no other island or area in the United States was more devoted to plantation economy than St. Simons.[14]

To the south and west of St. Simons Island on the mainland of Georgia lies the town of Brunswick. The town was founded in 1771 and named Brunswick in honor of King George III, whose properties in Hanover, Germany, bore that name. The town's growth was interrupted by the Revolutionary War, but by 1789 Brunswick had established itself as a seaport and by 1797 had become the county seat of Glynn County. This growth continued until the Civil War.[15]

The St. Marys River was part of the "debatable land" during Oglethorpe's time, and only after the Spanish were defeated did permanent inhabitants come into it. But Spain still proved to be a menace. After 1763, however, when Florida was ceded to England, more people settled in southeastern Georgia.[16]

Just below Cumberland Island, on a high bluff overlooking the north side of the St. Marys River, is the town of St. Marys. It was built in 1787, by a group of businessmen who saw the possibilities of a port town at the mouth of Georgia's southernmost river. By 1802, the little town was thriving with her lumbering trade and support from the neighboring plantations. Though shelled from the sea by the British in the War of 1812, the community continued to prosper. Her only enemies seemed to be the smugglers from Florida and hostile Indians. These troubles were short-lived, for in 1819, the United States purchased Florida.

With her border secured, St. Marys entered into the golden age of the plantation era. Plantations dotted the river, growing the staple crops of rice, cotton, sugar cane, peaches and oranges. The port town became the social and cultural center for the river area, and during the summer months a festive atmosphere prevailed with the influx of visitors and the usual round of parties.[17] But when the Civil War came, the inhabitants of St. Marys, like those all along the coast, moved inland. Though shelled from the sea, little damage was done to the city, and the citizens returned after the war to rebuild and start anew. Recovery was slow, and in the late nineteenth century the town was a mere sleepy little fishing village.[18]

The coast of Georgia, with islands like pearls around her neck, is a study in contrasts. From Savannah to St. Marys one finds the past blended well with the present. The gray moss still hangs in abundance from the trees and sways in the sea breezes. Yet, it is not Indian moccasin, priest's habit, or planter's boot that passes underneath but busy lanes of traffic streaming down giant thoroughfares. The fields are not white with cotton nor does the rice ripen to a golden brown with Indian summer. It is a land wholly of the present. But it was once the land of James Hamilton Couper, who loved it dearly.

Notes

[1] Mary Granger, ed., *Savannah River Plantations* (Savannah: Georgia Historical Society, 1947) introduction, n.p.

[2] Kenneth Coleman, *Georgia History in Outline* (Athens: University of Georgia Press, 1960) 5.

[3] Burnette Lightle Vanstory, *Georgia's Land of the Golden Isles* (Athens: University of Gerogia Press, 1956) 37-42.

[4] Vanstory, *Georgia's Land of the Golden Isles*, 74-76; Granger, ed., *Savannah River Plantations*, introduction, n.p.

[5] Vanstory, *Georgia's Land of the Golden Isles*, 75-76.

[6] Vanstory, *Georgia's Land of the Golden Isles*, 75-76; Margaret Davis Cate, *Altama Plantation* (n.p.: Brunswick GA, n.d.) 1.

[7] Vanstory, *Georgia's Land of the Golden Isles*, 76.

[8] Vanstory, *Georgia's Land of the Golden Isles*, 79-80; James Hamilton Couper to Caroline Couper, 20 July; 14 August 1850, Mary Traylor Thiesen Private Collection, Atlanta GA.

[9] Vanstory, *Georgia's Land of the Golden Isles*, 80; Bessie Lewis, *Patriarchal Plantations of St. Simons Island* (Brunswick GA: self published, 1974) 20-23; Betsy Fancher, *Georgia's Golden Isles* (Garden City NY: Doubleday and Company, 1971) 153.

[10] Vanstory, *Georgia's Land of the Golden Isles*, 82-83; Medora Field Perkerson, *White Columns in Georgia* (New York NY: Bonanza Books, 1955) 118; Sir Charles Lyell, *A Second Visit to North America* 2 vols. (New York NY: Harper and Brothers, 1849) 2:263.

[11] Margaret Davis Cate, *Our Todays and Yesterday: A Story of Brunswick and the Coastal Islands.* (reprint, Spartanburg SC: Peter Smith, 1979), 154-55.

[12] Ibid.

13 J. D. Legare, "Account of an Agricultural Excursion Made Into the South of Georgia in the Winter of 1832," *Southern Agriculturist and Register of Rural Affairs* 6 (April 1833): 159.

14 Vanstory, *Georgia's Land of the Golden Isles*, 130-67; Cate, *Our Todays and Yesterdays*, 123-53.

15 Vanstory, *Georgia's Land of the Golden Isles*, 121; George G. Leckie, *Georgia: A Guide to Its Towns and Countryside* (Atlanta GA: Tupper and Love, 1954) 166-69; Margaret Davis Cate and Orrin Sage Wrightman, *Early Days of Coastal Georgia* (St. Simons GA: Fort Federicka Association, 1955) 95, 197; Allen D. Candler and Clement A. Evans, eds., *Cyclopedia of Georgia* (Atlanta GA: Brown Publishing Co., 1906) 258-59.

16 Vanstory, *Georgia's Land of the Golden Isles*, 192-93.

17 James Thomas Vocelle, *History of Camden County* (St. Marys GA: self published, 1914) 13-20; Vanstory, *Georgia's Land of the Golden Isles*, 194-200.

18 Vanstory.

CHAPTER II

Genealogy and a Wedding

The ancestral home of the Coupers was Formakin, an estate near
Glasgow, Scotland. The family was related by blood to the royal
house of Stuart. In 1750, one of its members, John Couper, was
ordained minister for the parish of Loch Winnoch, Renfrewshire,
Scotland. He was a man of excellent scholarship and irreproachable character. On 23 October 1751, he married Sarah McKell from Galloway,
Scotland. Couper was most attentive to his duties in the parish and to his
family. Two of his sons attained high positions in the learned fields of
philosophy and science. His eldest son, James Couper, born in 1752, was
appointed by the crown to the chair of practical astronomy at the
University of Glasgow, a position which he held until his death in 1836.
The second son, William Couper, became a distinguished surgeon in
Glasgow. He was also instrumental in the invention of chloride of lime,
which when used as a bleaching agent greatly aided the textile industry
in Britain.[1]

The third son named John Couper might be best described as the
prodigal son. He was born on 9 March 1759, at 1:00 A.M. during the
height of a violent snow storm. He was imbued with a carefree and rest-
less nature. He was an idle boy who "preferred fishing and running
about" to his studies. At an early age he became inseparable friends with
another boy, James Hamilton, who shared his adventurous spirit.[2]

These two free spirits, Couper and Hamilton, at the early age of sixteen, secured passage to America, arriving in the autumn of 1775 in
Savannah where they were indentured to a mercantile company. With
the beginning of the American Revolution, their loyalist employers
moved to Florida, taking young Couper and Hamilton with them, where
they remained until peace came in 1783. Free from indenture, the young
men returned to Georgia and opened stores under the name of Couper
and Hamilton in Savannah and Sunbury. This enterprise brought them
good returns. In 1792, John Couper married Rebecca Maxwell of Bryan
and Liberty counties.[3]

Rebecca came from an illustrious Scottish ancestry. Rebecca's great-
grandfather, James Maxwell, came from Scotland to America in the
1600s, settling in Pennsylvania and starting a family. His sons, Audley

and James, eventually came to St. Johns Parish, later Liberty County, Georgia. Audley Maxwell came first from Pennsylvania in 1748, and settled with his wife and two sons, Audley, Jr. and James, on the banks of the Midway River. He secured a royal grant of 500 acres from George II and gave his plantation the name Plum Orchard. James Maxwell married Anne Way and had two children, Audley and Rebecca. It was Rebecca who married John Couper in 1792, thus uniting the Couper and Maxwell families.[4]

In 1793, John and Rebecca Couper purchased Cannon's Point plantation, which was located on the northeastern part of St. Simons Island and bordered by the Hampton River on the west. In 1804, a residence was built near the river. The foundation and first floor were made of tabby. The second and a half story above it were of wood painted white with green blinds. A wide verandah circled the house on three sides, and large front steps led to the second floor where the parlor, library, and dining room were located.[5] It was about this time, too, that James Hamilton, John Couper's good friend, bought a tract of land on the southwestern side of St. Simons on Gascoigne Bluff which he styled Hamilton plantation. Thus, the two men who had been inseparable from youth remained so later in life.

In 1789, the Georgia legislature became involved in the notorious land scandal known as the Yazoo Fraud. When the Articles of Confederation were adopted in 1781, Georgia had agreed to give up her western lands. However, she still had not done so. After America had changed governments and adopted a Federal Constitution, Georgia still continued to claim millions of acres stretching to the Mississippi River, the entire present-day states of Alabama and Mississippi. But Georgia was pressed by the new government to make good her promise, given in 1781, to relinquish the western lands. So, in desperate need of money, the Georgia Legislature decided to sell the land in question to private land companies before turning it over to the Federal government, which would, in turn, carve out of it the states of Alabama and Mississippi. So the sales were made in 1789 and 1795, and many legislators accepted bribes from land companies to vote for the sale. John Couper was one of the voices crying for the ouster of the corrupt Yazoo legislators. In 1796, new elections were held, the old legislature was turned out, and a new "Reform Legislature" took its place. One of those new members was John Couper of St. Simons Island. Two years later, he represented Glynn County in the convention to draw up a new state constitution.[6]

By the early 1800s John Couper had become quite successful as a planter and businessman, and he and James Hamilton embarked on a new land venture. In 1805, they purchased jointly a tract of land on the Altamaha River delta, which they called Hopeton. The plantation was approximately eight miles from Darien and sixteen miles from Brunswick. Originally the tract was 2000 acres, but as they prospered they added other lands until the plantation included 4500 acres. The area at first was a wilderness, but 600 slaves were purchased, and the land was soon cleared. Long staple cotton was the principal crop planted; then sugar cane, and finally, rice were added.[7]

As John and Rebecca progressed in life, they began to raise a family. Their first born was James Hamilton; then came Anne, John Jr., Isabelle, and William Audley. John and Rebecca loved their children devotedly and recalled fondly special episodes in the lives of each. Two events especially remembered were the courtship and marriage of Anne and the personality and character of William Audley.[8]

During the last days of the War of 1812 the British occupied Cumberland Island and commandeered Dungeness plantation owned by Catherine Greene Miller. The occupation took place during the Christmas season when a large house party was in session. Many of the young people from neighboring plantations were present. Among them was pretty little Anne Couper from Cannon's Point. As the British officers took over, they banished the inhabitants to the upper stories. The British conquerors were young and not oblivious to the charms of the girls who would come down the stairs of the great mansion to peek at them. It was during this time that Anne Couper caught the eye of young Captain John Fraser. Following this encounter, the young officer made many trips to Cannon's Point to see Anne. In a letter from Anne Couper dated 25 February 1815, to Captain Fraser of Cumberland Island, she stated: "Ere this our President has ratified the peace, and good will not only to us but our whole country…the time is not perhaps very distant when if you are the amiable and noble being you appear to be, the sentiments of friendship which I now feel may be changed into reciprocal affection." A few months later Captain Fraser returned to Cannon's Point and made Anne Couper his bride. After living in London for several years, the Fraser's returned to Cannon's Point and remained there for many years, during which time most of their nine children were born.[9]

Then speaking of his youngest son, William Audley, John Couper wrote to his brother in Scotland in 1828:

My son William now nears eleven years, is an idle boy and would sooner walk a mile to race home on a plough horse than learn his lessons. I, however, intend to make a philosopher of him. Next year I shall send him to an academy at Northampton in Massachusetts, and when he has laid in a sufficient amount of Yankee cunning, I shall send him to Berlin to unlearn roguery and gain honor—German principles. At about 24 he may return home to plant cow-peas and pumpkins and eat fat meat as his father has done.[10]

John Couper was an avid horticulturist. He surrounded his home with orange and lemon groves, he imported date palms from Persia, and exotic plants from all over the world to fill his gardens. He was one of the first to plant long staple cotton successfully, and it was from his garden that Thomas Spalding secured the stalks of sugar cane which marked the beginning of the sugar industry in Georgia. At the insistence of Thomas Jefferson, who was greatly interested in producing olives in this country, John Couper imported from France two hundred olive trees. They were five months en route, but nearly all of them lived to produce oil at Cannon's Point.[11]

Life at Cannon's Point was a regular round of house parties. John Couper liked people and wanted to be surrounded by them. There was a saying that, "Cannon's Point was a resort for all who needed help or sought pleasure."[12]

John Couper was also known for his unique wit and dry humor. In responding to a letter written by two old maid Maxwell aunts inquiring whom Couper's new-born son resembled, Couper responded:

Girls,

I have just returned from an inspection of him. He was lying in his mother's lap, and regarding his upturned face, I was resolved to write you he was the image of myself.

At that moment he cried out as though in pain, and upon his mother's reversing him, for the removal of an intruding pin, I saw that from that position, he greatly resembled the Maxwells. So I am happy to state that in the front he is a Couper—in the back, a Maxwell.[13]

Another example of John Couper's personality was reflected in the so-called "Organ Crisis." The Coupers were Episcopalians and attended Christ Church, Frederica. This little church, the only one on the island, was well attended and supported by the island's fourteen plantation families. The building, constructed in 1820, was a simple white structure with green blinds and a belfry at the top. On Sunday morning service was held at 11:00 A.M., and in the afternoon a lecture was given for the Negroes. On one occasion there was dissension in the church as to whether or not to buy an organ. Couper had taught his slave Johnny to play the bagpipes, and on the next Sunday morning following the dispute, he sent Johnny with his pipes to ask the congregation to "try the pipes as a compromise."[14]

John Couper was an epicure and boasted of having the second best cook in Georgia named Sans Foix. The best chef, by common acclaim, was Cupidion of Le Chatelet on the Sapelo Island estate of the Marquis de Montalet, a royalist exile from France. On one occasion when John Couper was visiting the Marquis, he was so delighted with the meal served him that, before leaving, he asked Cupidion, if he ever had a chance, to come to Cannon's Point and instruct Sans Foix. Years later when the Marquis died, his will freed Cupidion, his wife Venus and son Hercules, and the latter's wife Ceres. They immediately went to Cannon's Point to stay with the Coupers. And for years Cupidion instructed Sans Foix in the preparation of exquisite cuisine. John Couper could then boast of having the two best chefs in Georgia. Cupidion ran a regular cooking school at Cannon's Point. He trained chefs for the other planters, particularly the Wylly's cook, Davy, from the Village, and Abraham-Fire-All, the cook at Hopeton. After Cupidion's death, Sans Foix was acknowledged as the master chef on the coast. His method of preparing boned turkey that returned the bird to its original shape was a closely guarded secret. When preparing this dish, he ordered the kitchen cleared. The master chef kept a white cloth nearby to conceal his secrets should someone unexpectedly enter his domain. Working closely with Sans Foix was Rebecca Maxwell Couper, the elegant mistress, who ran the house at Cannon's Point as graciously as a queen dispensing favors. She was as serious and elegant as her husband was jovial and practical. Her recipe for orange cordial was legendary.[15]

In the summer of 1804, Aaron Burr, wishing to withdraw from public view after killing Alexander Hamilton in a duel, accepted an invitation from Major Pierce Butler to visit that gentlemen's residence at Hampton Point on St. Simons Island. Except for the servants, he occupied the house alone, for the Butler family was then living at Philadelphia. However, Burr soon became acquainted with a neighbor, John Couper, of whom he wrote his daughter Theodosia:

> I am at the house of Major Butler, comfortably settled, a very agreeable family within a half mile... Yesterday my neighbor, Mr. Couper, sent me an assortment of French wines, all excellent. Madame Couper added sweetmeats and pickles... The plantations of Butler and Couper are divided by a small creek... The cotton crop in this neighborhood has been entirely destroyed. The crop of Mr. Couper was supposed to be worth one hundred thousand dollars... He will not get enough to pay one half of the expense of the plantation. Yet, he laughs about it with good humor and without affection...[16]

As time passed, John and Rebecca Couper moved into middle age and their children began to make their own places as arbitors of society and contributors to coastal life and culture. They were intelligent, well educated, industrious, and sophisticated. They loved the land as much as their father.

Of all the children of John and Rebecca Couper, the one destined for greatness was the eldest, James Hamilton Couper, who was born at Sunbury on 4 March 1794. At the age of eight, James was sent to school in New Haven, accompanied by his slave Sandy. In his first letter he wrote, "Dear Pappa. I have the opportunity of writing you a few lines. I am well and hope you are well also, and my mother and brother and sister. My boy Sandy is well. I like the place very well but I don't like it so well as St. Simons." At age fourteen James Hamilton Couper was sent to St. Marys' College in Maryland, and eventually he went to Yale, where he was graduated in 1814, sharing honors with his roommate and best friend, John Lord of New York. Upon returning to Georgia, he began to work for his father, and at age twenty-two, in 1816, he was given the entire charge of Hopeton, the Couper-Hamilton plantation on the Altamaha.[17]

In 1825, James Hamilton Couper made a grand tour of Europe, visiting such places as England, Scotland, Holland, France and Italy. He stopped first in England to view Parliament in session. He received letters from his uncle, James Couper, Professor of Astronomy at Glasgow University. These letters gave him names of persons he should visit in London and were supposed to introduce him to London society. They also gave him a gracious invitation to visit Scotland, the home of his ancestors. After seeing London and the sights there, James Hamilton Couper went to Scotland, where he stayed with his uncle. He then went on to Holland, where he studied the diking systems in order to improve the ditching of his rice fields. He also toured many farms in Europe, discussing and learning about crop rotation.[18] In a letter to John Couper concerning his nephew's recent visit, James Couper wrote: "If I am not mistaken, he will, to stores of knowledge uncommon even in most that are double his age, be daily adding to his attainments so long as he lives; and I am much disposed to think that you will live to see him one of the most eminent characters in his age and country."[19]

Upon returning from Europe James Hamilton Couper found his father in desperate financial straits. He had begun planting without sufficient capital, and had to go into debt, and the 8 percent compounded interest was an overwhelming burden. Farming was always a gamble. In some years he was quite successful, while in others he made nothing. Before and during the War of 1812, the Embargo and Non-Intercourse acts reduced his profits. In addition, the British carried off sixty prime slaves which amounted to a loss of $15,000. To replace them, he bought 120 slaves at $450 each. After the war, several bad crop years followed. In 1824, he lost a $90,000 cotton crop to hurricane. The following year he lost his crop to caterpillars, while cotton and slave prices tumbled downward. Hence, in 1826, John Couper transferred all his land and slaves, except the Cannon's Point property, to his chief creditor, James Hamilton. In turn, the latter sold one-half interest in Hopeton Plantation to its manager, James Hamilton Couper, for $80,000. In addition, the younger Couper purchased half of the Hopeton slave force at current prices. The elder Couper paid his debts in full and had "a competence left."[20]

By 1827, James Hamilton Couper was a successful young planter with a rising reputation. He had been given the management of all the Couper-Hamilton properties, including the Hopeton and Barrett's Island plantations along the Altamaha and the plantations of Hamilton and Cannon's Point on St. Simons. His chief creditor, James Hamilton, was living in Philadelphia.[21] James Hamilton Couper was now thirty-three years of age and felt it was time to take a wife. He would marry Caroline Wylly of the Village Plantation.

The Wyllys were a distinguished low country family. Alexander Wylly came from Belfast, Ireland, to Savannah in 1750 and married Susannah Crook of that city. He became master of the great Colerain plantation on the Georgia side of the Savannah River. He was elected Speaker of the Commons House of Assembly (1763-1768) and served as clerk of Governor James Wright's Council from 1773 until the British Government ceased to exist in Georgia. The Wyllys were ardent Loyalists. His son, Alexander Campbell Wylly (1759-1833), was educated at Oxford and became a captain in the King's Rangers and was with the British forces at the siege of Savannah, September-October, 1779. His map, "Plan of Attack and the Fortifications at Savannah," greatly aided the British in their successful siege. After the war, with the Tory cause lost, the family estate of Colerain was confiscated by decree of the Georgia Provincial Government, and the Wyllys moved in exile to the Bahamas. Alexander Campbell Wylly became Royal Governor of the Island of Nassau, where he married Margaret Armstrong of that Island, formerly of North Carolina. They resided in Nassau until 1806, when his tenure as governor expired. They then returned to Georgia and eventually purchased The Village plantation on St. Simons Island. The Wyllys had one son, John, and four daughters—Susan, Matilda, Heriot, and Caroline, who was engaged to marry James Hamilton Couper on Christmas night, 1827.[22]

As the time for the wedding approached, all was astir at the Village. It was late December, and guests had been arriving for days. The house was a great rambling place fronting the river. The large yard was covered with a lawn of Bermuda grass neatly trimmed. Great live oaks stood with gray moss streaming from the branches. The sides and back of the yard was bordered with Spanish bayonet.[23]

One of the visitors was Mary Houstoun from Marengo plantation in McIntosh County, who wrote letters to her mother describing the occasion.[24] Of Margaret Armstrong Wylly she wrote: "Aunt Margaret is as lovely and stately as ever. Years cannot alter her, so perfect is she, in figure and bearing. She is truly the Lady of the Manor." Of John Couper she wrote, "He is in a class quite by himself with his innate humor and good sense. He jokingly refers to his serious son, the groom, as the 'Old Gentleman.'" Mary described Caroline as a beautiful girl but fancied she saw a "resignation of expression" as they spoke of the wedding. Was it because Caroline was only sixteen, her future husband thirty-three and already one of the most important planters of the coast?

At 4:00 P.M. on Christmas Day, the firestands were lighted on the lawn. There was a faint hint of haze, the sea breeze rustled the live oaks, and the moss moved in the soft wind. It would have given one an eerie feeling had the occasion not been such a happy one. Almost every plantation on the island was represented with many kin and friends from the mainland. The house was so crowded that there was no room for dancing, and the party moved to the lawn where Johnny, John Couper's slave musician, entertained the guests with renditions on his fiddle, clarinet and bagpipes on the piazza, while a group of slave gymnasts performed on the lawn.

The groom was not seen on the plantation until that morning when he came "to sign some papers Captain Wylly thought necessary." According to Miss Houstoun, he was "very tall, well made, for endurance not activity, of the Roman type, a broad and high forehead and sensitive mouth." He wore whiskers close trimmed with no mustache. His manner was stiff and formal but very courteous. "His fund of information, practical and literary is immense, but he is rigidly correct in speech, tone and thought, so much so that one cannot help wishing he were less so. He is so perfectly proper that impropriety gains a charm to those thrown with and associated with him."

The wedding took place at 7:30 P.M. in the drawing room; the couple stood between portraits of the Duke of Wellington and Admiral Nelson, the portraits quietly reflecting the Wylly's Political allegiance. There was also a portrait of Susan painted by Gilbert Stuart. Susan privately hinted to Miss Houston that the portraits were the real reason Mrs. Wylly refused to allow a church wedding. "The Reverend Mr. Matthews officiated. Captain Wylly wore regimentals, the first and only time he has donned them since leaving Nassau." Caroline's wedding dress, made at Madame Beaulard's Shop in Savannah, was of "'crepe de lisse' over a white satin slip. The corsage (bodice) full and rather high in front edged with a narrow rouleau of lace. The sleeves are very short puffed full, and set in a satin band, giving the effect of the calyx of a flower. The skirt has two rows of graduated satin leaves, arranged in two rows from the hem to the waist. In front of the waist is finished with a satin sash." Caroline's reception gown was equally impressive. It was of 'gros de Naples' of a brownish rose color, and trimmed in white. It fastened in the back, finished in front with two rows of interlaced crescents. The sleeves were long; the bodice was ornamented by the continuation of the double crescents diverging from the skirt's center to each shoulder. The crescents were in silver braid.

At 11:00 P.M. supper was served in the dining room with an overflow table on the piazza. The guests dined on cold roast and boiled turkey, stuffed hams, shrimp and crab pate, with a various assortment of breads and cakes. Syllabub was served "by the hundred glasses," and the punch bowl was filled twice. At midnight, toasts were raised to the happy couple. They left for Cannon's Point. From there the next morning they would go to Hopeton. The guests however remained at the Village until morning, when they were served a sumptuous breakfast of crisp hot waffles, fish caught just the hour before, honey, hominy and orange and peach preserves served with Cafe creme.

When James Hamilton and Caroline Couper went to Hopeton, there was no great house for them to live in. Consequently, they stayed in one of the "other houses" until a suitable residence could be constructed. It was not long, however, until the Hopeton mansion was built. It was designed by Couper himself. Approached from the river via a large canal, the house was impressive. It was of tabby construction with three stories and twenty-four rooms. The outside was painted white. The mansion was of Italian motif with curved windows at the top. Large steps led to the second floor where the library, study, drawing room and dining room were located. The drawing room opened in the back on to a large, circular porch with steps leading into formal gardens where magnolias, oleanders, cape jasmine, japonicas, yuccas, tea olive, crepe myrtle, English dogwood, wisteria, and many other trees and shrubs native to the region grew.[25]

It was in this house that James Hamilton and Caroline Couper reared their family. It was also here that the Coupers entertained American and foreign dignitaries who came to consult Couper on such various subjects as plantation management, scientific agriculture and geology. It was always James Hamilton Couper's home, despite the diverse interests and activities which drew his mind and talents into so wide an orbit.

Notes

[1]An Ecclesiastical Sketch of Loch Winnoch Parish, Scotland, John Couper Family Papers, Southern Historical Collection, University of North Carolina, Chapel Hill; George M. White, *Historical Collections of Georgia* (New York NY: Pudney and Russell, 1855) 469.

[2]John Couper to Hamilton Couper, 14 March 1839, Mary Traylor Thiesen Private Collection, 1804-1977, Atlanta GA; White, *Historical Collections of Georgia*, 469; Memories of Charles Spalding Wylly, Mackay Stiles Papers, Southern Historical Collection, University of North Carolina, Chapel Hill; T. Reed Ferguson, *The John Couper Family at Cannon's Point* (Macon GA: Mercer University Press, 1994) 5-6.

[3]Memories of Charles Spalding Wylly, Mackay Stiles Papers, Southern Historical Collection, University of North Carolina, Chapel Hill; White, *Historical Collections of Georgia*, 469; Ferguson, *The John Couper Family*, 1-2, 23; John Solomon Otto, *Cannon's Point Plantation, 1794-1860: Living Conditions and Status Patterns in the Old South* (New York NY: Academic Press, 1984) 20.

[4]Letter of Joseph E. Maxwell, 2 July 1885, in John Couper Family Papers, Southern Historical Collection; also in Mary Traylor Thiesen Private Collection, Atlanta GA; Maxwell Genealogy typescript, Mackay Stiles Papers, 1-3, Southern Historical Collection.

[5]Bessie Lewis, "Cannon's Point Plantation, 1793," *Savannah* (GA) *Morning News*, Magazine Section, 16 May 1965, 6.

[6]Ibid.

[7]John Couper Family Papers, Thiesen Collection, Atlanta GA (microfilm, Georgia Historical Society, Savannah); White, *Historical Collections of Georgia*, 469; James C. Bonner, *The Georgia Story* (Oklahoma City: Harlow Publishing Co., 1961) 164-69.

[8]Children of John and Rebecca Couper. Mackay Stiles Papers, Southern Historical Collection.

[9]Burnette Lightle Vanstory, *Georgia's Land of the Golden Isles* (Athens: University of Gerogia Press, 1956) 139-40, 187-88.

[10]John Couper to James Couper, 24 May 1828, Thiesen Collection, Atlanta GA.

[11]Ibid.; James Hamilton Couper to Mitchell King, n.d., Mackay Stiles Papers, Southern Historical Collection; John Couper to J. D. Legare in *Southern Agriculturalist and Register for Rural Affairs* 1, 302; Thomas Jefferson to M. Cathalan, fils., 22 March 1804, Thiesen Collection, Atlanta GA.

[12]Lewis, "Cannon's Point Plantation, 1793," 6.

[13]Typescript account of St. Clair Festivities, 7 December 1821, Mackay Stiles Papers, Southern Historical Collection.

[14]Caroline Couper Lovell, *The Golden Isles of Georgia* (Atlanta GA: Cherokee Publishing Company, 1970) 133.

[15]Ibid., 111-15; Vanstory, *Georgia's Land of the Golden Isles*, 138; typescript account of St. Clair Festivities, 7 December 1821, Mackay Stiles Papers, Southern Historical Collection.

[16]Aaron Burr to daughter Theodosia, 28, 31 August 1804, Mackay Stiles Papers, Southern Historical Collection.

[17]Early life of James Hamilton Couper, Mackay Stiles Papers, Southern Historical Collection; James Hamilton Couper to parents, 1 June 1808, Mackay Stiles Papers, Southern Historical Collection; Mills B. Lane IV, ed., *Neither More Nor Less Than Men: Slavery in Georgia* (Savannah GA: The Beehive Press, 1993) 60.

[18]James Couper to John Couper, 15 June 1825, Mackay Stiles Papers, Southern Historical Collection.

[19]James Couper to John Couper, 28 September 1825, Mackay Stiles Papers, Southern Historical Collection.

[20]John Couper to James Couper, 24 May 1828, Thiesen Collection, Atlanta GA.

[21]Early life of James Hamilton Couper typescript, Mackay Stiles Papers, Southern Historical Collection.

[22]Wylly Genealogy typescript in John Couper Family Papers, Georgia Historical Society, Savannah GA; Frank Screven to Charles Mills and Margaret Screven Duke, reproducing material in a letter written much earlier by Charles Spalding Wylly, John Couper Family Papers, Georgia Historical Society; Wylly Genealogical Record, Thiesen Collection, Atlanta GA.

[23]Mary Williamson Houstoun to Mrs. Jonathan Thomas, 22, 26 December 1827, microfilm copies in John Couper Family Papers, Georgia Historical Society; see also Bessie Lewis, *Patriarchal Plantations of St. Simons Island* (Brunswick GA: self published, 1974) 20-23.

[24]The following account of the wedding of James H. Couper is drawn from the letters of Mary Williamson Houstoun 1827, John Couper Family Papers, Georgia Historical Society.

[25]Mary Traylor Thiesen, interview with author, Atlanta GA, 6 May 1972; see also J. D. Legare, "Account of an Agricultural Excursion Made into the South of Georgia in the Winter of 1832," *Southern Agriculturist and Register of Rural Affairs* 6 (May-November 1833): 360, 362; Lovell, *The Golden Isles of Georgia*, 208; Lewis, *Patriarchal Plantations of St. Simons Island*, 6-8; Una Pope-Hennessy, ed., *The Aristocratic Journey: Mrs. Basil Hall's Account During Her Sojourn in America 1827-28*.

CHAPTER III

Public Service and a Manufacturing Venture

In the early 1800s, as the Creek and Cherokee Indians were being steadily pushed out of Georgia, great amounts of land were opened for white settlers. As a result, the up country began to mushroom in population. The great middle section of Georgia became the short staple cotton belt with low country planters moving into the area in hordes. With this influx of population also came problems. Farmers with plantations far removed from rivers had difficulty in transporting their crops to market. Various schemes were suggested to remedy the situation.[1]

At first the plan was to clear the many Georgia rivers to make them navigable and then establish roads connecting the rivers. Elaborate plans were devised for the dredging and deepening of rivers, and many Georgia rivers which had not been navigable were now opened to commerce. But turnpikes to connect the rivers proved too costly and too time consuming to construct. And often those that were in service became impassable in wet weather and almost impossible to keep in repair.[2]

One alternative scheme which many advocated was the abandonment of turnpike construction for canals. Indeed, canal fever was running high all over the country in the 1820s. The success of the New York and Erie canals had led many in Georgia to believe this was the most promising transportation mode for the future of the state. Since Georgia was blessed with a fine network of rivers, an equally fine system of canals could be constructed to connect all the major rivers, and farmers could use barges and flatboats to send their produce via canal to the nearest river and thence to a coastal port such as Savannah, Sunbury, Darien, Brunswick or St. Marys.[3]

Planters began to pressure the governor and state legislature to find ways to alleviate their transportation problems and to take some definite action. In 1825, the state government was forced to act. The internal improvement fund was increased to $500,000 and the legislature created a Board of Public Works, to employ "artists, agents and laborers" to make surveys and estimates for canals, roads, and bridges.[4] In the same vein, the legislature, acting upon requests from Governor George Marion Troup, passed a resolution providing for the yearly appropriation of $10,000 to be paid to a competent civil and topographical engineer to work with the newly created Board of Public Works. Hamilton Fulton, an English engineer of considerable reputation, accepted the post in March 1826.[5]

The legislature, besides providing for the creation of the Board of Public Works and for a civil engineer to spearhead efforts in that direction, also passed a supplementary measure. It instructed the board and the state engineer to investigate the possibility of constructing a great canal running from the Georgia coast westward to the Mississippi or Tennessee rivers, with feeder canals connecting major Georgia rivers. The "Great Canal" idea was popular with legislators who felt they had solved the state's transportation dilemma. Before adjourning, the body elected the seven members of the Board of Public Works. Those selected were John Elliott, Joel Crawford, E. H. Burritt, Wilson Lumpkin, John Schley, John G. Pittman and James Hamilton Couper. Couper was designated chairman.[6]

Governor Troup convened this board in its first session at Milledgeville on 20 March 1826. He addressed the group, reminding them of their great responsibility, and added: "The Eastern and Western waters are to be united, and to the accomplishment of this every minor interest is made subservient. The large rivers are to be connected with each other with the sea, by a grand transverse canal, as nearly central as practical from which the lateral ones are to flow."[7] He exhorted the members to perform faithfully their duties and to apportion the work fairly among various sections of the state so as to prevent local prejudices and jealousies.[8]

After its initial meeting, the board began to work earnestly and stayed in session the greater part of twelve days. Upon suggestion of Couper, the board was divided into committees so that several projects might be carried on simultaneously. Each member of the board was assigned special duties. Burritt had the task of purchasing the surveying instruments; Couper and Crawford were assigned the responsibility of acquiring books, maps and office equipment and to act as a committee of correspondence. Lumpkin, Schley and the others were named as executive committee to carry on routine work when the full board was not in session.[9]

James Hamilton Couper was deeply concerned over the state's preoccupation with canal construction and felt from the beginning that the governor, legislature, the board and chief engineer were wrong to commit the state to a program of ruinous canal construction. Couper knew about canals. Small canals of short distance could be effective even on the Georgia coast, for Couper used them extensively at Hopeton. But he knew the problems involved and realized that success with them on one plantation and the success of the New York and Erie Canals did not mean the whole state of Georgia could expect the same results. Being a geologist of note, he recognized the fact that much of the Georgia terrain, especially in the coastal plain area, would not support such an extensive network of canals. In many places the land was too porous for so many canals, and frequent floods would literally destroy many of them. Moreover, construction costs for such a massive program would be prohibitive, and to keep such a system in repair would be almost an impossibility.[10]

Therefore, during the twelve-day session of the board, with Governor Troup and Chief Engineer Hamilton Fulton present, James Hamilton Couper labored long and hard to change the minds of those present. Because of Couper's reputation as a man of great knowledge and integrity and the cool logic he used in his arguments, the board, governor and chief engineer were swayed to his position. By November 1826, the board had approved a lengthy report prepared by Couper which he presented to an expectant legislature. The report was not at all what the legislators had expected, for it urged the state to turn away from launching an elaborate program of canal construction, which was not at all suited to the needs of the state, and instead to embark upon a general program of railroad construction which would be more advantageous to the state and more economical in the long run.[11]

The report convinced the legislature, and it was accepted. Couper, by powerful and persuasive arguments, had saved the state from a ruinous, expensive system of canals, worthless anywhere in comparison with railroads and especially in the Southern states.[12] Years later, Couper wrote E. J. Harden of the meetings he had with the board and his relations with Governor Troup. A portion of the letter, dated St. Simons Island, 14 August 1858, read: "After a very earnest conversation with Gov. Troup, he at last said to me: 'Well, Mr. Couper, I will go with you in favor of railroads; but what power do you contemplate?' My reply was 'locomotives, of course.' 'Good God,' said he, 'I cannot stand that; I will go to the extent of horse power.' This was in 1826, when there were only 22 miles of rail road in the whole world. What a contrast a *third* of a century has produced."[13]

The Board of Public Works was a short-lived agency, but as a result of the farsightedness of its members, Georgia was saved from pursing a course of grievous error. Instead, the state launched a comprehensive program of railroad construction which greatly aided her development. By 1850, Georgia's railroads had earned her the title "Empire State of the South," and by 1861, Georgia was the hub center of rail traffic in the Confederacy.[14]

In 1831, James Hamilton Couper was again able to perform invaluable service for his state. Since 1819, when the United States acquired West Florida from Spain by the Adams-Onis Treaty, there had been a dispute concerning the exact boundary between Georgia and Florida. Earlier attempts to find the line had been frustrated by failure. Consequently, in February 1831, Governor John Rockingham Gilmer appointed James Hamilton Couper to head a commission to ascertain finally the boundary between Georgia and Florida. Couper was instructed by the governor to use the St. Marys River as a starting point.[15]

The expedition was not scheduled to begin until May 1831, but already Couper had begun making plans, for there was much to be done. His commission would not be an easy one. He would lead a task force into a wild and uncivilized area, survey the elusive boundary and return home. Artists, surveyors, common laborers, pack animals, maps and a host of supplies and provisions had to be secured. In early May, just before he planned departure of the expedition, Couper received word from the governor that Major Joel Crawford had been appointed to assist him in the venture. The governor was sending maps and instructions by Crawford that had not yet been forwarded to Couper. Crawford was also instructed by the governor to aid Couper in procuring needed supplies.[16]

About the middle of May, Crawford arrived in Darien. Couper saw him and they made plans for their impending trip. Governor Gilmore had appointed E. L. Thomas as surveyor. Before they left, Couper surveyed his "entourage." From its size, it looked like an army: there were eight wagons, fourteen horses and mules and many attendants. They had an ample budget and provisions in abundance.[17]

Couper began his trip with good spirits. Caroline had gone to the Village with the children. She would remain there with her parents for a while, then would visit some of the other summer residences of the coastal planters. When her husband finished his commission, she planned to meet him at the Lodge, the Couper's summer house in Waynesville.[18] Hopeton would be abandoned for the summer by the family. The overseer and slaves would run it. In fact this was a usual procedure, since Hopeton was dangerous in the summer months when malaria was prone to strike the residents of the rice coast. The Negroes, however, rarely contracted the fever due to a genetic natural immunity.

Crawford and Couper became the "best of friends," though Couper felt Major Crawford's aide, a Mr. Terrence, to be a bore.[19] The task of Couper and Crawford was formidable. They were to begin at the mouth of the St. Marys River and go up the river until they found its source. Once this was ascertained, they would run a line due west to Alabama. The problem, however, was that the St. Marys had so many "feeding springs" that finding the principal source would be difficult.[20]

On 7 June the source was found, and the latitude and longitude of the spot calculated. The southern boundary of Georgia would run along the river to Lake Randolph, which lay at the river's source. From Lake Randolph, the line would run west to the junction of the Flint and Chattahoochee Rivers. Couper wrote his wife that he expected to find the western extremity—the junction of the Flint and Chattahoochee Rivers at the Alabama line—in about twenty days. He predicted it would be at least fifty days before he could rejoin her at the Lodge. Of Lake Randolph he wrote: "It is a very pretty lake…about four miles in diameter, nearly circular, with clear water about ten feet deep. There are no inhabitants within less than twelve miles."[21]

By 29 June they were about 30 miles from the western extremity. At this time Couper was having some difficulty with his staff. Thomas, the surveyor, had not yet arrived and his absence held up progress. Also, the artist appointed by the governor, James Camak, left the expedition for more pressing duties at the state capital. Hopefully, the surveyor would arrive shortly, and since Couper himself was an amateur architect, he would act as artist for the expedition. Crawford and his aide Terrance planned to return home as soon as the western extremity was reached. Then Couper himself would draw the boundary line eastward from the western extremity to the main source of the St. Marys. Finally, he would run the line along the river, ending at its mouth.

Those were the plans Couper had agreed upon at this point in their venture, and he realized that most of the responsibility would be on his shoulders.[22] Couper enjoyed his travels, however, and his inquiring mind took note of the environment. He found the country pretty, but the people were suspicious of the commissioners and rather inhospitable. As Couper related, "We were received by them with cool civility." The scenery was beautiful with many small hills, slopes, and valleys. There was an abundance of fish in the streams. He continued in good health and wrote his wife that he was getting a little fleshy.[23]

By 5 July the expedition had reached the north end of Lake Jackson, near Tallahapa, Georgia. At this time Couper heard that Caroline and children had left The Village to stay with the Thomas Butler Kings. The surveyor Thomas had finally arrived, which certainly made things easier. Of his companions, Couper wrote: "Mr. Crawford and I harmonize admirably, and Mr. Terrence's personality seems to be improving and has proved more helpful than I had anticipated or expected. However, he almost drowned when he fell off a barge we constructed to travel across the lake." Couper estimated Lake Jackson to be 37 miles in circumference. It was long and 3 miles wide with many bays. The water was clear and pure. The only distraction from its beauty was a growth of floating grass. It was filled with an abundance of fine trout, perch and bream. Wild geese and ducks also watered there.[24]

Couper could be literary even in the wilderness. His style is reflected in the following letter, written to his wife on 15 July from a site 20 miles east of the Chattahoochee River:

> It has been thirty-six days since it commenced raining, and during this long period we have not had twenty-four hours of dry weather. We have trouble passing the time. We have conversed until it has become tedious. I have read until the pattering rain on our canvas roof has put me to sleep. I have walked to and fro in the ten feet space of our tent until I have grown giddy by turning. I have sallied out umbrella in hand until I have become drenched:—and have roasted myself before a lightwood fire until I have become thoroughly smoked and dried and yet the heavy hours remain. What therefore is to be done? Luckily, I have pen, ink, and paper at hand,—and lucky still a tale to tell. If you find it a dull one, blame the gloomy day;—if badly told, be pleased to remember that there are a half dozen persons conversing around me and that I take part in the conversation.[25]

The tale Couper related to his wife that rainy night concerned a private exploration he had undertaken a few days earlier which had proved quite interesting. Before leaving the Lake Jackson area, he had gone out one day on horseback to pass the time away. The progress of Thomas, the surveyor, was slow and tedious, and since his work was of the utmost importance, all waited on him. So Couper went exploring alone. He came upon another lake called Iamonia. The forest was beautiful. But he was called away from his transcendental meditations and the contemplation of the wide beauty by an unusual site:

> On the summit of one of the highest hills overlooking the lake my attentions were directed to the remains of a fortification with much regularity by a circular ditch and a wall of earth. There was a well worn and masked road diverging in different ways and leading to lands which from their appearance were once expertly cultivated by a race who were quite different from the Indian aborigines of the area. There were the remains of a village and a well garrisoned fort. Who were these people and where did they come from?[26]

After much research Couper found the answer to this puzzling question. According to traditions in times long past, a large number of white men had arrived with gun, sword and cannon and furnished with axes and hoes. They came in large ships to the coast. After landing they had friendly relations with the Indians of the area. They intermarried with the natives of a particular tribe, cleared fields, built themselves a fort and became prosperous. Unfortunately, the surrounding tribes became jealous and united against them in a war. The whites garrisoned themselves behind the fort and repulsed many attacks by the Indians. However, the attackers changed their strategy and began a policy of attrition to starve out those besieged in the fort. Finally the fort surrendered, and the survivors were either killed or enslaved. From where did these people originally come? Again, tradition said they were buccaneers from the West Indies. After many years of daring and successful ventures, they landed on the coast of middle Florida. The area was uncolonized and here they began a new life, free from the restraints of any government. For a while they prospered only to meet ultimate disaster.[27]

Finally, on 18 July 1831, Couper and his party reached the western extremity, the junction of the Flint and Chattahoochee Rivers which marked the Alabama line. At this time Crawford and Terrence left for home, leaving only Couper and his party to draw the line eastward from Alabama to the coast of Georgia. July was the rainy season in Georgia, and it rained incessantly. Forty days had passed with but little sunshine. Because of the wetness, several of the men had slight chills but otherwise remained healthy.[28]

In late July, however, the weather changed abruptly, and days of clear weather followed. This helped everybody's spirits, the sick became well, and by 20 July the line had been drawn twenty miles east of Alabama. Thoughts of home occupied every mind, and an atmosphere of joviality prevailed, and Couper and his band were making progress. They hoped to be at Lake Randolph within twenty-five days. As the days continued into August they became as hot and dry as they had been cool and wet in July. The party reached Lake Randolph in mid-August. Couper's task was now finished. He had drawn the line from Alabama to the main source of the St. Marys River, which was at Lake Randolph. By the governor's own admission and that of the United States government, the boundary would follow the river to the coast.

By 20 August Couper was home at the Lodge with his wife and children. He was tired but much relieved that his task had been successful and that his duty to his state and nation had been done. Never again would the question arise as to where Georgia ended and Florida began. Couper and his commission had settled the question once and for all. Indeed, for many years the Georgia-Florida boundary was known as the "Couper-Crawford Line."[29]

In 1833, James Hamilton Couper embarked on a new venture. For some time he had known the utility of oil extracted from the seed of cotton. The oil could be used in all types of lubricants and salves, and also for cooking. Yet, little effort had been made to utilize cotton seed oil for these purposes. Farmers continued to cast away the seed from their ginning as useless. In Couper's mind the country should tap this resource, and a whole new industry could be developed. It would result in added income for the farmers, and the consumer would benefit also. Therefore, Couper became one of the pioneers in the extraction and use of oil from cotton seed. In 1833 he began construction on two cotton seed crushing mills, one located in Natchez, Mississippi, and the other in Mobile, Alabama.[30]

Couper left Georgia to initiate his industrial ventures in the lower South on 19 November 1833. He departed Savannah on the evening stage bound for Macon. He planned to go to Mississippi first and then to Alabama. While Couper was away, Caroline and the two little boys, Hamilton and Robert, would travel staying for a while at the Village and then going to visit other friends and relatives along the coast. Indeed, for the next three years Couper would spend much time away from Georgia tending to his business in "the West."[31]

As he departed Savannah, the weather was unseasonably cold for November, but his clothes were warm and the head cold that had been troubling him for the past several days was much better. Couper arrived in Macon on 21 November and found much progress everywhere. "Macon I have found much improved. It is in every respect a very respectable town for its age, and is prettily situated." That same day he boarded the stage for Montgomery, Alabama, and expected to be there in forty-eight hours. From there he would go directly to Natchez.[32] Couper arrived in Natchez on 2 December. He described the place as a "town of 3,000 inhabitants, most beautifully situated on a hill of 200 feet high, on a fine sweep of the river commanding a beautiful view of the river and opposite country. The surrounding country is rich, with a beautifully undulating surface, generally well wooded… There is s a good deal of wealth concentrated here, and an exclusive aristocratic class exists, living in much style and luxury."[33]

After getting settled, he took an eight-day tour up the Mississippi to examine the rich delta lands an acquaintance had described. He then left for New Orleans. Couper had taken as a partner in the Natchez mill a native Mississippian by the name of Sam Plummer. Couper had not known Plummer for very long and would regret the arrangement. His trip to New Orleans was strictly business. He proposed to sell patent rights of the cotton seed crushing process to the legislature so that mills could be established by the state of Louisiana to benefit its own planters. Couper had offered to sell the rights for $90,000. Couper outlined the proposal to the legislature, and a select committee was appointed to review the matter and report back to a joint session of the legislature on the matter. Although the committee reported in favor of purchasing the patent rights, the skeptical legislature rejected Couper's proposal.[34]

After failing to secure the patent sale, Couper concentrated on the Bellevue mill at Natchez where work had been slowed by failure of certain machinery to arrive. John Wylly, Caroline's brother, was managing

29

the Natchez mill. By the first week of January 1834, Couper had come to realize that his partner, Sam Plummer, was not entirely honest and Couper had terminated the partnership, buying Plummer's half interest in the Bellevue mill. In his letters to Caroline, Couper lamented that the dishonesty of Plummer, the precise details of which Couper never revealed, had upset him but that he was determined to extricate himself from the unhealthy relationship.[35]

With the establishment of John Wylly as manager of the mill and the acquisition of additional hands to help him, James Hamilton Couper set out for Mobile, the site of his other mill. He arrived there on 11 December 1834. His brother, John Couper Jr., was managing this mill for him, and, of course, the reunion with his brother lessened his homesickness. He found John and the mill operating rather well. The mill had been deficient in hands, but fifty-four Negroes had recently arrived from Hopeton to help with the operations. The Alabama mill, unlike the one in Natchez, was completed and already producing cotton seed oil of a very fine quality which sold for one dollar per gallon. After witnessing the operation in Mobile, he considered the experiment there a complete success and was optimistic that, with proper management, it would prove very profitable.[36]

Satisfied with the situation at the Mobile mill, he returned to Natchez to try to straighten out his affairs there. Upon his arrival on 12 January 1835, he found John Wylly absent, having gone up river looking for seed; however, the machinery had just arrived, and Couper hoped to get the mill in operation within six weeks.[37] Couper worked extremely hard to expedite construction of the mill, but he also enjoyed a full social life. As a distinguished member of the Georgia low country aristocracy, he was accepted without question by the Mississippi planters; and to his pleasure he found that his difficulties with Sam Plummer had not hurt his social standing.

After a quick trip to Mobile on 21 February 1835, he traveled to New Orleans to address a select committee of the Louisiana legislature to lobby for their acceptance of a charter bill which would establish one of Couper's mills in the state, for which Couper would receive $41,000 from patent rights. The legislature had earlier turned down the original offer of $90,000. While there he dined with Governor Edward Douglas White.

On 13 April 1835, the Bellevue mill at Natchez was finally in operation, and cotton seed oil was made for the first time. It proved to be of very fine quality. By this time, John Wylly had purchased for mill business a new steamboat, the *Bonita*, and he had gone up river again trying to secure seed.[38]

Although by the spring 1835 the Alabama and Mississippi mills were operating and producing oil of excellent quality, Couper began to experience a series of set-backs. Unexpected costs came without warning, and he had great trouble securing enough seed for his oil manufacture. The planters were so used to throwing their cotton seeds away that it was difficult to get them to save them for sale to the oil-crushing mills. John Wylly had to spend much of his time sailing up and down the Mississippi River searching for seed all to little avail and spreading the word to the farmers that seed must be saved for the production of oil was no easy task.[39] It was with a sad heart that he wrote to Caroline in December 1835: "I have found my affairs in a more unpromising state than I expected, as far as respects the debts incurred and the profits of the business—and there are yet heavy outlays required.... At present I am making an effort to sell out everything, namely mill, land, Negroes and patent right either to some individual or to a company of persons."[40]

Then the cruelest blow of all came when he received word that his brother, John Couper Jr., manager of the Mobile mill, had died unexpectedly. He would now have to assume more duties there until he could sell out. More than ever now he would have to run back and forth between Mobile and Natchez to tend to his properties. Understandably, he should write his wife: "This wandering life passed in steamboats and hotels, amidst crowds that one knows and cares nothing about;—amidst noise without amusement, is more irksome to me: and I most ardently look forward to the time when I can exchange it for that dearest of all places—'Sweet home.' Where the faces I meet, if but few, are the dearest, and where want of incident is supplied by warmth of feeling..."[41]

Also, in January 1836 came disquieting news from Georgia. The Seminole Indians in Florida were on the rampage again, and troops from Georgia were being called in to put down the uprising. One of the troops volunteering its service was the Glynn County Hussars, and James Hamilton Couper was captain of that troop. He had been appointed its head in December 1831, by Governor Wilson Lumpkin.[42] Again he lamented to his wife: "I observe with pain that the Indians have been

31

troublesome in Florida, and I do not doubt that had I remained at home, I should now be leading the Glynn Hussars through the forests of that territory. Without much fancying exposure at this season of the year, I shall regret if the troop should go into service without my being with them."[43] But the Glynn County Hussars did go into service without their commander, who decided to remain in the west to complete his business.[44]

Finally in March 1836, Couper shut down his mills and sold his properties in Alabama and Mississippi. He had lost $18,000 in the milling venture. His original investment was $48,000. His dream had become a failure. His problems had been many. The mills were so far from home that he had difficulty attending to them properly, and then back home to Georgia to check on his family. Had the mills been established in Georgia, the situation might have been different. In addition, there was the delay in the shipment of machinery to the Natchez mill, which postponed its opening and increased his costs. Also capital with which to begin the mill operations was harder to obtain than expected, and the procurement of seed was always a problem. The charter bill Couper had counted on to pass the Louisiana legislature never passed, and unexpected costs finally ruined the venture. Disappointed but perhaps a bit wiser, he returned to Georgia on 10 April 1837.[45]

Notes

[1] E. Merton Coulter, *Georgia, A Short History* (Chapel Hill: Univeristy of North Carolina Press, 1960) 249-53.
[2] Ibid.
[3] Ibid.; Edward J. Harden, *The Life of George M. Troup* (Savannah GA: E. J. Purse, 1859) 178.
[4] Coulter, *Georgia A Short History,* 253.
[5] Fletcher M. Green, "Georgia's Board of Public Works, 1817-1826," *Georgia Historical Quarterly* 23 (June 1938): 128.
[6] Ibid., 130-31.
[7] Harden, *Life of Troup,* 179.
[8] Green, "Georgia's Board of Public Works," 131.
[9] Ibid., 132.
[10] Harden, *Life of Troup,* 180-81; Coulter, *Georgia A Short History,* 251.
[11] Harden, *Life of Troup,* 180-81; Green, "Georgia's Board of Public Works," 134.
[12] Harden, *Life of Troup,* 182.

[13]James Hamilton Couper to E. J. Harden, 14 August 1858, published in Harden's *Life of Troup,* 180-81.

[14]Green, "Georgia's Board of Public Works," 118.

[15]Governor John Rockingham Gilmer to James Hamilton Couper, 5 February 1831, *Governor's Letterbook: Official Letters of the Governor of Georgia, 1829-1843,* Georgia Department of Archives and History, Atlanta GA.

[16]Ibid.; Governor Gilmer to James Hamilton Couper, 5 May 1833, 2 May 1831, *Governor's Letterbook*; John C. Upchurch, ed., *The Southeastern United States: Essays on the Cultural and Historical Landscape* 18 vols. (Carrolton: West Georgia College, 1979) 18:66.

[17]James Hamilton Couper to Caroline Couper, 11 May 1831, Mackay Stiles Papers, Southern Historical Collection, University of North Carolina, Chapel Hill.

[18]Ibid.

[19]Ibid.

[20]James Hamilton Couper to Caroline Couper, 8 June 1831, Mackay Stiles Papers, Southern Historical Collection.

[21]Governor John Gilmer to James Hamilton Couper, 12 April 1831, *Governors' Letterbook*; James Hamilton Couper to Caroline Couper, 8 June 1831, Mackay Stiles Papers, Southern Historical Collection.

[22]Governor Gilmer to James Hamilton Couper, 12 April 1831, *Governors' Letterbook*; James Hamilton Couper to Caroline Couper, 29 June 1831, Mackay Stiles Papers, Southern Historical Collection.

[23]James Hamilton Couper to Caroline Couper, 5 July 1831, Mackay Stiles Papers, Southern Historical Collection.

[24]Ibid.

[25]James Hamilton Couper to Caroline Couper, 15 July 1831, Mackay Stiles Papers, Southern Historical Collection.

[26]Ibid.

[27]Ibid.

[28]James Hamilton Couper to Caroline Couper, 18 July 1831 Mackay Stiles Papers, Southern Historical Collection.

[29]James Hamilton Couper to Caroline Couper, 18 July 1831, 1 August 1831, Mackay Stiles Papers, Southern Historical Collection; see also "The Couper-Crawford Line" (a manuscript account of the "establishment of the Georgia-Florida boundary"), Mackay Stiles Papers, Southern Historical Collection.

[30]Collective letters of James Hamilton Couper to Caroline Couper, 1833-1836, concerning cotton seed mills in Alabama and Mississippi, Mackay Stiles Papers, Southern Historical Collection.

[31]James Hamilton Couper to Caroline Couper, 17, 21 November 1833, Mackay Stiles Papers, Southern Historical Collection.

[32]James Hamilton Couper to Caroline Couper, 17, 21 November 1833, Mackay Stiles Papers, Southern Historical Collection.

[33]James Hamilton Couper to Caroline Couper, 5 December 1833, Mackay Stiles Papers, Southern Historical Collection.

[34]James Hamilton Couper to Caroline, 17 January 1834, Mackay Stiles Papers, Southern Historical Collection; James Hamilton Couper Plantation Records, 4 vols., 1:147, 152, 167, 183, Southern Historical Collection, University of North Carolina, Chapel Hill.

[35]James Hamilton Couper to Caroline Couper, 7, 8 January 1834, Mackay Stiles Papers, Southern Historical Collection; James Hamilton Couper Plantation Records, 1:76, 132, 147, 152, 167-71, 184-85, Southern Historical Collection.

[36]James Hamilton Couper to Caroline Couper, 14 December 1834, Mackay Stiles Papers, Southern Historical Collection; James Hamilton Couper Plantation Records, 1:147, Southern Historical Collection; manuscript concerning James Hamilton Couper's Mobile and Natchez cotton seed crushing mills, Margaret Davis Cate Collection, Savannah GA, n.d., n.p. (copy available at Fort Frederica National Monument, St. Simons Island GA).

[37]James Hamilton Couper to Caroline Couper, 21 January 1835, Mackay Stiles Papers, Southern Historical Collection; James Hamilton Couper Plantation Records, 1:76, 184-85, Southern Historical Collection.

[38]James Hamilton Couper to Caroline Couper, 13 April 1835, Mackay Stiles Papers, Southern Historical Collection; James Hamilton Couper Plantation Records, 1:76, 171.

[39]James Hamilton Couper to Caroline Couper, 9 February 1836, Mackay Stiles Papers, Southern Historical Collection; James Hamilton Couper Plantation Records, 1:147, 152, 168, 171, Southern Historical Collection.

[40]James Hamilton Couper to Caroline Couper, 24 December 1835, Mackay Stiles Papers, Southern Historical Collection.

[41]James Hamilton Couper to Caroline Couper, 31 January 1836, Mackay Stiles Papers, Southern Historical Collection.

[42]*Military Record of Georgia, 1829-1841*, Georgia Department of Archives and History, Atlanta, 33; James Hamilton Couper Plantation Records, 1:125, Southern Historical Collection.

[43]James Hamilton Couper to Caroline Couper, 31 January 1836, Mackay Stiles Papers, Southern Historical Collection.

[44]James Hamilton Couper to Caroline Couper, 31 January 1836, Mackay Stiles Papers, Southern Historical Collection; see also "Seminole War" (manuscript

account of the Indian activities in Florida in 1831-1832), Mackay Stiles Papers, Southern Historical Collection.

[45]James Hamilton Couper to Caroline Couper, 10, 17, 24 March 1836; 13 April 1936; 17, 23 March 1837, Mackay Stiles Papers, Southern Historical Collection; James Hamilton Couper Plantation Records, 1:132 152, Southern Historical Collection; manuscript concerning James Hamilton Couper's Mobile and Natchez cotton seed crushing mills, Margaret Davis Cate Collection.

CHAPTER IV

The Sinking of the *Pulaski*

An ill wind blew through Georgia in 1838, bringing disaster. It was in early summer, a festive season when wealthy Georgians took sea excursions up the Atlantic coast to Northern resorts. On one such pleasure jaunt, Georgia's newest and most elegant passenger ship went to her death carrying with her many of the state's most prominent citizens. Almost every well-to-do family along the Georgia coast was affected. If one of their family members had not perished in the tragedy, one of their friends had.

A year earlier the steamship *Home* had sunk while on a run from New York to Charleston. After that disaster, the Savannah and Charleston Steam Packet Company appointed Gazaway Bugg Lamar, a wealthy Savannahian, to spearhead a move to construct an elegant and "luxurious coastal vessel that would be stronger, faster, and safer" than the *Home*.[1] The new ship was constructed in Baltimore and named the *Pulaski*. The ship operated out of Savannah, headquarters of the steamship company. In early spring the vessel began making regular trips from Savannah to New York via Charleston.[2]

The *Pulaski* was an impressive ship of 687 tons and beam wider than usual. She "sat low in the water," and her crew numbered thirty-seven.[3] The *Savannah Georgian* boasted proudly to its readers that no expense had been spared by the owners in the ship's construction. The paper continued: "Her engine is one of the best ever made in this country, and of great strength. She has ample accommodations and everything that is requisite for the comfort of passengers. Her qualities as a sea vessel, for ease, safety, and speed, are superior to any steamer that ever floated on the American waters."[4] The ladies were comfortably accommodated on the top deck, where the affect of the sea breeze was best; the men were quartered on the lower deck.

The ship had made three successful trips on the scheduled route, and on 13 June, 1838, a fourth was planned. It was the height of the season when Southerners visited the North, and the trip promised to be a gala one. The newspapers of Savannah and Charleston advertised the voyage "one night at sea." The ship would leave Savannah early in the morning and stop that evening in Charleston where the passengers could enjoy the night life. All would then leave Charleston the next morning for Baltimore, spending only "one night at sea."[5]

The *Pulaski* departed Savannah as scheduled on 13 June, with many of the most prominent citizens of Georgia on board. The South Carolinians planning to make the trip would get on that night when the ship docked in Charleston harbor. Almost 200 passengers were scheduled to be aboard. Among the Georgians was James Hamilton Couper, who was traveling North on business. Also among the passengers and under his care were Mrs. Fraser, his wife's sister, with her little son Menzies, and Mrs. Nightengale (granddaughter of Rufus King of New York), with her baby Louisa. Mrs. Nightengale's Negro nurse Rhynah was also on board.[6] Also making the trip were the Lamars of Savannah. Gazaway Bugg Lamar, the ship's promoter, was taking his whole family North for the summer including "his wife, six children, a niece, and his sister."[7]

The *Pulaski* left Savannah precisely at 8:00 A.M. on Wednesday, decked out gaily in her flags. The day was beautiful with a cool, refreshing sea breeze blowing from the southeast. Truly this was to be a jaunt of pleasure, and all on board mirrored their anticipation with cheerfulness. The captain was an amiable man named Dubois, who, along with the ship and her crew, inspired confidence.[8]

The ship arrived in Charleston around 7:30 P.M. , almost an hour before dark. The passengers milled about the deck before going ashore. Charleston was beautiful at night. They toured the gas-lighted streets of the Battery, that elite residential section which fronted the harbor. They visited the taverns, the celebrated establishments of the city.[9] The gala excursion departed Charleston harbor at 6:00 A.M. on Thursday, 14 June, after picking up sixty-five additional passengers.

The day dawned bright and sunny. But as the hours progressed, the wind increased and began to blow in force from the east, requiring the ladies to retire to their berths. Fearing that a gale might be brewing, the men became increasingly uneasy.[10] This alarm, however, was needless, for by nightfall the clouds disappeared and the stars shone brightly. The sea remained less than calm, so Captain Dubois ordered "a full pressure of steam" to enable the vessel to overcome the resistance of the waves. This she did admirably and by 10:00 P.M. was steaming at a rate of 11 mph. By this time most of the passengers had retired from the deck to the cabins below, assured that all was well. They anticipated a good night's rest after the late hours kept in Charleston the night before.[11]

James Hamilton Couper had retired at 10:30 P.M. , having lingered a little longer than most on deck, and had fallen asleep almost immediately.[12] At 11:00 P.M. all were awakened by a deafening explosion. The starboard boiler had exploded. The second engineer had allowed the water to run low in the boiler and then admitted fresh water into the heated copper container. Forty minutes after the explosion the ship began to break in two, with the midpart sinking into the ocean and the bow and stern rising into the air.[13]

Immediately after the first explosion, Couper sprang from his bed. The lights were extinguished in his quarters, and he was forced to fumble around in the dark. He made his way upstairs to the women's cabins which, fortunately, were lighted. He met the ladies under his care, Mrs. Fraser and Mrs. Nightengale, who were frightened but composed. He requested that they remain where they were until he could find out what had happened.

As he walked over the wreckage of the deck, fragments of glass cut his feet, and he heard voices crying out that the ship was on fire and calling for buckets of water. He continued to the center of the vessel where the engine was located. He ascertained that the "vitals" of the ship were injured beyond repair and that the vessel was about to sink. He met a poor man who was dragging himself along and crying out pitifully, "O God, both my legs are blown off!" It was the barber whose shop was near the boilers. Returning to the ladies' cabin and deck, he witnessed a heart-rending situation: men, women and children were grouped together in their nightclothes with the most hideous expressions of fear on their faces. Couper recounted that as he reached the companionway of the gentlemen's cabin:

> I stood still for a moment to rally myself. I felt the final hour of my existence had arrived, that there was no possible escape, and I summoned up all my energies to meet my fate with calmness and fortitude. The images of my wife, children, father and mother, flashed before my mind; the bitter pang of the last separation wrung the soul for an instant; the struggle was over and I was collected and ready to meet the emergency

At the same moment Rebecca Lamar, Gazaway Bugg Lamar's sister, reported:

> Just after the explosion I heard groans proceeding from the darkened passage. I stepped a few paces and found a Negro man on his hands and knees in agony. I said, "Daddy, what is the matter?" "Oh Miss's, my feet done burnt off!"[14]

Couper now turned his attentions to the ladies and children under his care. He shed his nightshirt and drew on his britches and shirt, rejecting his boots as too cumbersome for swimming. He grabbed a large camlet cloak for the protection of the women and the children and proceeded onto the deck. He could not see his charges anywhere but noticed two men lowering a rowboat. He could get into that boat with those two men and escape with his life. If he took time to search for those under his care, he might lose the one chance for his life, but honor dictated that he search for them.

He soon found his charges and instructed them to follow him. As they reached the side of the ship, two sailors were lowering a rowboat into the water. Couper took the infant from Mrs. Nightengale and instructed her to jump into the boat, now settled on the sea. The force of her ten-foot leap was broken by one of the men in the boat. Couper then jumped with the baby in his arms. However, the boat pulled away as Couper jumped, and his feet struck the gunwale, throwing him into the sea. Recovering himself, he threw the baby to its mother. After climbing into the boat, he instructed Mrs. Fraser to throw down her son. Couper caught him, and his mother soon followed. By this time the little boat was filled to capacity. As the boat shoved off, people were thronged on the side of the ship calling out, "Hold on to that boat—don't shove off that boat!" Had they not shoved off when they did, more people would have jumped in and it would have capsized. Later, Couper wrote of the situation:

> There are moments in life when the escape from impending danger has exceeded all possible hope, that the belief in an overriding Providence is felt with irresistible force. The heart then overflowing with gratitude vows with deep felt thankfulness to the hand that has stretched out to save. Never were persons in a situation more calculated to inspire such a feeling than we were at this moment.[15]

Having escaped the sinking vessel, the group turned their attention to their own condition. It was agreed that the boat should follow behind the Pulaski at a distance of about 150 yards—far enough not to be affected if the ship sank suddenly but close enough to regain her if she did not sink. The two sailors manned oars.[16]

The rowboat was small, 16-18 feet long, and crowded with twelve persons. Besides Couper and his party, there were four white men, a Negro waiter named Solomon and two Negro women. For a while they wondered whether the boat would survive in the sea, for it leaked a great deal and they had only a dipper with which to bail. The sea was rough, and they had but two oars with which to manage her. The two seamen rowed, and one person bailed continuously. From their vantage point these twelve persons watched the Pulaski. Although her galley lights were still on and the ship gave the appearance in the darkness that nothing was wrong, the huge mass was sinking gradually.[17] Suddenly the lights went out, and after a few moments of deadly black silence a heavy cracking sound was heard, followed by a shrieking wail from those on board. The ship had broken in half.[18]

Presently, another rowboat from the Pulaski approached and called to those in Couper's boat. The other boat was under the charge of the Pulaski's first mate, Hibbert. It was agreed that the two boats should stay close together but not desert the wrecked ship until morning. Mate Hibbert's boat contained only five persons, and he wanted to ply around the wreckage to pick up a few of those who were clinging to fragments of the wreck. The first to be rescued was a man named Bird from Georgia. Next were two firemen who had been scalded during the explosion. Then a raft was sighted with ten persons on board. The two boats turned away from it, for ten additional passengers would have sunk both boats. Hibbert next picked up a young German, a son of the Duke of Leuchtenberg, who was found floating on a settee. The last to be picked up was an elderly gentleman from New York, Judge Rochester.[19]

After rescuing as many as possible, both boats turned toward land, deserting the wrecked Pulaski. The time was 3:30 A.M. on Friday, 15 June. The moon was up, and the "first faint streaks of the morning light were just appearing in the east. The sky was gloomy and threatening, and the sea under a fresh wind was heaving in long inky waves, the crests of which broke incessantly into sheets of white spray." The survivors assumed that land lay to the northwest about 35 miles away, and they turned in that direction with Hibbert steering one boat and Couper the other. As they traveled on, few spoke and the silence was complete save for the continuous moans of the two scalded seamen.

At length, day broke and all eyes searched for land, but nothing was seen but the seemingly endless and boundless ocean. The sun rose brilliantly and soon became oppressive, blistering everyone's skin. They erected a makeshift sail out of the one coat on board. The wind was blowing toward the shore, and with the aid of the oars they made a speed of approximately three miles an hour. The moaning of the two scalded seamen intensified as the sun added to their miseries. One of them died and his body was dropped overboard. Then the boat commanded by Hibbert came alongside the boat directed by Couper and, as the Couper boat was overloaded, relieved them of three of their passengers.

The men in the boats took turns at the oars as sunburn worsened. There was no food or water on board, and the only relief was keeping feet and arms wet with salt water. All in the boat were earnestly looking for land, and many false reports were given. Fortunately, at about noon land was sighted by the mate, who waved his handkerchief and pointed to the west. The spirits of the persons in both boats revived immediately, and conversation became lively. The men began to manage the oars with greater effort.[20]

As the survivors approached land, they found a long, sandy beach which skirted the shore. In their dazed condition they thought they saw houses and villages, but as they drew nearer, these mirages disappeared, melting into barren hills and a deserted shore. At about 3:00 P.M. they were a quarter of a mile from the shore and they looked for some bay or inlet to afford them a safe landing. But none was seen, and between the boats and the shore was a line of dangerous breakers which made landing extremely perilous. Beyond the shore at a distance of about two miles, woods were seen and a few buildings distinguished.[21]

Both Couper and Hibbert believed that a landing should not be attempted at that time and that both boats should move down the coast in hopes of finding a safer place to land. But the men in both boats, exhausted from the rowing and suffering from acute hunger and thirst, refused to row any further and demanded that they attempt a landing.

Thus overruled, Couper and Hibbert reluctantly consented. Because there were women and children in the boat directed by Couper, Hibbert suggested that his boat try the first landing.[22]

The Sinking of the *Pulaski*

In pursuance of the plan, Couper steered his boat about 150 yards from the breakers to await the outcome of Hibbert's attempt. As those in Couper's boat watched, the other boat rose to the summit of the first breaker but disappeared beneath it, and they realized it had been upset. Presently, two figures emerged from the surf and struggled ashore. After resting for a moment, they returned to the water and dragged two others to the beach. Once again, the first two entered the water and dragged out another. Finally, a sixth was carried to safety. Eventually, they secured their boat from the water. Six of their party had perished. They were Judge Rochester of New York, Bird of Georgia, the two scalded firemen and the two Negro women.[23]

Sobered by the fate of the other craft, Couper persuaded the men in his lifeboat to delay landing until a more propitious moment, and they had several hours until sunset, plenty of time in Couper's judgment to row along the coast looking for a safe inlet or bay. But the men refused to row any further; they were too exhausted and any exertion had become painful. They preferred to stay where they were and attempt a landing before nightfall. Those on land urged that a landing not be tried at this time under any circumstances. But the weary party insisted on landing. Couper argued against this, but at length he was compelled to enter into a compromise with them. He agreed that if no aid had come by sunset, he would steer them to shore.

Time weighed heavily upon them, and no aid was in sight. Finally, as the sun began to dip in the West, Couper made preparations to land. He asked the young sailor, Barney, to save Mrs. Fraser in case they were upset. Solomon, the Negro man, was instructed to save her child. Another man named Robertson was asked to save Mrs. Nightengale, but when he refused, Couper accepted Mrs. Nightengale's suggestion that she tie her baby around her waist and he should save them both. Couper then gave general instructions to all on how to act if they capsized. He then suggested to Barney and Solomon that they lie down in the bottom of the boat to get some rest in preparation for the ordeal of landing. They agreed and Couper rested also. After a short nap the three men rose. Barney and Solomon rowed while Couper took the helm.

Just before sunset Couper gave the order to proceed headlong into the breakers. The first breaker came, and they road it well; the second came, and they survived it. But a third struck them with such force that the boat capsized. Couper felt a severe blow on the back of his head and

43

another on his chest. He found himself below the water and under the boat. Holding his breath, he "dove down perpendicularly, struck off horizontally until the light was seen above, and then rose to the surface." He saw the boat a few yards away, and the men who had just surfaced were swimming for shore. [24]

He glanced rapidly around for the women and children, but, at first, none was in sight. In a few moments, however, the back of Mrs. Fraser came slowly to the surface. Her head and feet were under water and she appeared to be struggling. As Couper reached her and pulled her head above water, he found that she had her son by the wrist, "having convulsively retained the grasp she had of his arm as she sat by him before the boat upset." Keeping their heads above water, he maneuvered them over to the boat and threw them across the keel. He then called Barney and Solomon and reminded them of their pledge to save this lady and her child. They quickly responded and assumed responsibility for their charges. Couper then returned his attention to finding Mrs. Nightengale and her baby. He dove down and began searching the area under the boat when he felt something brush against his feet. It was Mrs. Nightengale's body. He grabbed her by the hair and brought her to the surface. She was conscious, and the baby was still tied around her waist and alive. He placed them across the upturned bottom of the boat and then began to push it ashore. As they proceeded toward land, the breakers lashed them, three times submerging them completely in the water. Each time Couper had trouble keeping hold of the boat and his charges on it. As a fourth wave broke over them, he felt his feet touch ground. He then took Mrs. Nightengale from the boat, and they waded ashore with Couper holding the baby in one arm and supporting Mrs. Nightengale with the other. The bottom was lined with ridges, and the sand which moved about them with each wave made it slippery. They had not gone very far when Mrs. Nightengale slipped and fell. Couper tried several times to get her up but failed. Finally he reminded her that if she did not get up she would die. Thus encouraged, she rose and they made it to the edge of the beach.[25]

The men in the first boat had been watching, and as Couper and his charges reached the shallow waters near the beach, they rushed to assist Couper. Why additional aid had not come earlier was not known, but Couper was thankful that he and those under his care were alive. He was also consoled by the fact that the occupants of his boat had escaped with their lives. With the excitement over, Couper's strength vanished and he fell insensible on the sandy beach.[26] At 10:00 P.M. that night Couper was aroused by shouts from those who had gone for aid. They brought warm clothes and food. By 11:00 P.M., Couper and the survivors from both boats were comfortably situated in the home of Tigler Kedd of Onslow County, North Carolina.[27]

The wreck had occurred about 45 miles south of Cape Look Out, North Carolina, 30 miles from land.[28] The survivors traveled to Wilmington, North Carolina. The next morning thirty more Pulaski passengers arrived in that city. They had been picked up by a passing schooner after having drifted about the ocean, clinging to fragments from the wrecked ship, for several days without food or water. Rhynah, Mrs. Nightengale's nurse, was among them. Eventually, fifty-nine persons were saved from the wreck.[29]

Couper and his group then went to Norfolk, Virginia, and on to Baltimore, Maryland. No innkeeper, upon hearing who they were, would accept money for accommodations. In Baltimore they were met by John Alsop King of New York, the father of Mrs. Nightengale. Of King's daughter, Couper said, "She behaved most heroically. Neither of the ladies uttered an exclamation of fear when death seemed inevitable. Had they lost their presence of mind, I could never have saved them."[30]

After a brief stay in Baltimore, Couper journeyed to Philadelphia and finally to New York where he stayed with his good friend John Lord, who had been his roommate at Yale many years earlier. By this time Lord was a very successful lawyer. The two remained life-long friends and named their sons for each other. While in New York, James Hamilton Couper also visited the Kings at their residence near Jamaica, Long Island. When he arrived in Jamaica, the town turned out in celebration to thank Couper for what he had done for "their valued citizen and his family."[31] Concerning this and all the praise he had received lately, he wrote his wife, "It is very well that you are not inclined to jealousy, for I assure you that I am much made of by the ladies at present. It is not often that any one is so well rewarded for the performance of a duty, as I have been in this instance."[32]

Notes
[1] Joseph Frederick Waring, *Cerveau's Savannah* (Savannah: Georgia Historical Society, 1973) 53.

[2]*Savannah Daily Georgian*, 1 March 1838. On file at Georgia Department of Archives and History, Atlanta GA.

[3]Waring, *Cerveau's Savannah*, 54.

[4]*Savannah Daily Georgian*, 10 April 1838.

[5]*Savannah Georgian*, 12, 13, 14 June 1838; Waring, *Cerveau's Savannah*, 54; William Hardin, *A History of Savannah and South Georgia* (Atlanta GA; Cherokee Publishing Company, 1969) 337.

[6]"The Ordeal of the *Pulaski*" (typescript concerning the ordeal of Mrs. Fraser and Mrs. Nightengale during the sinking of the *Pulaski*), Mackay Stiles Papers, Southern Historical Collection, University of North Carolina, Chapel Hill.

[7]Waring, *Cerveau's Savannah*, 54.

[8]*Wilmington* (NC) *Advertiser*, 18, 22 June 1838, ; Mrs. Hugh McLeod "The Loss of the Steamer *Pulaski*," *Georgia Historical Quarterly* 3 (March 1919): 65-66. This article is a primary account of the sinking of the *Pulaski*, for Mrs. Hugh McLeod was the former Rebecca Lamar, one of the survivors of the wreck of the *Pulaski*. To my knowledge, Couper and McLeod were the only two survivors who have left detailed accounts of the diaster to posterity.

[9]McLeod, "The Loss of the *Pulaski*," 66; *Wilmington Advertiser*, 18, 22, June 1838; James Hamilton Couper, manuscript account of the sinking of the *Pulaski*, Mackay Stiles Papers, Southern Historical Collection. Couper wrote this for publication in the various newspapers of the coastal states. Published accounts may be found in George M. White, *Historical Collections of Georgia* (New York NY: Pudney and Russell, 1855) 353-64, and Caroline Couper Lovell, *Golden Isles of Georgia* (Atlanta GA: Cherokee Publishing Company, 1970) 157-81.

[10]McLeod, "The Loss of the *Pulaski*," 63; Couper, manuscript account of *Pulaski* sinking; *Wilmington Advertiser*, 18, 22 June 1838.

[11]McLeod, "The Loss of the *Pulaski*," 63-66; Couper, manuscript account of the sinking of the *Pulaski*, Mackay Stiles Papers, Southern Historical Collection.

[12]Couper, manuscript account of the sinking of the *Pulaski*, Mackay Stiles Papers, Southern Historical Collection.

[13]McLeod, "The Loss of the *Pulaski*," 63-64; *Charleston* (SC) *Courier*, 19 June 1838; *Savannah Daily Georgian*, 21 June 1838; Frances Anne Kemble, *Journal of a Residence on a Georgian Plantation in 1838-1839* (New York NY: Alfred A. Knopf, 1961) 337.

[14]McLeod, "The Loss of the *Pulaski*," 69; Couper, manuscript account of *Pulaski* sinking, Mackay Stiles Papers, Southern Historical Collection; see also Waring, *Cerveau's Savannah*, 54. This fourteen-year-old boy, Charley Lamar, was Charles Augustus Lafayette Lamar, who grew into "one of the most swaggering young bucks ever to grace Savannah Society." He and William C. Corrie were involved in the *Wanderer* affair in 1859. Gazaway Bugg Lamar, his sister Rebecca

and his son Charley survived, but Mrs. Lamar, her niece and five Lamar children did not.

[15]Couper, manuscript account of *Pulaski* sinking, Mackay Stiles Papers, Southern Historical Collection.

[16]Ibid.; McLeod, "The Loss of the *Pulaski*," 9.

[17]Couper, manuscript account of *Pulaski* sinking, Mackay Stiles Papers, Southern Historical Collection.

[18]Ibid., McLeod, "The Loss of the *Pulaski*," 63-64.

[19]Couper, manuscript account of *Pulaski* sinking, Mackay Stiles Papers, Southern Historical Collection; Hardin, *History of Savannah and South Georgia*, 338; *Charleston Courier*, 19 June 1838.

[20]Couper, manuscript account of *Pulaski* sinking, Mackay Stiles Papers, Southern Historical Collection.

[21]Ibid.; McLeod, "The Loss of the *Pulaski*," 85; *Wilmington Advertiser*, 18, 22 June 1838.

[22]Couper, manuscript account of *Pulaski* sinking, Mackay Stiles Papers, Southern Historical Collection; McLeod, "The Loss of the *Pulaski*," 90-95.

[23]Couper, manuscript account of *Pulaski* sinking, Mackay Stiles Papers, Southern Historical Collection; McLeod, "The Loss of the *Pulaski*," 90-95.

[24]Couper, manuscript account of Pulaski sinking, Mackay Stiles Papers, Southern Historical Collection.

[25]Ibid.; Kemble, *Journal*, 341-42.

[26]Couper, manuscript account of *Pulaski* sinking, Mackay Stiles Papers, Southern Historical Collection.

[27]Ibid.;White, *Historical Collections of Georgia*, 363-64.

[28]Hardin, *History of Savannah and South Georgia*, 338.

[29]Couper to Caroline Couper, 19, 23 June 1838, Mackay Stiles Papers, Southern Historical Collection; McLeod, "The Loss of the *Pulaski*," 90-95. In *Cerveau's Savannah*, however, Waring states (p. 54) that "of the 131 passengers 77 were lost."

[30]Couper to Caroline Couper, 19, 23 June 1838, Mackay Stiles Papers, Southern Historical Collection.

[31]Couper to Caroline Couper, 3 July 1838, Mackay Stiles Papers, Southern Historical Collection.

[32]Couper to Caroline Couper, 5 July 1838, Mackay Stiles Papers, Southern Historical Collection.

CHAPTER V

Sea Island Cotton

James Hamilton Couper was one of the antebellum South's foremost
agriculturists, and his farming operations were held up for emulation
by agricultural editors throughout the region who applauded his experimentation with the major staples of cotton, sugar cane, and rice. They
praised his attempts to ameliorate the soil through a systematic plan of
crop rotation, the proper use of fertilizers, and the application of the
principles of deep plowing. They were encouraged by his pioneering
efforts in new uses for Bermuda grass and for his enterprising culture of
the date palm and the olive. After a visit to Hopeton in December 1832,
J. D. Legare, editor of the *Southern Agriculturist*, wrote in his
publication:

> We hesitate not to say *Hopeton* is decidedly the best plantation
> we have ever visited, and we doubt whether it can be equaled in
> the Southern States; and when we consider the extent of the
> crops, the variety of the same, and the number of operatives
> who have to be directed and managed, it will not be presump-
> tive to say that it may fairly challenge comparison with any
> establishment of the United States, for the systematic arrange-
> ment of the whole, the regularity and precision with which each
> and all of the operations are carried out, and the perfect and
> daily accountability established in every department.[1]

It was not by accident that Couper became a planter. In fact, his
father had groomed his eldest son for that vocation, which was also a
social position as well. Growing up on his father's plantation of Cannon's
Point on St. Simons Island, young Couper had indicated, an early interest in agricultural pursuits. Consequently, upon his graduation from Yale
in 1814, he returned home to work with his father. He showed such
promise in plantation management that in 1818, at the age of twenty, he
was given the entire charge of Hopeton, the Couper-Hamilton plantation on the Altamaha River.

In 1826, when John Couper went bankrupt, he transferred his property with the exception of Cannon's Point to his partner and chief

creditor, James Hamilton. In turn Hamilton sold one-half interest in Hopeton to its manager, James Hamilton Couper. From that time until 1856, Couper managed Hopeton for himself and the Hamilton heirs, for James Hamilton died in 1829. After 1856, Francis Porteus Corbin, who had married James Hamilton's only child Isabella (the Corbins had been living alternately in Virginia and Paris), took over the management of the Hamilton interest in Hopeton. Thereafter, Couper and Corbin supervised the Hopeton-Altama properties as co-managers.[2]

Eventually Hopeton was transformed from a diversified farm, growing the major staples of cotton, sugar cane, and rice, into one on which rice was the dominant crop. This was accomplished by 1841, when 714 acres were planted in rice, 40 acres in sugar cane and none in cotton. Clearly rice by that decade had surpassed cotton and sugar cane as the main staple at Hopeton. Couper began with cotton as the major crop and gradually shifted to sugar cane and finally to rice. In examining Couper's crop record book for the period 1818-1841, one can see a definite pattern of conversion from sea island cotton to rice. In the early 1820s, cotton received the major interest with respect to acreage, the peak year being 1822. By the early 1830s, however, cotton had been replaced by sugar cane in emphasis, the chief year being 1831. By the early 1840s, however, rice had become dominant, replacing substantially both cotton and sugar cane.[3] Couper realized that if he prepared his fields so that they could grow either cotton, sugar cane or rice, separately or in rotation, that in case a major shift was deemed expedient for any or various reasons, the switch could be accomplished rather easily. While Couper was slowly converting his acres into the productive rice lands that Hopeton boasted by 1841, cotton and sugar cane were planted in the interim.

This conversion of primitive tide swamplands into properly banked, ditched and leveled rice fields was a laborious process that often stretched over decades on a given plantation. The first step was the construction of a massive bank or levee designed to keep the tidal river waters off the fields. This was usually accomplished by digging an enormous drainage ditch along the entire border of the field. The dirt from this ditch was used to construct the bank or levee. Wooden trunks, which were designed to control the waters flowing in or out of the fields, were built into the levees. Once this initial step was accomplished, one could plant cotton and cane in these low tidelands.

Before the planter could raise a rice crop on the same land a tremendous amount of of work was required. The land had to be leveled within the field to insure a uniform water level over the rice plants when the fields were flooded. Also, numerous ditches and cross-ditches had to be dug in the field to facilitate the rapid flooding and draining of the rice at specific intervals of the plants' development.[4]

Besides a well-devised network of fields and subfields within a great levee, Couper constructed a large canal and a railroad on his plantation that facilitated work at harvest time. The canal ran in snakelike fashion past many of the important buildings at Hopeton, past the sugar mill, the rice mill, and mansion house, meandering through the fields and emptying back into the Altamaha. The canal was 3 miles long, 15 feet wide and 4 1/2 feet deep. At its entrance on the Altamaha was a giant lockgate 75 feet long and 12 feet wide consisting of four pairs of gates, calculated to pass flatboats 45 feet long and 11 feet wide at any stage of the tide. At the other end of the canal was a floodgate 35 feet long and 11 feet wide, with two pairs of gates. This arrangement, by allowing the water to enter at one end of the canal and leave by the other, prevented it from stagnating. The canal required about 10,000 man-days of labor for a number of slaves and their supervisors. It served the purposes of draining and flowing the interior fields and of harvesting the crops and transporting produce and plantation supplies to and from the river. The railroad, one of the first of its kind to be constructed on a plantation, consisted of movable wooden rails, and was used principally to haul cane from the fields to the canal where it was transported by flatboats to the river.[5]

As Couper's conversion process from sea island cotton to rice had barely begun in 1818, when he assumed the management of Hopeton, the early years of his tenure as manager saw the plantation primarily devoted to the production of sea island cotton. This remained true until 1825. In 1818, Couper planted over 544 acres in the staple with no lands devoted to either sugar cane or rice. His production that year was 147,543 pounds (147½ bales) of seed cotton. His peak year of production came in 1819, when 261,383 pounds (261 bales) of seed cotton were produced from 566 acres. In 1825, the last year of major cotton emphasis, he planted 516 acres in the staple from which he received 91,498 pounds (91½ bales) of seed cotton.[6]

The type of cotton that Couper produced was not the short staple variety made famous by Eli Whitney's gin, but rather a more delicate, more restricted type of higher quality. This cotton surpassed all other varieties in length and strength of fibre and in fineness and silkiness of texture. It brought prices double that of short staple or upland cotton. Moreover, it was ginned in a different way for a different market. While short staple cotton was manufactured into a commonplace fabric with many uses, the aristocratic long staple variety was used only to make the fine cambric and laces for the wealthy.[7]

There were several varieties of long staple cotton, but the type grown in the southern United States took its name from the place where it was first grown—the sea islands. This introduction came as an indirect result of the American Revolution. Following the British defeat, a number of Georgia planters made their home in the Bahamas. But as planters what could be grown there? A benevolent British government came to their aid and introduced the seed of a variety of cotton which was already flourishing on the island of Anguilla, a British possession in the Caribbean Sea. The Georgia expatriates prospered in the cultivation of this new cotton. They also kept close ties with their friends and kinsmen back in Georgia. Consequently, in 1785-1786 Colonel Roger Kelsall, a planter in the Bahamas, sent a bag of the Anguilla cotton seed to his former business partner, James Spalding, on St. Simons Island, Georgia. Spalding planted the seeds the next spring. They came up having luxuriant foliage, bloomed, but bore no fruit. When winter came, Spalding cut the stalks back. The next spring, 1787, new sprouts came up from the roots, bloomed and produced excellent cotton. During the same time other Georgians received more bags of the new seed from friends or relatives in the Bahamas and witnessed similar results. Hence, Anguilla cotton became sea island cotton and spread from Georgia to the coast of South Carolina, thereby beginning the first cotton belt in the United States.[8] This first cotton belt, however, was destined to become restricted due to the delicate nature of the plant. It needed a saline atmosphere and a certain temperature. Hence, the cotton would thrive only from the Georgetown district of coastal South Carolina to the St. Marys River in Georgia. The sea islands were its favorite habitat, and it could be grown successfully no further than 15-30 miles inland from the coast.[9]

In planting sea island cotton, like any other crop, the first requirement was to prepare the land for the seeds. Hence, Couper like the other planters, began in early winter by plowing under the stubble of the previous crop. Shortly thereafter, a manure consisting of rice straw and cane trash, which had been seasoned in the stock pens and mixed with mud from the marshes, was applied to the land and mixed in well with the plow. During the winter the land was plowed and cross-plowed to pulverize it. In the early spring the final plowing was done. In this procedure the fields were marked off in rows of ridges approximately 10 inches high extending in straight lines across the entire field and spaced 4-6 feet apart. The ridge was about 3 feet wide with a smooth, flat surface. Then drainage ditches were dug between the ridges to let off excess amounts of water during a heavy thunderstorm or hurricane. After this was accomplished, a trench was made along the middle of the ridge from 2-4 inches deep. When this was completed the field was ready to receive the seed.[10]

The time of planting came between 1 March and 1 May. However, Couper preferred to plant from 10 March to 10 April. His friend Thomas Spalding of Sapelo Island believed the optimum time to be from 1 April to 15 April. These two men were beyond doubt the foremost scientific agriculturists along the Georgia coast and they felt that extremely early or late planting was hazardous. Early planting invited a freeze, while late planting delayed maturity of the bolls. Experience had taught Couper to plant many more seed to the hill than could grow there. Hence he planted at least one bushel of cotton seed to the acre. For planting, Couper divided his slaves into groups of five each. Two slaves would work along the prepared cotton beds and mark off holes in the ridges at intervals of approximately thirty-six inches to receive the seed. A third slave then sowed the seed while two others covered them. In this last process of covering the seeds Couper used the hoe, but Spalding and a number of other planters in his area felt a slave's foot could accomplish the same result in less time.[11]

Once the young plants came up, the process of thinning the cotton and hoeing the weeds from it became most important. As soon as the plants could be seen above the ground the first hoeing commenced. The hoe was always used on the sea islands, because the plow, which was used for upland cotton, was thought to be injurious to the delicate root system of this coastal variety. Also the hoe was used mainly in the alleys or furrows between, never on the top of the row or cotton bed. Here where the tender plants grew all the grass was picked carefully by hand to avoid bruising the delicate stalks, for once a sea island cotton stalk was bruised it never recovered. The number of hoeings differed with the planter and crop, but usually six were sufficient. They were continued until about the middle of July when the crop was "laid by." To cultivate past this time tended to stimulate growth and thus retard maturation of the cotton bolls. The process of thinning was begun with the second hoeing about two weeks after the crop came up, when the plants were about 4 inches tall or in their "fifth leaf," as Couper liked to express it. At this time the center plants were taken out of each hill. As soon as the remaining plants crowded each other, they were again thinned to about seven plants per hill. A third thinning was then given when the plants closed the spaces between them, and their number was reduced to three or four. At this time a little earth was drawn up around the plants from the furrow to support them. When 6-8 inches high, the plants were thinned to two plants per hill, and when 15-18 inches high, they were reduced to a single stalk.[12]

Another method of enhancing the maturation of the plant besides discontinuing the hoeing was topping. About the middle of August the extreme shoots were nipped off. During the months of August and September, suckers which appeared were removed when from 3-6 inches long. This operation completed the cultivation. The only planters along the Georgia coast who practiced topping were Couper and Spalding. The advantages of topping were earlier, larger bolls, the direction of the sap into the lower branches which were more fruitful, and less dropping of the bolls before maturity. Opponents of topping, however, contended that this process made the cotton grow so thick as to make picking difficult, for slaves with their cotton sacks had problems proceeding down the rows. Both Couper and Spalding apparently were able to live with this difficulty, for both testified to the usefulness of the operation.[13]

Around 1 July, the cotton began to bloom. On the first day the blossom was a delicate yellow, but during the night it changed into a brilliant crimson and on the third day turned to a rich chocolate brown. The fourth day it fell off, leaving a pod already 1/2 inch in diameter. The pods ripened at various intervals from four to six weeks.[14]

About the first of August the cotton pods or bolls, as they are now called, began to open. From this time until the first of December the planter's attention was directed toward picking the cotton as the bolls opened daily. When a "full blow"[15] was achieved the slaves were sent into the fields, each having a portion of the field as his task to pick. Each slave was equipped with a large bag that hung from his neck which he dragged along the ground behind him and into which he deposited the cotton.

Much care was taken to insure that the cotton put into the sacks was as clean as possible, for trash or extraneous matter lowered the grade or quality of the cotton. Each slave was given a large cotton sheet which he spread at the end of one of the rows in his task, or portion, to be picked. When his cotton sack was filled, its contents were emptied onto the open sheet. At the end of the day the cotton was weighed and the amount each slave picked carefully recorded.

If the weather were favorable, each slave was expected to bring in at least 50 pounds of seed cotton during the first picking. However, in subsequent gleanings 25 pounds was the expected quota per hand, and as the season waned 10 pounds was considered a day's work. Picking sea island cotton was a tedious business. The delicate fibre had to be gathered as soon as the bolls opened or it was likely to be injured by dust, wind and rain. Moreover, sea island cotton opened more slowly and over a longer period of time than short staple cotton. Therefore, it required from ten to twelve pickings as compared to three for short staple cotton. The amount of sea island cotton a slave could pick was much less than that harvested by a slave on an upland cotton plantation. For example, numerous accounts from short staple planters show that a prime field hand could be expected to pick 200-600 pounds per day. This discrepancy in the expected amount to be picked was due to the fact that each sea island cotton stalk had fewer bolls than upland cotton and often times refused to open sufficiently for rapid extraction. Also the bulk yield from a sea island cotton field was about half that for the same size field of short staple cotton.[16]

When night came the cotton gathered during the day was transferred to cotton houses where it was kept until the next morning. At that time it was carried out of doors and spread onto drying floors raised upon posts three feet from the ground. The cotton was allowed to dry in this manner for about one day. When dried it was put through a whipper, a barrel made of slats or wire which revolved, allowing sticks, sand, leaves, or other extraneous matter to sift out. When the cotton was thoroughly whipped, it was returned to the cotton house.[17]

The next step in the process of preparing the cotton for market was moting. The cotton was again taken from the cotton house and spread on large wooden frames located out of doors or in an adjacent building. Moting was the process of picking from the cotton with the fingers all the stained cotton, cracked seed or visible specks not removed by the whipper. Great care was necessary in this process not to handle the cotton too much, particularly that it was not pulled or torn apart; otherwise, the staple would be injured and the quality lowered. In the task of moting, a slave could finish 30 pounds of cotton a day.[18]

Next came the ginning process and, contrary to popular opinion, the planters of the sea island cotton kingdom did not use the gin invented by Eli Whitney. The latter was used exclusively for upland cotton. Prior to 1793, the year of Whitney's invention, various gins were already in use in the Bahamas and in Georgia. They all operated on the same principle— two wooden rollers revolving upon each other. In rapid motion, handfuls of cotton were cast upon them and were immediately drawn in. But with no room for the seeds to pass, they were left behind, while the cotton was pulled through and delivered clean on the other side of the rollers. While this worked well in extracting the slick black seed of the sea island variety, the rollers were inept at loosening the hairy green seed of the short staple type which clung tenaciously to the cotton wool. While attending a party at Mulberry Grove, the Savannah River plantation of Mrs. Nathaniel Greene, Whitney listened to a group of upland cotton planters present at the party complain about the existing gins. Within ten days he had con- structed a device that would satisfy their purpose. He added iron combs called saws to loosen the seeds before they hit the rollers. Although this worked for short staple cotton, it was injurious to the sea island variety, for the saws tore the delicate long strands of the latter. Hence, the roller gins continued to be used on the Georgia and South Carolina coast where long staple cotton was grown, while the Whitney saw gin and oth- ers like it mushroomed in their use in middle Georgia and other areas of the short staple cotton kingdom.[19]

The particular gin used by Couper was called Eve's Horse Gin. It was invented by Joseph Eve in the 1780s, in the Bahamas. It was supposed to gin over 200 pounds per day, and by 1796, there were 140 operating in the Bahamas. It could be propelled by a small force either of wind, water, or horsepower, or could be attached to a rice mill, sawmill, or grist mill.[20]

After ginning, the cotton was again returned to the cotton house for the last moting. The newly ginned cotton lint was spread on framed tables resembling a modern billiard table and of about the same height. Slave women walked around it or sometimes sat on stools picking out any crushed seeds, any burnt fibre blackened by the ginning process, or any extraneous matter that had escaped previous searches. Again a slave's goal was thirty pounds per day. After this operation, the cotton was ready to be bagged for market.[21]

Interestingly enough, sea island cotton was not put in square or round bales like short staple cotton. It was not put in bales at all; it was put into bags made of hemp and large enough to hold approximately 300 pounds of compressed cotton. In this last process of packing or bagging the cotton, the method generally involved two men who usually packed two bags a day. The bag was laced around a hoop and suspended through a hole in the packing loft. One of the men got into the bag suspended from the loft, and the other stayed in the loft and funneled the cotton through the loft hole into the bag. The man in the bag packed the lint first with his feet and then used a heavy iron pestle. When this was accomplished the contents of the bag weighed 300 pounds, the cotton was ready to be sent to Savannah and from there to some foreign market.[22]

This tedious process was laborious and costly for the sea island cotton planter. R. F. W. Allston, famous agriculturist in Georgetown District, South Carolina, estimated that it took from fifty to sixty man-days of labor to prepare a bag of the finest sea island cotton after it was made in the field. Another planter estimated that the cost of preparing a bale for market was at least $27.00 while that for upland cotton was only fifty cents. The time-consuming methods of cultivation centering around the use of the hoe instead of the plow, and the laborious pickings and preparations for market severely limited the amount of cotton a planter could plant. Along the sea islands of Georgia and South Carolina the average acreage was 3 1/2 acres per hand. The yield was also low—about half that of short staple cotton. For example, it was common for the burgeoning short staple cotton fields of the Southwest to yield a bale to the acre. But this was rarely possible on the lands of the old long staple cotton kingdom. The usual yield there averaged from one-fourth to one-half bag of lint cotton to the acre, or 250-500 pounds of seed cotton to the acre respectively.

A distinction must be made between seed cotton and lint or ginned cotton. It took at least 1,000 pounds of seed cotton to equal 300 pounds of ginned cotton. Hence, from 1,000 pounds of seed cotton the planter received one bag. For example, James Hamilton Couper's average yield for the period 1818-1837 was only 318.9 pounds of seed cotton per acre or approximately one-third of a bag of ginned cotton. The highest yield was 617.3 pounds of seed cotton per acre in 1828; the lowest was 72 pounds of seed cotton per acre in 1837. The fluctuation in cotton yields was tremendous at Hopeton, the difference between the two extremes being 543.3 pounds of seed cotton per acre. Compared with other planters in his area his yields were about average. One particular problem that plagued Couper at Hopeton was the fact that his land was too fertile for cotton. Thus, in some years the plants would reach the uncommon height of 14 feet. While having luxuriant foliage, they had few bolls. Moreover, in the late fall when the first frost came, he occasionally found his cotton growing and blooming profusely with no mature bolls. In short, being a leguminous plant, cotton on rich lands will go to stalk and not mature bolls, no matter how long the growing season.[23]

One may well wonder why coastal planters planted long staple cotton if the cost of production was so great and the yield so low. Two reasons are paramount—exceptionally high prices and a guaranteed market. However, Couper slowly began to decrease his cotton acreage in the early 1820s, and drastically reduced it toward the end of the decade. This trend continued throughout the 1830s, and by 1840, he grew no cotton at all. This shift was not an isolated case. The same was true of Thomas Spalding, who was considered to be the "master planter" of sea island cotton in Georgia. It was also true of other less well known planters along the Georgia and South Carolina coast.[24]

The first reason for the shift away from cotton at the time was the price. Long staple cotton brought double the price of short staple cotton, and, at the beginning of the nineteenth century, prices were generally lucrative. However, in 1825, the bottom dropped out of the cotton market, and a severe cotton depression followed that lasted until 1837. Then prices improved slightly but did not recover substantially until the prosperity of the 1850s.[25] An examination of Couper's crop records shows that price was directly tied to his cotton production. For example, in 1825, the year the depression began, he planted 516 acres of cotton, but in 1826, he cut his acreage almost in half, planting only a little over 286 acres. The decline in acres continued each succeeding year until 1838, when he produced no cotton.[26] With these low prices, Couper and other sea island planters simply could not make the cotton culture pay. Moreover, the vicissitudes of growing sea island cotton did not diminish; the hazards of a late frost, caterpillars and hurricanes were ever-present dangers. Also, in the late 1820s, partly due to the cotton depression, a sugar craze swept the Georgia coast and numerous planters rushed to reap a profit from a new money crop.[27] And finally, all the while since 1821, James Hamilton Couper had been converting his plantation slowly but surely into a rice plantation. He seemed to realize that his lands were best suited for rice. One thing is clear, however; Couper did not shift from sea island cotton to other staples because of the competition from the productive short staple cotton fields of the Southwest. Indeed, they were two different industries supplying totally different markets. One gave the aristocrat his lace and cambric, the other the common man his shirt.[28]

Notes

[1]J. D. Legare, "Account of an Agricultural Excursion Made into the South of Georgia in the Winter of 1832," *Southern Agriculturist and Register of Rural Affairs* 6 (May-November 1833): 359; J. D. B. De Bow, "Cultivation of the Olive in the Southern States," *De Bow's Review* 3 (March 1847): 265-66.

[2]Charles Spalding Wylly, typescript concerning James Hamilton Couper's entry into planting, Mackay-Stiles Papers, Southern Historical Collection, University of North Carolina Press, Chapel Hill.

[3]James Hamilton Couper Plantation Records, 4 vols. 3:1-54, Southern Historical Collection, University of North Carolina Press, Chapel Hill.

[4]Legare, "Account of Agricultural Excursion," 362-65; James Hamilton Couper Plantation Records, 3:15, 20, 44; 4:59, Southern Historical Collection; R. F. W. Allston, "Rice," *De Bow's Review* 4 (December 1847): 506-11.

[5]Legare, "Account of Agricultural Excursion," 362-65; J. Carlyle Sitterson, *Sugar Country* (Lexington: University of Kentucky Press, 1953) 135.

[6]James Hamilton Couper Plantation Records, 3:1-54, Southern Historical Collection; Thomas Spalding, "Cotton—Its Introduction and Progress of Its Culture in the United States," *Southern Agriculturist and Register of Rural Affairs* 8 (January 1835): 45-46.

[7]E. Merton Coulter, *Thomas Spalding of Sapelo* (Baton Rouge: Louisiana State University Press, 1940) 63-64, 72-73; Lewis Cecil Gray, *History of Agriculture in the Southern United States to 1860* 2 vols. (Washington DC: Carnegie Inistitution, 1933) 2:731; Ulrich Bonnell Phillips, *Life and Labor in the Old South* (New York NY: Grosset and Dunlap, 1929) 91.

[8]Spalding, "Cotton," 35-38; Coulter, *Thomas Spalding*, 65-69; US Department of Agriculture, "The Sea Island Cotton of the South, Its History, Characteristics, Cultivation, Etc.," *De Bow's Review, After the War Series* 3 (January 1867): 84; *Savannah Georgia Gazette*, 7, 21 February 1793. On file at the Georgia Historical Society, Savannah GA; John Couper, "On the Origin of Sea Island Cotton," *Southern Agriculturist and Register of Rural Affairs* 4 (May 1831): 242-45; Thomas Spalding, "On the Introduction of Sea Island Cotton into Georgia,"

Southern Agriculturist and Register of Rural Affairs 4 (March 1831): 133. Others besides Spalding experimenting with the introduction of sea island cotton into Georgia were Alexander Bisset, Richard Leake, Josiah Tattnal, Nicholas Turnbull, and Francis Levitt.

[9]Spalding, "Cotton," 39-46; Gray, *History of Agriculture*, 2:731, 733; US Department of Agriculture, "Sea Island Cotton of the South," *De Bow's Review, After the War Series* 3 January 1867: 84.

[10]Legare, "Account of Agricultural Excursion," 460-61; James Hamilton Couper Plantation Records, 3:1, 10, Southern Historical Collection; Spalding, "Cotton," 39-40; Gray, *History of Agriculture*, 2:675-77, 734-35; Ulrich Bonnell Phillips, *American Negro Slavery* (New York NY: D. Appleton and Co., 1918) 153; James C. Bonner, *A History of Georgia Agriculture, 1732-1860* (Athens: University of Georgia Press, 1964) 51.

[11]Legare, "Account of Agricultural Excursion," 461-62; James Hamilton Couper Plantation Records, 3:10-15, 34, 38, Southern Historical Collection; William Allister Noble, "Sequent Occupance of Hopeton-Altama, 1816-1956" (Master's thesis, University of Georgia, 1956) 65; Spalding, "Cotton," 40-41; William Henry Capers, "On the Culture of Sea Island Cotton," *Southern Agriculturist and Register of Rural Affairs* 8 (August 1835): 402-407.

[12]Manuscript concerning Couper's 1820 cotton crop, Margaret Davis Cate Collection, Georgia Historical Society, Savannah GA; Legare, "Account of Agricultural Excursion," 462; James Hamilton Couper Plantation Records, 3:10, 30, Southern Historical Collection; Capers, "On the Culture of Sea Island Cotton," 407-408; Spalding, "Cotton," 40-42; Gray, *History of Southern Agriculture*, 2:734-35.

[13]Capers, "On the Culture of Sea Island Cotton," 408; Legare, "Account of Agricultural Excursion," 463, 465-66; Coulter, *Thomas Spalding*, 71; James Hamilton Couper Plantation Records, 3:24, Southern Historical Collection.

[14]Spalding, "Cotton," 42.

[15]A "full blow" was the term used when enough cotton bolls had opened sufficiently to warrant the first picking.

[16]Captain Basil Hall, *Travels in North America, 1827-1828* 3 vols. (Edinburgh, Scotland: Cadell and Company, 1829) 3:220; Gray, *History of Agriculture*, 2:702-703, 735; Spalding, "Cotton," 42-43, Capers, "On the Culture of Sea Island Cotton," 408-409; "Sea Island Cotton of the South," *De Bow's Review, After the War Series* 3 (January 1867): 85; Phillips, *American Negro Slavery*, 154.

[17]Spalding, "Cotton," 43-44.

[18]Capers, "On the Culture of Sea Island Cotton," 411; R. F. W. Allston, "Sea Coast Crops of the South," *De Bow's Review* 16 (June 1854): 598.

[19]Hall, *Travels*, 3:211; Coulter, *Thomas Spalding*, 63-64, 72; Phillips, *American Negro Slavery*, 156-57; Spalding , "Cotton," 44, 82-83; Allston, "Sea Coast Crops of the South," 597.

[20]Coulter, *Thomas Spalding*, 161-62; *Savannah Georgia Gazette*, 21 April 1796.

[21]Spalding, "Cotton," 45; "Ginning and Packing Cotton" (manuscript account of Couper's ginning and bagging [packing] of cotton at Hopeton), Mackay Stiles Papers, Southern Historical Collection, University of North Carolina Chapel Hill; Legare, "Account of Agricultural Excursion,"161-62, 465.

[22]"Ginning and Packing Cotton," Mackay Stiles Papers; Capers, "On the Cultivation of Sea Island Cotton," 412.

[23]Gray, *History of Agriculture*, 2:736-37; James Hamilton Couper Plantation Records, 3:1, 54, Southern Historical Collection; Noble, "Sequent Occupance of Hopeton-Altama," 52.

[24]Coulter, *Thomas Spalding*, 73, 75.

[25]Gray, *History of Agriculture*, 2:697-98, 738; Bonner, *History of Georgia Agriculture*, 56-57, 73.

[26]James Hamilton Couper Plantation Records, 3:1-54, Southern Historical Collection.

[27]Bonner, *History of Georgia Agriculture*, 57, 73, 83-84; Spalding "Cotton," 40-41.

CHAPTER VI

Sugar Cane

Sugar cane cultivation spread to the South Atlantic coast in the 1820s, as a direct result of the success of the Louisiana sugar plantations and because certain planters, like Couper, sought to promote diversification and looked for a third crop to plant with cotton and rice.[1] The cultivation of sugar cane for the purpose of making sugar is limited in the United States geographically to three separate areas. The first is the area in Louisiana extending northward to the city of Alexandria on the Red River. The second is the Atlantic coast including the states of Florida, Georgia, and lower South Carolina. The last is the area of Texas in the region of the Brazos and Colorado River valleys.[2] Actually, none of these regions is ideally suited for sugar cane cultivation because the plant needs a year-round average temperature of seventy-five degrees Fahrenheit with at least sixty inches of rainfall a year and abundant sunshine together with fertile soil. However, in the above semi-tropical areas its cultivation was possible, and with hard work, good management and luck, fortunes could be made.[3]

Sugar culture was first introduced into North America by the French and Spanish in Louisiana, but it did not become an important crop until 1794, when Etienne de Bore, a New Orleans Creole, produced a crop of sugar of the Creole variety which he sold for $12,000. Sugar cane had been an important crop in the West Indies prior to this time, and it was its success there that prompted de Bore to experiment with it on a large scale.[4]

In 1806, the culture spread to the Atlantic seaboard. In that year Thomas Spalding received his first stalks from his neighbor, John Couper, who had some plants growing in his garden on St. Simons Island. The cane stalks Spalding received from Couper were of the Otaheite variety, first brought by a Lieutenant Blight to Louisiana in 1797, from the island of Otaheite (Tahiti). Spalding planted the canes, saved the seed, and the next year was able to plant 1 1/2 acres. For several years before, Spalding had been interested in sugar culture and felt that the climate of southern Georgia was as conducive to cane as that of Louisiana. From 1805-1813, Spalding continued to experiment with the culture and each year extended his acreage. Finally, in 1814, he produced a crop that grossed $12,500.[5]

In the same year that Spalding made his impressive crop, a new variety of sugar cane was introduced that would greatly enhance the sugar industry in the United States. In 1814, John McQueen of Savannah brought the ribbon cane from Jamaica and distributed it to some of his friends in Georgia, where it replaced both the Creole and Otaheite varieties. Ribbon cane received its name from its striped appearance. One type had a green and yellow stalk, while another had a green, and red, blue or purple stalk. This new variety grew rapidly and ripened earlier than the Creole or Otaheite, and its thicker bark increased its resistance to cold. In 1825, John J. Coiron, a former resident of Savannah, introduced the plant on his plantation at Terreaux-Beoufs in St. Bernard Parish, Louisiana. Coiron received the cane transported by schooner from Savannah to New Orleans and sent to him by his friend, Roswell King of St. Simons Island. Here, as in Georgia, ribbon cane became the dominant variety, replacing all others.[6]

By the late 1820s, sugar culture was expanding in Georgia due to low cotton prices and success stories from Louisiana. Along the Altamaha River those most closely connected with it were Pierce Butler of Hampton Point plantation, Jordan Wood of Potoir, and James Hamilton Couper of Hopeton. Of these, Couper was the last to pursue the culture. The years when sugar cane was most important at Hopeton were 1829-1836. Couper first grew cane in 1825, when 5½ acres were planted. His crop records show no sugar production, so it must be assumed that the product was turned into syrup for home consumption. The next year 3½ acres were planted in cane, but again there was no record of a yield. In 1827, he planted cane on nineteen acres, and, as before, the product was unrecorded. It is likely that Couper was experimenting during these years to determine whether to include sugar cane as one of his major staples. By 1828, however, he seems to have been convinced of its profitability, for his record shows that in that year he planted 48 acres from which he received 5411 pounds of sugar and 650 gallons of molasses. During the next few years the amount of land devoted to sugar cane constantly increased.[7]

The cultivation of sugar cane with the idea of producing sugar called for a well-disciplined agricultural program with meticulous scheduling. Time was of paramount importance. For the sugar farmer almost every day in the year was filled with the ritual of sugar production.

The first step was careful preparation of the land. In early winter fields were sub-divided into plots of two acres each to facilitate harvest and to provide work division for the slaves. Drainage ditches criss-crossed the network and emptied into canals that led into a nearby river, bayou, or inland swamp. The whole area was plowed deep to pulverize the soil and then harrowed smooth. The plows were utilized again to lay off the plots into beds or ridges in which the cane would be planted. The ridges (rows) were generally low, rising about 4-5 inches in height and flat on top. A trench two inches deep was opened in the center of the row and cane stalks of about two feet in length were laid in the center of the ridge so that they touched each other and formed a complete line of seed cane. Some planters preferred to construct a wider bed that would accomodate two lines of cane stalks instead of one. In this case the lines of cane within the ridge would be spaced from 2-4 inches apart. Also, in this method, the stalks would not touch end to end but had a space of about one half of a cane stalk between them. The canes, whether planted in single or double file, were then covered with 1-2 inches of dirt and packed thoroughly.[8]

There was some debate between Louisiana and Atlantic coast planters as to the proper distance between rows. Louisiana planters had long advocated rows with alleys of from 2 1/2 to 4 feet between them. They claimed that "narrow rows" resulted in larger tonnage and a greater quantity of sugar. However, Atlantic coast planters advocated a wider alley between rows. Thomas Spalding, the dean of sugar planters in that area, set the practice in 1814, on the Atlantic coast by having his rows spaced 5-8 feet apart, depending on the richness of the soil. This "wider row" allowed more air and sun to reach the cane which was so necessary to the maturing of the plant. Moreover, Atlantic coast planters pointed out that the extra tonnage brought about by narrow rows required more labor in harvesting and that the additional weight or cane bulk received was due to a larger proportion of water than sugar. Atlantic coastal planters found that cane did better in rows spaced widely apart; it matured quicker resulting in a high sugar content. By the 1840s, the trend toward the wider row was becoming more popular and the Louisiana planters accepted the dictum. Valcour Aime, a well known Louisiana planter from St. James Parish, felt that the change to the wider row was one of the most significant recent advances in sugar culture, for the slaves could then do with the plow what they had done previously with the hoe.[9]

Another difference on the cane culture on the Atlantic Coast and in Louisiana was in the time of planting and the method of saving seed. Spalding on the Georgia Coast had early established the practice of fall planting. This was an outgrowth of the fact that Spalding had trouble saving seed to plant in January or February. When he followed the practices in Louisiana or the West Indies, he lost his cane. Hence, he experimented with the idea of planting his cane crop as soon as it was cut. In 1813, he began planting on 20 October and continued to plant as rapidly as possible until he had his whole crop in the ground. By this method he did not "lose one plant in a thousand." The only difficulties with this system, however, were that he was pressed for time and labor shortage was a problem. This was the busiest time of the year, for, from October to December, the cane must be cut, hauled from the field and made into sugar. To alleviate this problem Spalding devised a method of saving seed somewhat different from that used in Louisiana. He devised the "standing mattress" to preserve the cane until spring planting. Into the middle of each field intended for spring planting, he would place enough cane to plant it (a single acre of cut cane could plant 20 acres). He would make a long stack fourteen feet wide and as high as the cane would make it. The cane was stood upright, butts down. When the stack was finished, he would throw dirt mixed with cane blades to the sides nearly to the top. The stack stood this way until about 20 December. Then 2-3 inches of dirt were thrown over the top of the stacks. The reason for not doing this earlier was that heat generated by the green cane would cause the buds to sprout in the stack and materially damage the cane.[10] Spalding's method of planting and preserving cane soon became widely accepted on the Atlantic coast.

In Louisiana planting was usually done in January or February. Hence, mattressing was quite prevalent there; the canes were laid flat in piles and covered with dirt. Spalding found that this would not work in Georgia for the heat generated in the green stack greatly damaged the buds. Louisiana planters hesitated to plant in the fall, contending that the seed cane frequently rotted in the ground. This, however, was most likely due to improper drainage, as Spalding found canes would not rot on well-drained land. Also, James Hamilton Couper counseled that planting too deep would cause cane seed to rot. Seed cane should be planted no deeper than 1-1 1/2 inches.[11]

Another method of preserving seed cane was the practice known as windrowing. This came into vogue on the Atlantic coast by 1830, and was the method most often used by Couper. Indeed, by the mid-thirties this method had replaced the "standing mattress" in Georgia. Windrowing was the practice of placing the cane in trenches in the fields and covering it to a depth of 3-4 inches as soon as it had been cut in the fall. The leaves stuck out and formed a thatch over the canes. They remained in this position until spring.[12] It is interesting to note that, although windrowing was first devised as a practice in 1828, by John Anderson of Houmas plantation in Louisiana, the local planters were slow to accept it. Not until the 1840s, a decade after its acceptance in Georgia, did the practice gain any degree of acceptance in Louisiana. Given the numerous instances of cane spoiling in mattresses from dry and wet rot, it is puzzling that Louisiana growers did not follow the example of Georgia planters in preserving their cane in windrows, the accepted method today. By the 1850s, a few Louisiana farmers were windrowing cane with success, but it was not until the decade following the Civil War that the method became general in that region. In all probability this was due to the exodus of cane planters from the destroyed plantations of the Atlantic coast to the Louisiana area where cane could be grown more profitably.[13]

Still another difference between these two sugar-producing regions was the ratooning of cane. In both Georgia and Louisiana, after cane was planted the first year and harvested, the stubble was left in the ground and allowed to come up again in the spring from the roots. Sugar cane is a perennial plant and will sprout from the roots every year if allowed to do so. Hence, cane grown from the previous year's planting was known as ratoon cane. However, in both regions planters noticed that each successive crop harvested without replanting was inferior to the former, and this inferiority increased with each year cane was ratooned. In Louisiana, cane generally was replanted after the third year, giving after the initial planting two ratoon crops. Some planters even allowed the cane to ratoon a third year. But in Georgia planters replanted every other year, allowing the cane to ratoon only once. Like other planters in his region, Couper found that because of their particular soils and climate ratoons were not as profitable as in Louisiana.[14]

In the spring, when the ground became warm and the danger of frost was over, the cane joints sprouted and sent up their green shoots. The first plowing and hoeing of the crop came in the early spring when the first grass appeared. The rows were plowed to stimulate growth, and the tops of the beds were hoed or hand-picked free of grass. After two weeks the operation was repeated. These plowings and hoeings were continued until the plants were 3 1/2-4 feet high. After that time, they were left alone because further plowing retarded the maturation of the crop, and weeds and grasses had ceased to become a problem because of the luxuriant growth of the cane. No further attention was given the cane until harvest time, and the crop was said to be "laid by" or made.[15]

During the spring and early summer, Couper generally flooded his cane fields at least twice, or more often if the fields became dry. But from August until harvest time he kept the fields as dry as possible. This was the time when the cane matured and too much water would retard sweetness.[16]

Fall of the year was the busiest time on a sugar plantation, for the cane had to be harvested and the juice expressed and processed into sugar by the end of December. Cutting began around the middle or last of October. Gangs of Negroes were sent into the fields to strip off the leaves. Others cut the canes within a few inches of the ground and severed the unripe buds from the top of the cane stalks. As the canes were cut, they were put into piles. At Hopeton it was the rule for slaves to have some free time in the afternoons, but this was suspended during rolling time. The crop had to be cut and ground before the first hard freeze. If the weather remained moderate the pace was regular but not hurried, and the slaves worked all day instead of finishing at 3:00 P.M. as they usually did. But, with the first hint of cold weather the whole operation went into high gear and all available slaves were sent into the fields to windrow the cane to prevent it from being damaged by the cold. On occasion, if a freeze were imminent, the slaves were required to work a shift every third night. It was the rule on most plantations in both Georgia and Louisiana to have the slaves work on Sunday during this period of intense activity from October through December. However, Hopeton was the exception in this case. Only on rare instances did Couper ask his slaves to work on Sunday, and this was done when a freeze threatened to destroy the cane crop. During rolling time at Hopeton work usually stopped at midnight on Saturday, and Sunday was reserved for rest and worship.[17]

The Negroes usually welcomed the coming of harvest season. Work was hard and steady but not without certain gaieties of life that attended the whole operation. They enjoyed the hustle and bustle of the occasion and sensed their added importance at this crucial time. They went about their work busily, oftentimes singing and chewing cane. Sugar planters generally found that their slaves worked better, seemed happier and healthier during the grinding period than at any other time in the year. Couper observed that at no other time were his slaves in better general health or more cheerfully disposed to work. Spalding wrote that "the health of the gangs of Negroes employed, is much greater in this species of cultivation than in any other." Also, typical of prosperous Louisiana planters were Valcour Aime and Dr. John P. R. Stone, who noted similar responses in their records.[18]

One of the main problems in the cane harvest was transporting the cut cane from the field. This was an expensive and time-consuming operation. To help alleviate the problem some planters constructed railroads on their plantations. Two of the first to do so were James Hamilton Couper of Hopeton and Madame Poefaire of St. James Parish, Louisiana, both of whom had railroads in operation by 1830. Couper constructed nearly two miles of movable wooden rails at the cost of $100 per mile. Horse-drawn carts moved along the rails, transporting the cane to the canal where it was loaded onto large rice flatboats and taken to the mill which was situated near the banks of the canal. Madame Poefaire' had one main permanent rail line made of iron running through the middle of her plantation leading to her sugar mill. Portable wooden feeder lines connected to the main line supplied the cane from various fields that was then transported to the mill. By the 1840s, many sugar planters with large plantations had constructed horse-drawn rail lines on their property.[19]

As early as 1814, John Couper had built a sugar mill on his plantation at Cannon's Point, but his losses during the war with the British prevented him from proceeding with the sugar culture. The mill remained unused until 1825 when his son, James Hamilton Couper, repaired it to grind cane he did not use for seed. This mill was used by Couper until 1830. Since 1825, the first year he planted cane, Couper had steadily increased his acreage, and several years of experience in the culture had convinced him that sugar cane could be grown profitably at Hopeton. Consequently, he decided to build a more modern sugar plantation. Couper began by giving the matter intensive study. He engaged in voluminous correspondence with sugar makers in Louisiana, the West Indies and Europe to decide what type of mill he should construct. He studied many drawings of different mill designs and in 1829, he began the construction of his own mill. It was completed in 1830, and used for the first time in the fall of that year.[20]

Couper's new sugar mill was quite elaborate and was reported at that time to have been "the finest ever erected in Georgia and equal to any in the West Indies or Louisiana." It was made of tabby, which was a common building material along the Georgia coast, although in Louisiana most mills, even as late as the 1850s, were made of wood. Also, in Georgia the sugar mill and boiling kettles were usually in separate but adjacent houses; in Louisiana and the West Indies they were always housed under the same roof. Couper visited Louisiana, Jamaica and British Guinea, and since his mill was patterned after designs he saw in those locations, his mill and kettles were housed together.[21]

The sugar mill was the universal instrument used for extracting the juice from the cane. There were two kinds of mills—those powered by horse, mule or oxen and those relying upon steam power. By 1830, a majority of the mills in Louisiana were still animal-powered and it was rare indeed to find one of steam along the Atlantic coast. Thomas Spalding and Pierce Butler, two of Couper's principal sugar-producing neighbors, had mills driven in the typical manner by animal power; Couper's used steam. The sugar mill consisted of three rollers, made of wood or iron, turning upon each other. They were fluted to hold the cane firmly as the turning motion drew in the cane. The cane was fed into the mill by hand. The usual size of the rollers was 30-40 inches in length and 20-25 inches in diameter. Couper, however, constructed rollers 60 inches long and 28 inches in diameter. Quite frequently the smaller rollers were rotated too fast, not leaving the cane under pressure long enough. Couper enlarged the size to solve this problem. His roller revolved five times per minute and expressed 1000-1200 gallons of juice per hour, while Spalding's horsepowered mill expressed a maximum of 300-360 gallons per hour.[22]

The cost of the sugar establishment, of course, varied with the individual and region. The average cost of an animal-powered mill in both Georgia and Louisiana was around $1000. This was the cost of Spalding's which had the regular wooden rollers. Pierce Butler's mill, however, was equipped with iron rollers and cost $2500. In Louisiana in 1831, the average cost of a steam-powered establishment was $4500. Couper's, however, cost $21,984.67.[23]

The size and shape of the sugar structure varied as much as its cost. In Georgia most of the mills, like those of Spalding and Butler, were octagonal in shape due to the fact that the structure housed vertical rollers around which a team of four horses moved. Hence, the movement of the horses around the rollers perhaps suggested the polygonal construction. In the West Indies and Louisiana, however, the mills, whether run by steam or animal power, were normally rectangular in shape. The typical Louisiana sugar house was a two-story building 100-160 feet long and 50-60 feet wide. The Georgia sugar house was normally much smaller. However, Couper patterned his sugar works after those in Louisiana and the West Indies. His facility's dimensions were 39 feet in width and 240 feet in length. The height of the two-story building was 26 feet from floor to rafters with three chimneys from the boiling room rising to a height of 50 feet.[24]

The steam engine was imported from Liverpool, manufactured by Bolton and Watt. It was 15 horse-power and was used to drive the rice threshing and pounding mills when not used for grinding cane.[25]

The process of manufacturing sugar was a complicated one. The cane was transported on flats by way of the canal and deposited in a pile in front of the sugar house which was located near the canal. From there the cane was placed neatly in cane carts running on wooden rails and propelled up an inclined plane to the mill house which was slightly elevated. The carts were drawn up the plane by a rope wound around a drum. When the cart arrived at the mill door, the canes were deposited into a hopper and the cart was allowed to descend on another rail that returned it close to its original starting point. In the meantime another cart had been filled and the process continued. The cane in the hopper was then placed onto a "cane carrier" which was a wooden trough which served to convey the canes into the rollers which expressed the juice. When this was accomplished, the expressed cane stalk leavings or "bagasse" was conveyed into little rail cars. At the same time the juice fell into a wider pan beneath the rollers called a millbed.[26]

The juice then was transferred by wooden spouts into four large receivers or vats which held several hundred gallons each. At the end of the spouts sieves of fine brass wire were placed to strain the coarser impurities from the juice. The receivers held the large amounts of raw, squeezed cane juice. After being heated in the receivers, the juice made its way through copper spouts into kettles for the final cooking stage.

Usually a sugar mill had only two such receivers to service four kettles, an arrangement common in both Georgia and Louisiana. However, because of the scale of the Hopeton establishment, four receivers were needed, since the Couper works had two sets of kettles with six kettles to each set instead of the usual four, making a combined grouping of twelve kettles and four receivers. Also, in Georgia and Louisiana the receivers were generally made of wood—Couper's were made of copper. And instead of having one furnace, he had three. Essentially, Couper had two mills in one.[27]

While the juice remained in the receivers it went through a process known as clarification or purification. This process began when lime was added to the raw juice. A dedicated furnace heated the juice in the receivers to a temperature of 200 degrees Fahrenheit until it bubbled and frothed, a condition called "yawing." At this point the fire was checked and the solution was not allowed to boil. The scum or foam, which appeared on the surface and contained impurities, was ladled off. This was called skimming. When this stage was completed and if the juice had been purified properly, the liquid would be of a clear amber color.[28]

The next stage in the process of making sugar was to boil the juice so that the water would be evaporated and the saccharine[29] content in the juice would granulate into sugar crystals. For this process the juice was conveyed by copper pipes into what would normally have been four kettles. However, in this case twelve iron kettles held stationary in heavy masonry were used. Not until all twelve boilers were filled was the fire kindled in the kettles' furnace. The purified juice then boiled for approximately one to two hours. The boiling process was the most crucial and precarious point in the entire sugar-making process, for there was no set rule as to how long the juice should boil or at what point it would granulate; the answers to these questions depended on the quality of the cane (saccharine content) and on the degree of ripeness. This knowledge only came from experience. If the syrup was not boiled long enough it would not granulate when cooled, but if boiled too much, the sugar would be of inferior quality. Many failures resulted from this uncertainty, and to acquire a reputation as a "good sugar-boiler" was a distinction for both slave and planter.[30] In any event, two methods could be employed to determine the quality and readiness of the syrup. One way was to dip a heavy copper spoon with wooden handle into one of the kettles and if, when it was drawn out, the syrup covering it was thick and had a "grained appearance," it was said to be sufficiently boiled. Yet another way was to put a little of the syrup on the thumb and press it with the forefinger. If, when the fingers were separated, the syrup drew into a thread and broke dry, the boiling was said to be good.[31]

When the boiling was completed, the thick sugarproof syrup (syrup ready to crystallize into sugar) was piped into coolers made of cypress wood measuring 6-7 feet long, 4-5 feet wide, and 12-14 inches deep. Since there were usually six coolers to a set of kettles, Couper had twelve. The cooling process took from six to fourteen hours, the syrup granulating into sugar crystals as it cooled.[32]

When granulation had taken place, the "thick turbid mass" combined with its molasses was conveyed into the draining or curing room by wooden buckets or tubs. On most sugar plantations in Georgia and Louisiana, it took two men to carry each of these 5-8 gallon containers to the next room. However, Couper utilized his railroad for that purpose, and movable wooden rails located inside the sugar establishment conveyed the tubs placed in carts to their next destination.[33]

In the draining room there were slatted beams elevated over two inclined planes which projected a funnel-like appearance. The sugar mass was emptied from the buckets into hogsheads of 1000 pounds capacity which were placed on top of the wooden beams. Several auger holes were made in each barrel and plugged with cane stalks or bullrushes. When the sugar mass had hardened sufficiently or "set up," which took from one to two days, the canes or reeds were withdrawn and the molasses slowly drained from the hogsheads into the triangular inclined plane below. From there the molasses emptied into two large cisterns holding 7000 gallons each and located below ground level. Because of the size of Couper's establishment, his cisterns were larger than those of the other sugar planters along the Georgia coast. Spalding's molasses cisterns, for instance, held 2000 gallons each.[34]

In the same room but constructed above the sugar hogsheads were slatted rafters just like those below. Here were placed empty molasses hogsheads. The molasses which collected in the cisterns below ground was pumped to this high elevation and filled the barrels in assembly-line fashion. Then they were sealed and ready for market. This double-decker curing room held 350 hogsheads of sugar and the same number of molasses barrels holding 31 1/2 gallons each. Gangways were constructed on both levels from which the sugar and molasses kegs were rolled down to the canal, which meandered by the sugar house. Most sugar, when it had been drained of its molasses for three or four months, was ready for market. However, the finer sugars were ready in from four to six weeks. From forty to fifty-five gallons of molasses were drained from each hogshead.[35]

It is evident from examining Couper's detailed sketches of his sugar works and reading his comments concerning it that for a few years the process of sugar production occupied a great deal of his time and thought. Without a doubt his sugar works, when finished in 1830, was the most impressive establishment of its kind on the Atlantic coast. In a number of ways he was more progressive than most planters in Georgia and Louisiana. He was one of the first planters in either state to use bagasse in conjunction with wood to fuel his furnaces. By the 1840s, and 1850s, however, this practice gradually began to catch on, particularly in Louisiana. In 1854, it was greatly accelerated by Mose Thompson of Jefferson Parish, Louisiana, who developed a new furnace for burning wet bagasse. His invention was successful, and by the end of the decade the use of bagasse became quite acceptable as an alternative to wood and coal. But in the early 1830s, Couper was utilizing the idea at Hopeton. In addition, he developed a method of saving time and expense by deleting one of the recognized steps in the process of making sugar. It was customary after grinding to run the raw cane juice into wooden receivers to clarify or purify the juice by adding lime. Then when the solution was thoroughly mixed, it was piped into the "grande," the largest of the kettles. The juice was then heated to a temperature of 200 degrees Fahrenheit until the impurities rose to the top as foam or scum, to be skimmed off. Couper, however, combined these two steps into one, cleverly saving precious time in the busiest of seasons. Instead of wood receivers, he had copper, so that instead of running the juice and lime solution into the "grande" for heating, he could heat the mixture in the receivers. Hence, the juice was clarified in one operation instead of two, and the juice was then ready to be sent into all the kettles for the next step of boiling. The time saved was significant. For example, normally it took more than five hours to reduce the raw juice to a condition of sugarproof syrup; Couper by deleting one step, was able to produce syrup of sugarproof in a little over three hours.[36]

In like manner Couper was the only sugar planter on the Atlantic coast ever to construct so elaborate a plant with three furnaces and two sets of kettles of six kettles each. Usually there was only one furnace and one set of kettles, with only four kettles to the set. And even in Louisiana, the principal sugar-producing area in the country, an establishment of these proportions was not common.[37]

Moreover, Couper saved time and labor by constructing a railroad on his plantation. It was utilized, among other ways, in transporting the cane from the field which would have been otherwise a back-breaking task. What is more unusual and quite novel was his use of movable rails inside his sugar establishment to cart the granulated syrup from the cooling room into the curing room for drainage, perhaps the first evidence of such an innovation in the history of sugar culture in the United States.[38]

In addition, Couper deviated from the practice prevalent in both Georgia and Louisiana of having separate curing rooms for both crystallized sugar and molasses. Departing from the standard practice Couper had only one room—the molasses hogsheads being located just above the sugar hogsheads on elevated rafters or beams. The object in this arrangement was to save space, and in Couper's words, "give more air to the cooling—to admit the laying of rails in the most advantageous manner from the cooling vats to the hogsheads in the curing room—and to adapt it to the course of a canal, which runs parallel to the length of the building."[39]

In May 1831, after trying his mill out for the first time in the fall of the previous year, Couper summed up his opinion of his sugar establishment by saying that "the performance of every part of it was satisfactory." He further commented that in his opinion it "combined economy and simplicity with rapidity of execution, in a greater degree than any other offered as a substitute; it may be received as the best, for the purposes of the planter, of any as yet sanctioned by experience."[40]

Couper tried in 1829 to construct one of the most modern, up-to-date sugar establishments in the United States for his time, and he succeeded. However, before long progress would render it obsolete, for Couper used the open kettle system by which the juice was cooked in open kettles. Much heat was lost in this process, thereby lengthening the time of boiling. It was only a year after Couper completed his sugar works that Thomas Morgan of Plaquemines Parish, Louisiana, introduced on his plantation a new method of boiling cane juice. Instead of cooking the juice in open kettles as had always been customary, he cooked it in a vacuum pan, an idea he borrowed from Europe. His first attempt was quite successful, producing more sugar of better quality, resulting in a higher price, than the older method. However, the planters in the sugar-producing districts were slow to adopt this new practice. It remained for Norbert Rillieux, a brilliant Creole Negro, to improve upon it and perfect it to the point that the vacuum pan system eventually replaced the old method of using open kettles.[41]

Sugar yields were determined by a number of factors including the suitability of the land, effectiveness of the sugar manufacture, saccharine richness of the juice, and the experience of the planter in the culture. Prior to the introduction of the steam mill, an output of 800-1000 pounds per acre was considered average; after steam was introduced the average was set at 1500 pounds.[42]

Despite Couper's elaborate sugar works and his devotion to the culture, his fields did not produce abundant yields of sugar. For example, in 1828, the 48 acres he planted in sugar cane yielded 5411 pounds of sugar and 650 gallons of molasses, an average of only 113 pounds of sugar per acre. Over the next three years his acreage increased dramatically, until 1831, when he secured 166,061 pounds of sugar and 14,735 gallons of molasses from 376 acres in cultivation. This was his largest product and the largest number of acres of cane ever planted at Hopeton. After 1833, when 311 acres were planted in cane, the amount of land planted in that crop dropped off. Although a few acres were cultivated for home consumption as late as 1840 and 1841, no cane was grown for market. During his peak period of sugar production, 1828-1839, the average yield per acre was only 374 pounds, and the highest, attained in 1835, was just 718 pounds.[43]

Even compared to his neighbors, Couper's yield was not impressive, and in comparison to Louisiana planters it was miserable. For example, in 1814 Major Pierce Butler produced 140,000 pounds of sugar from 110 acres on his Hampton Point plantation. Ten acres was put up for seed and some dwarf cane was not fit for the mill. Therefore, his per-acre yield amounted to about 1400 pounds.[44] Moreover, in 1824, Roswell King Jr., managing the same plantation for Butler's grandson, Pierce Mease Butler, produced thirty nine hogsheads of 1200 pounds each from 56 acres, an average of 835 pounds per acre—and this was the year of the hurricane that destroyed so many crops along the Georgia coast.[45] And, in 1814, Thomas Spalding planted 80 acres from which he secured a yield of 644 pounds per acre.[46] The next year, he planted 184 acres from which he succeeded in getting only 500 pounds to the acre.[47] But collectively, a score of planters in the Altamaha region averaged 961 pounds of sugar per acre for the ten-year period 1815-1825.[48] From 1820-1840, the average yield in Georgia was 850 pounds of sugar and 45 gallons of molasses per acre.[49]

These low yields experienced by Couper were due substantially to two main reasons—climate and suitability of land. It is apparent from examining Couper's plantation records that the climate of the Georgia coast was not conducive to sugar cultivation. Typical of his entries were: 1829, "heavy rains in March and cold weather in April injured the cane, and the spring altogether most unfavorable;" in 1830, "a dry summer and fall checked the growth of the cane... A very severe black frost on the 21st of December froze the cane of about forty acres of standing cane, and rendered it necessary to grind them into syrup."[50] Georgia's weather is most fickle. Excessive and unexpected rains, droughts, and cold weather, plus the hurricane menace took their toll and depleted the profits of sugar planters.[51] Moreover, the second reason, suitability of soils, was of even more consequence to the sugar planter in Georgia than the weather.[52] What Couper and the other planters did not fully realize was that their lands were working against them. The alluvial delta lands of numerous coastal rivers of Georgia were fertile, but when planted in cane their richness went to stalk, making tall, luxuriant plants, but with little sucrose content.[53] Couper had witnessed this same phenomenon when planting sea island cotton.[54]

The *Southern Review* of Charleston gave a bleak view of the future of sugar production on the Atlantic coast when its editor wrote in 1829:

It cannot be concealed that from some peculiarity of soil or climate there has been great difficulty in procuring sugar of good quality from the cane along the Atlantic border of the Southern States. If a few have succeeded, many have failed. Sugar makers from the Mississippi have been brought to the Altamaha, and have disappointed their employers; planters from the West Indies have not been more successful. While syrup, molasses, rum, have been produced in great quantities sugar has been but sparingly obtained. Hence has arisen a common opinion in the country, that the juice of the cane is too weak to yield sugar advantageously in our climate.[55]

Unsuitable soils and climate were not the only factors discouraging Georgia sugar planters. The protective tariff and the price growers received for raw sugar greatly influenced their decision to abandon the culture. By 1840, the sugar craze that had swept the Atlantic coast in the two preceding decades had ended.

Many Southerners did not like the idea of protective tariffs, for in many instances they saw themselves selling their agricultural products in an unprotected market and buying manufactured articles in a protected one. However, sugar, because of the competition from Cuba and the West Indies, was one of the few agricultural staples to receive protection. And it was the general consensus among sugar planters that without such protection their industry would be doomed. Hence, the three cents per pound duty levied on foreign raw sugar in 1816, which continued until 1832, provided ample encouragement to Southern cane growers, and the sugar industry experienced sixteen years of profitable expansion. But the tariff of 1832 lowered rates on foreign sugar imported into the United States by half a cent per pound, making foreign competition easier. And in 1833, a new tariff further reduced the rate of protection over an eight-year period culminating in a much lower rate by 1841. This action, taken in 1833, did not immediately affect the sugar growers adversely because of the graduated nature of the tariff. But, by 1838-1840, they began to feel the pinch. It was during this time that many planters along the Atlantic coast began their wholesale abandonment of sugar cane as a marketable commodity.[56] However, an examination of Couper's cane production shows that he began to abandon sugar culture in the mid-1830s, presumably in response to changes in the tariff. For in 1834, the year after the passage of the Compromise Tariff, he reduced his acreage drastically. In 1833, 311 acres were planted in cane at Hopeton, but in 1834, only 165 1/2 acres were planted. He continually reduced his acreage over the next several years until, in 1841, he only planted 40 acres of cane and this was only for home consumption.[57]

As a direct result of the tariff of 1833 more foreign sugar found its way into the American domestic market and prices began a gradual decline. To combat this situation, American growers began increasing acreage and production which in effect accelerated the downward spiral of prices. In fact, the sugar depression continued until rescued by the general rise of all agricultural commodities in the decade prior to the Civil War. Hence, it is understandable that sugar growers along the

Atlantic coast turned from an economically unproductive staple to another that offered a brighter prospect.[58]

Finally, Couper abandoned large-scale production of both sugar cane and cotton for rice because the latter was more profitable in his region.[59] However, he continued to plant both on a small scale, for in 1850 the agricultural census records show that he produced 37 1/2 bales (bags) of ginned cotton, fifteen hogsheads of sugar and 1400 gallons of molasses. And, in 1860, he produced 58 bales of cotton with no mention of sugar or syrup, but census records do show that in that year he produced 3911 gallons of molasses. Since it is impossible to have molasses without sugar (molasses is a by-product of sugar) Couper may have used the product for home consumption on his various plantations. A more plausible explanation, given the magnitude of the quantity produced, is that the "molasses" registered by the census of 1860 for Hopeton plantation was actually syrup, for in the 1850s the trend in Georgia was to produce syrup instead of sugar. In any event, the 1850s and 1860s saw the continuation of the trend established by 1841, of the gradual conversion of Hopeton from a multi-crop farm into principally a rice plantation. Rice certainly was dominant by 1841 and continued to be so until the Civil War disrupted Hopeton's agricultural operations.[60]

Notes

[1]J. Carlyle Sitterson, "Ante-Bellum Sugar Culture in the South Atlantic States," *Journal of Southern History* 3 (May 1937): 175, 187.

[2]J. Carlyle Sitterson, *Sugar Country* (Lexington: University of Kentucky Press, 1953) 13-14, 17; Ulrich B. Phillips, *Life and Labor in the Old South* (New York NY:Grosset and Dunlap, 1929) 119.

[3]Sitterson, *Sugar Country*, 13.

[4]Lewis Cecil Gray, *History of Agriculture in the United States* 2 vols. (Washington DC: Carnegie Institution, 1933) 2:739-40; Merton E. Coulter, *Thomas Spalding of Sapelo* (Baton Rouge: Louisiana State University Press, 1940) 111-12; Ulrich Bonnell Phillips, *Life and Labor in the Old South*, 119-20.

[5]Coulter, *Thomas Spalding*, 112; Thomas Spalding, "On the Cultivation of the Sugar Cane, Erecting of Proper Buildings, and Manufacturing of Sugar," *Southern Agriculturist and Register of Rural Affairs* 2 (February 1829): 55; Sitterson, "Ante-Bellum Sugar Culture in the South Atlantic States," 175-76; Sitterson, *Sugar Country*, 31, 119; Gray, *History of Agriculture*, 2:748.

[6]Coulter, *Thomas Spalding*, 113; Sitterson, *Sugar Country*, 120; "Tribute to James Hamilton Couper," *Interstate Sugar Cane Growers Association Report, 1908*, 71, Mackay Stiles Papers, Southern Historical Collection, University of North

Carolina Press, Chapel Hill; D. G. Purse and W. C. Stubbs, *Cultivation of Sugar Cane, Part Second. Sugar Cane: Its History in Georgia, Florida, and South Carolina, 1767-1900...Recollections of Hopeton Plantation*, vol 2. of *Cultivation of Sugar Cane* (Savannah GA: D. G. Purse, 1901) 3.

[7]Sitterson, "Ante-Bellum Sugar Culture in the South Atlantic States," 177-78; James Hamilton Couper Plantation Records, 4 vols., 3:54, Southern Historical Collection, University of North Carolina, Chapel Hill; Sitterson, *Sugar Country*, 31-32.

[8]J. D. Legare, "Account of an Agricultural Excursion Made into the South of Georgia in the Winter of 1832," *Southern Agriculturist and Register of Rural Affairs* 6 (May-November 1833): 515-17; James Hamilton Couper Plantation Records, 4:14, Southern Historical Collection; Sitterson, *Sugar Country*, 113-14.

[9]Sitterson, *Sugar Country*, 114-15; Coulter, *Thomas Spalding*, 115.

[10]Thomas Spalding, "Observations in the Method of Planting and Cultivating the Sugar-Cane in Georgia and South Carolina, Together with the Process of Boiling and Granulating; and a Description of the Fixtures Requisite for Grinding and Boiling," in a letter from Thomas Spalding, Esq. to Major General Thomas Pinckney, with an Appendix (Charleston SC: 1816), reprinted in E. Merton Coulter, *Georgia Disputed Ruins* (Chapel Hill: University of North Carolina, 1937), 231-32; Coulter, *Thomas Spalding*, 113-14.

[11]Sitterson, *Sugar Country*, 116-22; James Hamilton Couper Plantation Records, 4:14, Southern Historical Collection; Legare, "Account of Agricultural Excursion," 515-17.

[12]Legare, "Account of Agricultural Excursion," 518; Sitterson, *Sugar Country*, 39, 123.

[13]Sitterson, *Sugar Country*, 125; Ulrich Bonnell Phillips, *American Negro Slavery* (New York: Appleton and Co., 1918) 244.

[14]James Hamilton Couper Plantation Records, 4:14-15, Southern Historical Collection; Sitterson, *Sugar Country*, 119-23.

[15]Legare, "Account of Agricultural Excursion," 515-17; James Hamilton Couper Plantation Records, 4:14, Southern Historical Collection.

[16]Legare, "Account of Agricultural Excursion," 519.

[17]Ibid., 526-27; Sitterson, *Sugar Country*, 134; Coulter, *Thomas Spalding*, 115-16.

[18]Legare, "Account of Agricultural Excursion," 528-29; Spalding, "Observation," 263; Sitterson, *Sugar Country*, 133-34; Phillips, *American Negro Slavery*, 242-44.

[19]Jordan Wood, "An Account of the Process of Cultivating, Harvesting, and Manufacturing of Sugar Cane," *Southern Agriculturist and Register of Rural Affairs* 3 (May 1830): 227.

[20]Purse and Stubbs, *Cultivation of Sugar Cane, Part Second.*, 54; Sitterson, "Ante-Bellum Sugar Culture in the South Atlantic States," 177; James Hamilton

Couper Plantation Records, 3:54, Southern Historical Collection.

[21]Purse and Stubbs, *Cultivation of Sugar Cane, Part Second.*, 24, 34; manuscript concerning the sugar establishment of Hopeton, n.d., n.p., Margaret Davis Cate Collection, Georgia Historical Society, Savannah GA; Sitterson, *Sugar Country*, 32-33, 135; Julia Floyd Smith, *Slavery & Rice Culture in Low Country Georgia 1750-1860* (Knoxville: University of Tennessee Press, 1985) 225.

[22]Sitterson, *Sugar Country*, 137, 139; Spalding, "Observations," 236-39; James Hamilton Couper, "Account of, and Directions for Erecting a Sugar Establishment," *Southern Agriculturist and Register of Rural Affairs* 4 (May 1831): 227.

[23]Spalding, "Observations," 239-50; Sitterson, *Sugar Country*, 138; Purse and Stubbs, *Cultivation of Sugar Cane, Part Second.*, 3-4.

[24]Spalding, "Observations," 50-52; Coulter, *Thomas Spalding*, 115-16; Sitterson, *Sugar Country*, 137; Couper, "Directions for Erecting a Sugar Establishment," 227; Purse and Stubbs, *Cultivation of Sugar Cane, Part Second.*, 24-25.

[25]Couper, "Directions for Erecting a Sugar Establishment," 227.

[26]Ibid., 227-28; Spalding, "Observations," 235-39; Sitterson, *Sugar Country*, 137-140; Coulter, *Thomas Spalding*, 116-17; J. D. B. De Bow, "Manufacture of Sugar In Louisiana," *De Bow s Review* 3 (May 1847): 376-79.

[27]James Hamilton Couper Plantation Records, 4:23, 29, Southern Historical Collection; Couper, "Directions for Erecting a Sugar Establishment," 226, 228-29; Sitterson, *Sugar Country*, 140-41.

[28]James Hamilton Couper Plantation Records, 4:16-20, 26, Southern Historical Collection; Couper, "Directions for Erecting a Sugar Establishment," 229; De Bow, "Manufacture of Sugar in Louisiana," 384-85.

[29]The adjective saccharine ("of or relating to sugar") should not be confused with the artificial sweetner saccharin discovered in the late 1800s.

[30]Spalding, "Observations," 241-42; Couper, "Directions for Erecting a Sugar Establishment," 229; Sitterson, *Sugar Country*, 140-43; James Hamilton Couper Plantation Records, 4:23, Southern Historical Collection; De Bow, "Manufacture of Sugar in Louisiana," 386-87.

[31]Legare, "Account of Agricultural Excursion," 524-25; Sitterson, *Sugar Country*, 142-43.

[32]Legare, "Account of Agricultural Excursion," 524-25; Couper, "Directions for Erecting a Sugar Establishment," 229; James Hamilton Couper Plantation Records, 4:15-22, Southern Historical Collection.

[33]Sitterson, *Sugar Country*, 142; Coulter, *Thomas Spalding*, 118; Couper, "Directions for Erecting a Sugar Establishment," 227, 230.

[34]Couper, "Directions for Erecting a Sugar Establishment," 230-31; Legare, "Account of Agricultural Excursion," 526-27; Coulter, *Thomas Spalding*, 118; De Bow, "Manufacture of Sugar in Louisiana," 395.

[35]Legare, "Account of Agricultural Excursion," 526-27; Couper, "Directions for Erecting a Sugar Establishment," 230-31; De Bow, "Manufacture of Sugar in Louisiana," 395-96.

[36]Couper, "Directions for Erecting a Sugar Establishment," 228-29, 231-32, 285-88; Sitterson, *Sugar Country,* 140, 146, 149, 152-53.

[37]Couper, "Directions for Erecting a Sugar Establishment," 226-27, 230; Sitterson, *Sugar Country,* 141-43.

[38]Couper, "Directions for Erecting a Sugar Establishment," 226-27, 230; Sitterson, *Sugar Country,* 141-43.

[39]Couper, "Directions for Erecting a Sugar Establishment," 226-27, 230; Sitterson, *Sugar Country,* 141-43.

[40]Couper, "Directions for Erecting a Sugar Establishment," 225-31.

[41]Gray, *History of Agriculture,* 2:742; Sitterson, *Sugar Country,* 146-50; De Bow, "Manufacture of Sugar in Louisiana," 392-93.

[42]Gray, *History of Agriculture,* 2:751; Coulter, *Thomas Spalding,* 119; Sitterson, *Sugar Country,* 155.

[43]James Hamilton Couper Plantation Records, 3:1-54, Southern Historical Collection; Sitterson, "Ante-Bellum Sugar Culture in the South Atlantic States," 177-78.

[44]Spalding, "Observations," 244-45.

[45]Sitterson, "Ante-Bellum Sugar Culture in the South Atlantic States," 177; Roswell King Jr., "On the Management of the Butler Estate, and the Cultivation of the Sugar Cane," *Southern Agriculturist and Register of Rural Affairs* 1 (December 1828): 527-28.

[46]Spalding, "Observations," 244.

[47]Coulter, *Thomas Spalding,* 119.

[48]Sitterson, *Sugar Country,* 32; King, "On the Management of the Butler Estate and the Cultivation of Sugar Cane," 527; J. D. Legare, "On Our Southern Agricultural Concerns," *Southern Agriculturist and Register of Rural Affairs* 1 (October 1828): 448.

[49]Purse and Stubbs, *Cultivation of Sugar Cane, Part Second.,* 6.

[50]James Hamilton Couper Plantation Records, 3:48, 52, Southern Historical Collection; Sitterson, "Ante-Bellum Sugar Culture in the South Atlantic States," 178.

[51]Wood, "An Account of the Process of Cultivating, Harvesting, and Manufacturing of Sugar Cane," 231; Blachette Zoega, "On the Manufacture of Sugar," *Southern Review* 3 (May 1829): 330.

[52]Purse and Stubbs, *Cultivation of Sugar Cane, Part Second.,* 6.

[53]Ibid.; Zoega, "On the Manufacture of Sugar," 330.

[54]"Tribute to James Hamilton Couper," *Interstate Sugar Cane Growers Association, 1908,* 72-73, Mackay Stiles Papers, Southern Historical Collection.

[55]Zoega, "On the Manufacture of Sugar," 330.

[56]Sitterson, *Sugar Country*, 170-72, 175-77.

[57]James Hamilton Couper Plantation Records, 3:1-54, Southern Historical Collection.

[58]Sitterson, *Sugar Country*, 170-77.

[59]"Tribute to James Hamilton Couper," *Interstate Sugar Cane Growers Association, 1908*, 73, Mackay Stiles Papers, Southern Historical Collection; James Hamilton Couper Plantation Records, 3:1-54, Southern Historical Collection.

[60]James Hamilton Couper Plantation Records, 3:1-54, Southern Historical Collection; Bureau of the Census, *Seventh Census of the United States, 1850. Agriculture.*, prepared by Robert Armstrong (Washington DC: Government Printing Office, 1853); Bureau of the Census, *Eighth Census of United States, 1860. Agriculture.*, prepared by Robert Armstrong (Washington DC: Government Printing Office, 1864).

CHAPTER VII

Rice

While the cultivation of sea island cotton and particularly sugar cane was diminishing in Georgia by 1841, rice planting was considered "gold" by coastal planters. The master of Hopeton first planted rice in 1821, as an experiment to find a crop that could be successfully grown in rotation with sea island cotton. Although he had planted his first cotton in 1818, and his first sugar cane in 1825, Hopeton developed into a great rice plantation because of the location of the plantation and its climate and soils. At the height of his planting career, he was reported to have been directing the cultivation of 2600 acres of rice and working 1142 slaves in the culture. These figures included land and slaves he owned plus others under his care.[1]

Rice production in the United States in the antebellum era was limited geographically to the area known as the "Rice Coast." This area extended from its northernmost limits of the Cape Fear River in North Carolina to the St. Marys River on the Georgia-Florida border. As the tide was a determining factor in rice culture, the regions of the upper Atlantic, lower Florida, and the Gulf coast were unsuited, because the tide was not high enough to flood the fields; for it was by the rise and fall of the tides that the rice fields were flooded and drained. In this respect, Georgia and South Carolina were the most favored states, having 6-7 feet tides over most of the area. The planters found this level to be most satisfactory for the flooding and draining of their rice fields. The tides around most of Florida's coast were 3-4 feet and only 2 feet in the Gulf of Mexico. North of Cape Hatteras, North Carolina, the rise and fall of the tide was only 3 feet.[2]

Within this area of the Atlantic coast, the region was further restricted to a limit of from 9 1/2 to 20 1/2 miles inland from the ocean. Because of the necessity of using the tidal flow method of irrigation, the area of cultivation was further confined to the banks of rivers and major creeks. The coast of Georgia is well watered by a network of rivers and their tributaries, plus numerous creeks. Beginning with the Savannah River which divides Georgia from South Carolina, the other rivers that crisscross the state from South Carolina to Florida are the Ogeechee, Altamaha, Satilla, and St. Marys. There was a persistent problem, however, attending the tidal flow method of rice cultivation which worried all planters. As the rise and fall of fresh river water levels were affected by salt water tides from the Atlantic Ocean, a great fear of planters was the threat of salt water getting into the rice fields. This was particularly true during hurricane season of late summer and early fall.[3]

The earliest history of rice cultivation in the United States is rather obscure. It is known that rice was one of the crops with which the early colonists experimented. In 1647, Governor Berkeley of Virginia initiated experiments with the crop and during the last decade of the century Governor Edmund Andros attempted to promote rice culture. These experiments, however, met with little success and were relatively futile, for no rice industry of any consequence was ever established in Virginia.[4]

Early introduction of rice culture into South Carolina is clouded by misconceptions and contradictions. The traditional story has it that a Madagascan sea captain was forced to land in Charleston harbor in 1694. Here he met Landgrave Thomas Smith to whom he gave a bag of rice. Smith is reported to have distributed the seed among his friends and from this incident the cultivation of rice began. However, records show that rice was grown in the colony along with cotton and indigo in 1691, and as early as 1677, the proprietors of Carolina wrote that they were in the process of securing rice seed for the colony. Be that as it may, the industry appears to have been firmly established in 1695. It is likely that the sea captain simply introduced a superior quality of rice seed into the colony which greatly aided the industry.[5]

The rice industry flourished in South Carolina during the next century and became a major export of that colony. The success of its cultivation contributed to the rise of a powerful aristocracy based on talent and wealth which centered around Charleston and the Georgetown district. However, by the 1790s, South Carolina planters realized that continuous cropping of the staple had to a degree exhausted the fertility of their soil. In direct response to this fact, they moved south into the virgin lands of Georgia, securing by their wealth and developing some of the choicest rice lands in the state. Examples of prominent South Carolina families who migrated into the Georgia rice region include the Butlers, Manigaults, Heywards, Hugers and Grants. The culture spread quickly until the Georgia coast became an extension of the South Carolina low country. The counties involved in the production of this new staple in Georgia ringed the coast and included Chatham, Bryan, Liberty, McIntosh, Glynn and Camden.[6]

Rice

In the late seventeenth century when rice was first introduced into South Carolina, the inland swamp or brook swamp was used almost exclusively in the growing of rice. It was known that rice grew best on lands receiving upwards of 60 inches of rainfall a year, amply dispersed during the summer months. While coastal South Carolina generally received an annual rainfall of 60 inches, it was oftentimes not well divided during the summer months and dry periods were always a possibility. Hence, the earliest rice planters chose inland swamps as sites for their rice fields because of the ample water supply. To prepare an inland swamp for rice cultivation, one had to drain the swamp, level it and clear the area of all stumps. At the headwaters of the swamp a large reservoir had to be constructed by the use of dams or dikes. When a dry season threatened, water could be let in to irrigate the fields. At first there was no systematic flooding of rice fields but simply irrigation to carry the crop through dry periods. But as the culture progressed, it was noticed that rice could be grown "in water" as well as out of it and that during rainy seasons when the water stood in the swamp for days, even weeks, the rice received no ill effects. It was also noticed that all other vegetation died during these occasional natural floodings. Hence, planters constructed a second dam at the other end of the swamp and began periodic floodings to reduce the number of time-consuming hoeings required of the crop. But this brought on added difficulties, for available land became a problem. It was found that the water reservoirs of even the largest swamps were insufficient to meet the needs of three or four lengthy floodings. Moreover, the small size and scattered location of these swamp fields, their poor adaptation for drainage, coupled with their shallow soils and small yields caused the rice planter to look for a new and different area in which to grow rice. In 1758, McKewn Johnstone of Winyah Bay, South Carolina, pioneered in removing his rice culture from the inland swamp to the tidal swamp lying alongside the rivers and smaller fresh water streams. So successful was the relocation that by the end of the century the inland swamp was abandoned for rice culture and replaced by the tidal swamp. And, in time, all the major rivers and creeks of coastal South Carolina and Georgia were utilized to some degree in rice culture, and rice plantations dotted their banks.[7]

The preparation of such tide-swamp lands for the rice culture was complicated, time-consuming and expensive. Moreover, the land had to be low enough to be flooded at high tide and high enough to be drained when the tide was out. When such a tract was selected a great bank or levee was constructed to separate the new area from the river and to surround the entire rice field. Then a main ditch was dug on the field side of the levee and, like the levee, surrounded the entire proposed rice field. Then all the trees were felled and stumps and other debris removed. The entire tract was then made as level as possible so that flooding and draining would be uniform. The next step was to sub-divide the large area into numerous smaller fields, each enclosed within a smaller bank with an accompanying ditch. These fields were usually 14-50 acres in size. Robert F. W. Allston felt that 20 acres was an optimum size for one of these sub-divided fields. However, Couper felt that a fifty-acre plot was more suitable to his purposes.

For flooding and draining purposes several great floodgates or "trunks" were built into the side of the great bank or levee that fronted the river. By careful utilization of these floodgates or sluice gates the entire area could be flooded or drained at will. Likewise, each individual field separately ditched and banked was supplied with floodgates to allow for individual flooding or draining. Each trunk had two doors, one at each end, called an inner and an outer door, to control the ingress and egress of the water. To flood or "flow" a field, the outer door was raised and the inner one lowered to close the trunk's mouth.[8] "At high tide the pressure of water from without would open the inner door, and a stream would flow through until the water levels inside and out were equalized. But when the tide fell, the beginning of any return current would promptly close the door and keep the water impounded upon the crop. When drainage was desired, the inner door was raised and the outer one lowered," thus reversing the process and draining the fields.[9]

Because of the complexities involved in the water control system of rice culture and in order to improve the diking and drainage of his rice fields, James Hamilton Couper went to Holland in 1825, to study that country's system of water control. Upon his return he put into operation the irrigation system he had studied there. Sometime later his father, John Couper, wrote to a daughter, "Your brother has just put into operation his Dutch floodgates—perhaps the only thing of the kind in America." In January 1846, Charles Lyell, president of the Geological Society of London, and his wife spent two weeks with the Coupers. In his *Second Visit to North America* Lyell wrote of watching two "carpenters putting up sluices and a lock in a canal of a kind unknown in this part of the world."

Lyell further commented that a black foreman was directing the construction of the floodgates from a plan drawn for him by Couper who had observed it himself many years before in Holland.[10]

The next step in the cultivation of rice after reclaiming the tidal swamp and instituting a water control system was preparing the land for planting. This was done during the winter months when the stubble from the previous year's crop was either turned under or burned off. At this time the ditches were cleaned and such plowing, harvesting and thinning of the soil as was necessary was accomplished. The fields were kept dry during the winter months and immediately before time to plant, trenches were dug to receive the seed. The trenches were long straight rows 3-5 inches wide and 13-15 inches from center to center. Slaves planted the seed by hand, broadcasting the kernels in the rows. From 2-3 bushels of seed rice were needed to sow one acre, depending on the fertility of the soil. Workers carrying light wooden bats then covered the seeded trenches with dirt to a depth of about two inches. Seed was planted from 10 March to 10 June depending on the weather and tides. Planting earlier than this would subject the crop to a possible freeze which would materially damage the crop and require replanting. And planting later than 10 June would throw the harvest late into the fall, subjecting it to the perils of hurricanes and early cold weather.[11]

Immediately after sowing, the fields were flooded from three to six days, just long enough to swell the grain and prepare it to sprout. This was called the sprout flow. After this initial flow the water was withdrawn and the fields dried for a period of approximately ten days. During this time the rice sprouted above ground and received its first hoeing. With this accomplished, the fields were again flooded with the point flow, which lasted from eight to ten days. By this time the plants had grown to a height of 6-8 inches. Again, the water was withdrawn, this time for two weeks, and the rice received another hoeing. For the next three weeks the third flooding (stretch flow) was put on, with the water rising approximately ten inches above the tops of the rice plants. Then the fields were drained slowly and remained dry for about a month. During this interval the rice plants usually received one or two hoeings. Following this, the last flooding (harvest flow) was let in, and the fields remained inundated until just before the grain was ready for harvest.[12]

The culture just described was the traditional mode of rice cultivation and was referred to as the "dry culture, closed-trench method." But by 1850, the South Carolina rice plantations were dropping in their yields due to worn-out lands from continuous cropping, and planters in that state were turning to a new method of cultivation which promised higher yields. This method was called "open planting." It had probably been developed in the 1820s, in South Carolina but had taken some time to come into general use. Planters were hesitant at first to use the method because risks were greater than in the traditional way.[13]

For this culture the land was prepared for planting in the same way as for the traditional method. The difference came, however, in the fact that the seed was not covered, but had been "clayed." Claying was a process the seed went through before planting. Seed were placed in a large flat wooden vat or earthen container and sprinkled lightly with powdered clay. Then a small amount of water was added, just enough to make the clay particles adhere to the individual seed. After mixing thoroughly, the clayed seed were spread out and allowed to dry for about a day or two prior to planting. After the seed were strewn in open trenches, water was let in to a depth of 1 1/2 feet. The seed ordinarily would have floated to the top had it not been for the clay which tenaciously clung to the hairy fuzz surrounding the husk of each seed. The seed in this condition adhered to the earth when water was let on and, consequently, were able to germinate properly.[14]

The sprout flow was kept on the field for about twenty-one days. The water was then drawn off and the land allowed to dry for fifteen days. At this time a light hoeing was done. This period was one of anxious waiting for the planter, for the gamble was great. At anytime during these early weeks a high wind or rainstorm could tear out the plants which had not yet taken firm root and pile them up in a tangled mass against the embankments of the field, or rice birds could nip the new-green shoots, pulling the plants from the field. In either case the planter had to replant. After the first light hoeing, water was again returned to the field, remaining on it for the next twenty days. The water was then withdrawn and the land stayed dry for forty days. During this time two hoeings were usually required. At the end of this period the harvest flow was put on and the water remained on the crop until time for the sickle.[15]

There were many advantages to this system, such as a better stand and higher yields. Also, labor was saved, for, instead of the usual five hoeings for the older covered-trench culture, only three were required for the open planting method. Moreover, the fields were noticeably freer from grass and volunteer rice—seed that had fallen from last year's crop and sprouted. Yet, the Georgia planters never accepted this new method of planting. They were not pushed to it, for their lands were not yet suffering from soil exhaustion and their yields were still high. The only Georgia planter who seems to have had signal success with the new method was Louis Manigault on his two Savannah River plantations, Gowrie and East Hermitage—and he was originally from South Carolina. He used the method almost exclusively in the Savannah basin from 1850 until the early 1860s. In 1852, Manigault recorded that Allston had informed him that all the planters in the Georgetown District of South Carolina had switched to the open planting method. To be sure, open planting could have been as successful in Georgia as in South Carolina had the planters wanted to employ it. Both Hugh Fraser Grant and James Hamilton Couper tried it in the Altamaha delta but abandoned it for the simple reason that the end did not justify the means. The risks were too great; the weather was too fickle to warrant the gamble when it was not necessary. Likewise, their labor force was adequate to perform the extra hoeings required. The refusal of the Georgia planters to accept this new method of planting introduced by the South Carolina planters was a key difference between the two rice regions.[16]

Two of the most troublesome and persistent of pests plaguing the rice planters were the rice birds and red rice. The rice birds were Bobolinks which, following their yearly migratory cycle, arrived in the Altamaha basin by mid-April, shifted to the Savannah River area by 25 April, and moved on into South Carolina by May. They remained for four or five weeks to consume any rice dropped in planting. They would even scratch up the seed from the lightly covered trenches after the sprout flow was lifted. Then in the fall, on their way south, they would appear in the rice fields, just before harvest time, to feed on the ripened grain. To protect their fields from this menace, planters often would employ children or old Negroes to frighten them away. A favorite sport in the fall was the shooting of these birds for game, for when cooked, these fat, rice-fed birds made a toothsome morsel.[17]

The other pest, red rice, was just as annoying. The traditional explanation for this was that it was volunteer rice. The first year the kernels were white, but the next year some turned a brilliant red and the evil perpetuated itself each year. Though of the same food value, size and taste as white rice, consumers shied away from it. According to then current standards, market rice could not have more than one kernel of red rice per one hundred kernels of the pure white strain. Hence, there was a desire to stamp it out. One of the best methods of doing this was crop rotation, substituting for a year or two a crop of dry culture such as oats, peas, cotton or sugar cane on a field that had been planted in rice for a number of years. But, unfortunately, since most planters generally did not rotate other crops with rice, this remedy was little used. A few planters were an exception though, and in Georgia there were two—Thomas Spalding and James Hamilton Couper. Spalding was never a large rice planter but recognized the necessity for the practice nevertheless. Couper used the remedy on a regular basis. Other planters, not so scientific, simply resorted to less effective methods such as harvesting the red rice before the rest and picking out the red kernels once the rice was threshed and milled.[18]

With the approach of fall, it was time for the harvest. Planters who caught the early March tides and had their crop planted by the end of the month could expect to begin reaping around 20 August. This was the policy of both Hugh Fraser Grant at Elizafield and James Hamilton Couper at Hopeton, for it was a rare occurrence when a freeze struck coastal Georgia after 10 March.

Harvesting rice in Georgia involved several distinct steps. First of all, a few days before the cutting, the harvest flow was let off and the ground allowed to dry. Then, the day before the rice was said to be ripe, the slaves went in with sickles to cut the shoulder-high grain. With rhythmic motion the field hand grasped a handful of stalks with the left hand and swung the sickle with the right, leaving a generous stubble of about a foot high. The cut stalks were then carefully laid across the stubble to dry for twenty-four hours. The next day the sheaves were collected, bound into bundles, and stacked in the field. When all the grain had been gathered in the field, it was transported in ox carts (or, in Couper's case, railroad cars) to the canal where it was loaded onto flats[19] and carried to the barnyard surrounding the rice mill for drying. When the rice was sufficiently dried it was ready for threshing. A dry fall was necessary for a successful season, for wet weather could seriously delay the harvest and damage the grain. With good weather harvesting was usually finished by the last of September in Georgia, but an unusually late planting in June was not ready for the sickle until October.[20]

After the harvest the rice had to be prepared for market, and this involved a complicated process which included threshing, cleaning and pounding. When this was done, the rice was said to be "milled" and was "clean rice" ready to be cooked for the table.

Threshing, the first step in the process, was the method by which the grain was separated from the sheaf but retained its husk. When this was completed the rice was called "rough rice" or "paddy." Most Georgia planters threshed their rice by very primitive means. The rice bundles were carried, carefully balanced on the heads of slaves or by hand, from the barnyard into a building which housed a threshing floor. A convenient size for such floors was 110 feet by 60 feet. The rice stalks were spread out on the floor and beaten by slaves wielding flat sticks. The separated grains fell through slits in the threshing floor onto a sub-floor made of two inclined planes which collected and funneled them into tubs of one-bushel capacity.

A few of the more affluent planters, however, had threshing mills complete with cleaning and pounding facilities and involving a capital investment of $6000-$10,000. Notable among these were James Hamilton Couper and Pierce Butler on the Altamaha and Charles and Louis Manigault on the Savannah.[21] The type of threshing mill used by these planters and those of similar station in South Carolina was one invented by Calvin Emmons of New York in 1829, and run by either animal or steam power. Prior attempts to devise a successful mill had largely come to naught. Emmons's machine "was equipped with beaters provided with teeth composed of serrated iron wire, so arranged as to comb the grain from the ears of rice."[22]

The output of these mills sometimes varied from plantation to plantation depending on the competency of the operators. The average daily production when run by horsepower was 200-300 bushels, but when powered by steam this average was raised to 450-700 bushels a day. Couper, whose steam mill was built in 1835, recorded in that year that its average daily production was 500 bushels. But in 1843, Allston reported that he knew of a mill in South Carolina with a daily output of 700 bushels. However, by 1851, the steam threshing apparatus had been so improved that mills were recording a daily average production of 1000 bushels.[23]

After threshing, the planter had to decide whether to sell his rice in the rough as "paddy" or to have it pounded. Pounding or milling was the process by which the rice had its brown outer husk or covering removed, revealing the pearly white kernel. Then after cleaning and polishing, the product was ready to be shipped abroad or consumed domestically. But since few plantations were equipped with rice mills which both threshed and pounded rice and since having rice pounded on another plantation or in far-away Savannah or Charleston was quite an expensive undertaking, most planters in both Georgia and South Carolina preferred to sell their rice in the rough. Exceptions in Georgia were, of course, James Hamilton Couper and Pierce Butler, both of whom, by 1835, had elaborate pounding facilities run by steam and sold their product as clean rice.[24]

The pounding process was a mechanical operation by which the rice was first fed in between two large grinding stones. This rubbing action loosened the husk which clung tenaciously around each rice kernel. Then the rice was fed into a set of fifteen to twenty wooden mortars, each holding about a bushel of grain. Above the mortars a like number of pestles, of slotted timbers, were thrust into "the deep contents of the mortars" below. This pounding action, which lasted for about two hours, finished the work the grinding stones had begun and delivered the unsheafed white kernel. The rice thus pounded was then elevated to the second story of the mill and forced to pass through "a long horizontal rolling-screen, slightly depressed at one end, where by means of a system of wire-sieves" the rice was graded into the various components while a fan blew the chaff away. The rice components included rice flour, small rice, broken rice and prime rice. The prime rice (the large unbroken grains) was then funneled into a "brushing screen," a vertical cylinder or drum two feet in diameter and from four to six feet in height. Inside, attached vertically, were strips of sheep-skin closely spaced. As this drum revolved with great velocity the grains were cleaned and polished to a shiny whiteness. The rice was then packed into tierces (barrels) holding 600 pounds each and stored ready for market in Savannah or Charleston.[25]

These pounding mills were remarkably productive. Allston recorded the product of a South Carolina mill operating with twenty pestles which pounded 3000 bushels of rough rice in sixty hours, or 600 bushels per day. Evidence is scarce as to the output of the Georgia mills. But it is likely that they did not approach the volume of the Carolina mills with the possible exception of those at Hopeton and Butler's Island. It is more likely that the majority of Georgia pounding mills were smaller with fewer pestles and operating at slower speeds and powered by the tides or small steam engines. An example of such a mill was at Gowrie, Charles Manigault's plantation on the Savannah River. The output of this mill was "8 to 10 barrels with each tide" or 460 barrels pounded in three months. A mill of this description, however, powered by a small steam engine could doubtless double this output.[26]

The prices rice planters received for their product fluctuated, as did those for other staples, and were dictated by world market prices. But rice was relatively freer from drastic depression periods that plagued the cotton and sugar industries. American rice competed successfully in the world market because of its superior quality when compared with Oriental or Mediterranean rice. Also, United States growers had ready-made monopoly in their homeland owing largely to the restricted nature of the culture geographically and to the fact that the United States did not import rice. Consequently, the tariff, so important to sugar growers, was of little importance to rice producers. From 1800 to 1860, prices ranged from two to seven cents per pound for clean rice with an average price during the period of from three to four cents a pound.

In the early antebellum period most rice was exported as clean rice. However, by 1830, some Europeans, notably the English, preferred to buy rough rice and mill it at home, for rice tasted better when freshly pounded, and rough rice could be kept indefinitely without losing its flavor. Most Georgia rice was exported from Charleston prior to 1835, but after that time it was marketed from Savannah. This was due to the fact that Savannah was becoming a more important commercial center by the late antebellum period and the Savannah River basin had developed as an emerging rice center. It is safe to say that because of their peculiar, situation with a crop restricted in geographic area, with a growing market both at home and abroad, added to an easy contact with Europe, the planters of the rice coast were among the most prosperous and progressive in the South.[27]

Couper planted his first rice crop at Hopeton in 1821, and gradually increased his acreage until it replaced cotton and sugar cane as the plantation's major staple. From that year through 1826, his acreage increased dramatically. In 1827, he recorded a yield of 17,571 bushels from 351 1/2 acres planted in rice. During these early years it is obvious that he was experimenting to see whether rice would indeed be a feasible crop on his plantation. Rice became important at Hopeton after 1825, and was the chief staple from 1834 when 487 1/2 acres were planted, to 1841, when 714 acres were seeded. His peak production during that period came in 1840 when 36,394 bushels were produced from 684 acres. Unfortunately, his plantation records cease with 1841, although it is known that he continued his rice-planting activities until the Civil War. It is inconceivable that such a meticulous and methodical man as Couper did not keep records of his agricultural activities during these later years, and it is unfortunate that these records are lost.[28]

Yields varied considerably within the rice region. They were generally lower in South Carolina than in Georgia because continuous cropping in the older region had led to soil exhaustion. In the newer lands of the Georgia rice region yield remained high throughout the antebellum era. The average yield in South Carolina was 40 bushels per acre; in Georgia it was around 50 bushels. An analysis of Couper's yields for the fourteen-year period 1827-1840 (no production figures were given for 1841 though he planted 714 acres in rice) reveals the following information. His average aggregate yield for all fields for those years was 53.3 bushels per acre. His maximum yield amounted to 60.4 bushels in 1839, with a minimum yield of 49.8 bushels in 1830. However, accounts show that on certain prime fields he repeatedly made 60, 70, and even 85 bushels to the acre. The master of Hopeton plantation knew that an average yield of at least 50 bushels per acre would be forthcoming year after year. The reliability of rice probably was the main factor responsible for its eventual dominance in Hopeton's land use system.[29] Allston recorded that in 1823, the average yield on his plantation in the Peedee River area of South Carolina was 30 bushels per acre. However, later his showing improved, for, in 1858, he recorded that on his plantation, Nightengale Hall, he received an average yield of 49 bushels per acre. Thomas Spalding maintained that he generally averaged 60 bushels to the acre. But Spalding was never a substantial planter of rice, and most of his acreage was devoted to cotton and sugar cane. Charles and Louis Manigault, who practiced the open planting method on the 500 acres of ricelands at Gowrie, recorded yields in 1852, 1855, and. 1857 of 946, 995, and 990 1/2 barrels, respectively, or, converted into bushels, 38, 40, and 39.5 respectively. These yields were about average for planters in South Carolina, but did not compare with Spalding, Couper or the Georgia average.[30]

James Hamilton Couper was certainly a successful planter when compared with his contemporaries. In 1841, the last year Couper recorded his acreage in existing plantation records, he was planting 714 acres in rice. Compared with other planters in Georgia this was a considerable amount. Charles Manigault was planting 500 acres at Gowrie at that time and Hugh Fraser Grant, Couper's neighbor at Elizafield, was planting 300 acres.[31] It is a fair estimate that most Georgia rice plantations had 250-600 acres planted in the staple with a median size of 400 acres devoted to the rice culture. As late as 1860, the average amount of land devoted to rice on the Savannah River plantations was 425 acres per plantation. To be sure, there were some plantations reported with as many as 1000 or 1200 acres of rice lands, but these frequently were divided into several plantations of 300 to 400 acres each, and operated as separate units.[32] Hence, by Georgia standards, Couper's acreage in 1841, was substantial. Even by South Carolina standards Couper's scale was respectable. William Aiken of Jehossee Island plantation, one of South Carolina's largest planters, had 1500 acres on the estate ditched and banked but planted only 1000 acres in rice annually. Also Nathaniel Heyward, the largest planter in the South, had at his death in 1851, fourteen rice plantations in South Carolina with a combined rice cultivation of 4390 acres. The maximum acreage on any one plantation was 600.[33]

The 1850 and 1860 agricultural census records show some interesting data. In 1849, five planters in Georgia produced over a million pounds of rice. The planter with the largest production was James Potter of Chatham County with 1,750,000 pounds. Next came Pierce Butler of McIntosh with 1,521,550 pounds, and James Hamilton Couper was third with 1,500,000 pounds. Hence, in 1850, Couper was the largest rice planter in Glynn County and the third largest producer in the state.

The 1860 returns for Georgia show an increased production for, in 1859, the number of planters producing over a million pounds of rice in the state had risen from five to twelve, more than double. Three of the planters, James Potter and R. E. Elliott from Chatham County and George Owens from Camden, produced over two million pounds of rice each, and a fourth, Augustine S. Jones, also of Chatham, produced more than three million pounds. Couper's production increased somewhat from 1,500,000 in 1849, making him the sixth largest rice producer in the latter year, his increase in 1860, was to 1,693,200 pounds of rice. It is also evident that Couper had increased his acreage by 1860, for 1910 acres were listed as improved in 1849, as compared to 2587 acres in 1859. Also, it is apparent that, had he not devoted considerable acreage to cotton and sugar cane in that year, his rice production would have been greater. The records show that those producing more than Couper in 1859 grew only rice. Another inescapable observation is that James Hamilton Couper was co-managing one of the largest agricultural units (Hopeton-Altama) in the state in 1859 with a combined estate of 8476 acres of improved and unimproved land. The term "improved" meant that the land was in a condition to be cultivated if the planter desired. "Unimproved" meant that the acreage was unreclaimed swamp or pineland and was not as yet suitable for cultivation. There is no record as to how many acres Couper actually planted in rice or any other crop in 1849 or 1859. However, converted into bushels, using the conversion formula of 45 pounds of rough rice to one bushel, Couper's production in terms of bushels in 1849 was 33,333, and in 1859, approximately 37,626, which is similar to his production in 1839 and 1840 of 34,359 and 36,394 bushels respectively.[34]

It has been a matter of historical debate as to whether the plantation system in the South was really profitable. For James Hamilton Couper it was. His account books showing profit and loss are not in existence, but the mere continuance and expansion of his operations suggest that his planting pursuits were profitable. As a young man he managed Hopeton so successfully that in 1826 he was able to purchase half interest in the plantation. And his continued success as a planter allowed his purchase of other plantations and slaves. In addition, in 1829, he was able to finance the building of one of the South's finest sugar establishments, and, in 1831, to underwrite the construction of his cotton seed crushing mills in Alabama and Mississippi. In both of these ventures he lost money, but the profits from his plantations enabled him to absorb the losses, and it goes without saying that these profits, in the main, came from his production of rice.

Rice cultivation was introduced into the colony of Georgia in the eighteenth century, but it did not spread rapidly until the late 1820s, when South Carolina lands began to show signs of soil exhaustion, and South Carolina planters as well as native Georgians rushed to control the choicest spots. Georgia was indeed considered the new frontier of tidal rice region. As late as 1852, it was declared that, "there are many thousands of acres of choice ricelands in Georgia still unsubdued."[35] The census records for 1839 show that Georgia planters produced 12,384,732 pounds of rice or twenty percent of the South Carolina crop, thereby making Georgia the second most important rice-producing state in the union. By 1849, the state's production had jumped to 38,950,691 pounds or 25 percent of the South Carolina crop. A survey in that year revealed that the rice plantations which produced as much as 20,000 pounds a year numbered 446 in South Carolina, 80 in Georgia, and 25 in North Carolina. In the decade of the 1850s rice production declined in South Carolina due to the ever-increasing soil exhaustion and the refusal of most planters to practice crop rotation and other measures to restore the soil. However, in Georgia during this same period the rice industry was experiencing rapid growing pains. This development was evidenced by the fact that in 1859 production had increased to 52,507,652 pounds of rice, which amounted to 45 percent of the South Carolina production.[36]

It is clear that James Hamilton Couper was one of the top rice planters in a region where the rice culture was expanding. It is also clear that he was one of the early substantial planters of Georgia. Rice became a serious crop at Hopeton in 1826 and was sustained increasingly in a dominant position for the next thirty-four years. In 1841 his production seems to have hit a plateau of about 36,000 bushels annually, which was maintained until 1860. Had the Civil War not intervened, Georgia's future in the rice industry would have been bright.

Notes

[1]"Tribute to James Hamilton Couper," *Interstate Sugar Cane Growers Association, 1908*, 73, Mackay-Stiles Papers, Southern Historical Collection, Univeristy of North Carolina, Chapel Hill; James Hamilton Couper Plantation Records, 4 vols, 3:54, Southern Historical Collection, University of North Carolina, Chapel Hill; J. Carlyle Sitterson, "Ante-Bellum Sugar Culture in the South Atlantic States," *Journal of Southern History* (May 1937): 181; "Rice Planter" (typescript concerning Couper as rice planter), n.p., n.d., Mackay-Stiles Papers, Southern Historical Collection; "Meteorology of Cotton and Cane Fields," *De Bow's Review* 18 (January 1855): 45-46.

[2]Lewis Cecil Gray, *History of Agriculture in the Southern United States*, 2 vols. (Washington DC: Carnegie Institution, 1933) 2:721-22; Merton E. Coulter, *Thomas Spalding of Sapelo* (Baton Rouge: Louisiana State University Press, 1940) 76-77.

[3]James Herbert Stone, "Black Leadership in the Old South: The Slave Drivers of the Rice Kingdom" (Ph.D. diss., Florida State University, 1976) 3-4.

[4]Gray, *History of Agriculture*, 1:227.

[5]Ibid.

[6]Burnette Lightle Vanstory, *Georgia's Land of the Golden Isles* (Athens: Univeristy of Georgia Press, 1956) 85; Mary Granger, ed., *Savannah River Plantations*, introduction, n.p. (Savannah: Georgia Historical Society, 1947); Coulter, *Thomas Spalding,* 211.

[7]Duncan Clinch Heyward, *Seed from Madagascar* (Chapel Hill: University of North Carolina Press, 1937) 11-14; Ulrich Bonnell Phillips, *Life and Labor in the Old South* (New York NY: Grossett and Dunlap, 1929) 116; Gray, *History of Agriculture,* 2:280-81, 721.

[8]R. F. W. Allston, "Rice," *De Bow's Review,* 1 (April 1846): 332; Allston, "Rice," 4 (December 1847): 506-11; Phillips, *Life and Labor in the Old South,* 116-17; J. D. Legare, "Account of Agricultural Excursion Made into the South of Georgia in the Winter of 1832," *Southern Argiculturist and Register of Rural Affairs* 4 (May-November 1833): 360-61; Gray, *History of Agriculture,* 2:726.

[9]Phillips, *Life and Labor in the Old South,* 117.

[10]Alfred W. Jones, *Altama: Then and Now* (Sea Island GA: self published, 1970) 3; Sir Charles Lyell, *A Second Visit to North America* 2 vols. (New York NY: Harper and Brother, 1849) 2:267.

[11]Albert Virgil House Jr., ed., *Planter Management and Capitalism in Ante-Bellum Georgia: The Journal of Hugh Fraser Grant, Rice Grower* (New York NY: Columbia University Press, 1954) 28-29; Allston, "Rice," 1, 334; Gray, *History of Agriculture,* 2:727; R. F. W. Allston, "Sea-Coast Crops of the South," *De Bow's Review* 16 (June 1854): 608-609; James Hamilton Couper Plantation Records, 4:33-35, Southern Historical Collection; Legare "Account of Agricultural Excursion," 413-14.

[12]House, ed., *Journal of Hugh Fraser Grant,* 32; Allston, "Rice," 1, 335-36; James Hamilton Couper Plantation Records, 4:33-34, Southern Historical Collection; Legare, "Account of Agricultural Excursion," 413-14; Gray, *History of Agriculture,* 2:728-29.

[13]House, ed., *Journal of Hugh Fraser Grant,* 33; Albert V. House, ed., Jr., "Charles Manigault's Essay on the Open Planting of Rice," *Agricultural History* 16 (October 1942): 184-90.

[14]Allston, "Rice," 1, 335; House, ed., *Journal of Hugh Fraser Grant,* 33-34; House, "Charles Manigault's Essay on Open Rice Planting," 186-90.

[15]House, ed., *Journal of Hugh Fraser Grant,* 34; House, "Charles Manigault's Essay on Open Rice Planting," 186-91.

[16]House, ed., *Journal of Hugh Fraser Grant,* 34; House, "Charles Manigault's Essay on Open Rice Planting," 186-91; James Hamilton Couper Plantation Records, 4:51, Southern Historical Collection; Gray, *History of Agriculture,* 2:728.

[17]House, ed., *Journal of Hugh Fraser Grant*, 35; Gray, *History of Agriculture*, 2:729; Heyward, *Seed from Madagascar*, 32-33; Phillips, *American Negro Slavery*, 90.

[18]House, "Charles Manigault's Essay on Open Rice Planting," 186-87; Legare, "Account of Agricultural Excursion," 413-14; Gray, *History of Agriculture*, 2:729. Recent scholarship has questioned the actual identity of red rice. James H. Stone, a careful scholar in the area of antebellurn rice production, maintains that red rice was not volunteer rice at all but a different species altogether which perpetuated itself each year as rice was planted. Be that as it may, "red" or "volunteer," its appearance was troublesome for planters.

[19]A "flat" was a flat-bottomed boat of shallow draft, 20-30 feet in length, square at both ends, narrow enough to use in the canals of the rice fields as well as on rivers, and usually manned by two to six slaves.

[20]Phillips, *American Negro Slavery*, 90; Gray, *History of Southern Agriculture*, 2:729-30; Legare, "Account of Agricultural Excursion," 413-14; Heyward, *Seed from Madagascar*, 40-41; Allston, "Sea-Coast Crops of the South," 611-12; Allston, "Rice," 1, 336; House, ed., *Journal of Hugh Fraser Grant*, 36-37.

[21]House, ed., *Journal of Hugh Fraser Grant*, 59-60, 68.

[22]Gray, *History of Agriculture*, 2:730.

[23]Ibid.; Allston, "Rice," 1, 340-341; James Hamilton Couper Plantation Records, 4:54, Southern Historical Collection.

[24]James Hamilton Couper Plantation Records, 4:49-55, Southern Historical Collection; House, ed., *Journal of Hugh Fraser Grant*, 68.

[25]Allston, "Rice," 1, 348-349; Allston, "Sea-Coast Crops of the South," 612; J. H. Easterby, ed., *The South Carolina Rice Plantation as Revealed in the Papers of Robert F. W. Allston* (Chicago: University of Chicago Press, 1945) 32-33; Phillips, "Life and Labor in the Old South," 116; Gray, *History of Agriculture*, 2:730; House, ed., *Journal of Hugh Fraser Grant*, 62-63.

[26]House, ed., *Journal of Hugh Fraser Grant*, 64-65.

[27]Gray, *History of Agriculture*, 2:724-26; House, ed., *Journal of Hugh Fraser Grant*, 57-81; Heyward, *Seed from Madagascar*, 43; Phillips, *American Negro Slavery*, 252.

[28]James Hamilton Couper Plantation Records, 3:1-54, Southern Historical Collection.

[29]Ibid.; Legare, "Account of Agricultural Excursion," 415; William Allister Noble, "Sequent Occupance of Hopeton-Altama" (Master thesis, University of Georgia, 1956) 53; Gray, *History of Agriculture*, 2:730; House, ed., *Journal of Hugh Fraser Grant*, 24; Albert Virgil House, "Labor Management Problems on Georgia Rice Plantations, 1840-1860," *Agricultural History* 28 (October 1954): 150.

[30]J. H. Easterby ed., *The South Carolina Rice Plantation*, 36; Coulter, *Thomas Spalding*, 79; House, "Charles Manigault's Essay on Open Rice Planting," 193.

[31]House, ed., *Journal of Hugh Fraser Grant*, 8-9; Phillips, *American Negro Slavery*, 254-56.

[32]House, "Labor Management Problems on Georgia Rice Plantations," 150; Stone, "Slave Drivers of the Rice Kingdom," 4.

[33]Phillips, *American Negro Slavery*, 250-52.

[34]Bureau of the Census, *Seventh Census of the United States, 1850. Agriculture.*, prepared by Robert Armstrong (Washington DC: Government Printing Office, 1853); Bureau of the Census, *Eighth Census of United States, 1860. Agriculture.*, prepared by Robert Armstrong (Washington DC: Government Printing Office, 1864).

[35]Gray, *History of Agriculture*, 2:724.

[36]Allston, "Rice," 1, 372; House, ed., *Journal of Hugh Fraser Grant*, 22-23; Stone, "Slave Drivers of the Rice Kingdom," 8; Gray.

CHAPTER VIII

The Progressive Agriculturist

Although Couper was primarily known for his rice planting, he achieved considerable distinction as one of the two leading scientific agriculturists on the Georgia coast. The other was Thomas Spalding. Both men felt that crop diversification was a most important ingredient for a successful plantation. Couper was well aware of the dangers inherent in a one-crop agricultural system. This was why he never allowed Hopeton to become exclusively devoted to one crop. Rice became dominant, but other crops were always planted in conjunction with it. As a capitalistic enterprise Couper felt that the plantation should be managed according to progressive methods rather than old habits. He had a broad program for diversified agriculture. First, staple crops should be grown; then there should be the secondary crops which contributed to sustenance and comfort; thirdly, new and valuable crops should be introduced and promoted. It was this last item that greatly separated him from the majority of planters who were content to concentrate on the crop most economically advantageous to them. And in this quest for diversification Couper periodically consulted such agricultural periodicals and general works as Home's *Principles of Vegetation*, Darwin's *Phylologia*, Hunter's *Agricultural Essays*, Anderson's *Essays*, and Lord Dundonald's *Connection of Chemistry and Agriculture*.[1]

Besides experimenting with the major staples, cotton, sugar cane and rice, Couper experimented with other more exotic plants. Those with which he became most closely identified were Bermuda grass, sweet and sour oranges, date palms and olives.

Bermuda grass had been a favorite cover for pasture land since its introduction into Georgia in 1751, by Henry Ellis, the colony's second royal governor. But it remained for James Hamilton Couper to introduce its use in rice culture to prevent soil erosion. He strongly recommended it for the cover of all rice banks as a sure protection against any breakage due to freshets. Couper cited many instances when water poured over such banks for days without doing the least damage, while those spots not protected were swept entirely away. However, the agriculturist warned that care had to be taken to prevent the grass from getting a foothold on high land, for, of all grasses with the exception of nut grass, it was the most difficult to eradicate. But if it were confined to rice banks, it would be kept in check by the water which killed it easily. In 1832, Couper showed a guest, J. D. Legare of Charleston, banks which had been covered with the grass for fourteen years without its having spread beyond their base. This practice proved so successful that by 1840, it was in general use in both Georgia and South Carolina.[2]

John Couper had imported a number of date palms from Persia which he planted at Cannon's Point. James Hamilton Couper continued their cultivation and even added to the stock but never pursued the culture on a large scale. The trees grew so slowly and produced fruit so irregularly that serious contemplation of the date palm as a crop was abandoned.

Similarly, James Hamilton Couper experimented with sweet and sour oranges. He planted large groves of each at Cannon's Point and, by 1835, they were bearing abundantly. However, in the winter of that year the thermometer dropped to 8 degrees Fahrenheit, the coldest recorded temperature in a century on the Georgia coast. The cold killed the sweet oranges. But Couper cut them back and they sprouted from the roots the next spring. The sour orange trees, however, were little damaged. This observation led Couper to believe that the orange culture, particularly that of the sour variety, could readily be pursued by sea island planters.[3]

But of all the exotic plants with which Couper experimented, his greatest success was with the olive culture. The olive was first introduced into this country in South Carolina in the early 1670s. However, the tree was never grown extensively and was found during its early history in this country growing in the gardens of Charleston mainly as a conversation piece. However, Thomas Jefferson, a scientific agriculturist himself, became highly interested in the olive as a crop that could be raised commercially for the fruit and oil. In 1804, he wrote a shipping company in Marseilles, M. Cathalan and *fils*, that John Couper of St. Simons Island, Georgia, would undertake an experiment to ascertain whether the olive could be grown extensively in America. Through his influence as President, Jefferson urged the French company to do all within its power to expedite a shipment of trees to Georgia. But because of worsening relations between the two countries over shipping and neutral rights on the high seas, the trees were never delivered. Years later, after the turbulence of the Napoleonic era had passed, contact between Couper and the French company was resumed. Two hundred trees finally arrived in May of 1825 having been five months en route. Most lived and began bearing fruit. During the severe winter of 1835 these trees were damaged so severely that they had to be cut down to the ground. When spring came, though, they all threw up shoots from the old stumps and, sixteen years later, many had attained a diameter of nine inches.[4]

James Hamilton Couper continued the experiments begun by his father and maintained that the climate and soils of the Atlantic coast from South Carolina to Florida, and extending to states bordering the Gulf of Mexico, were as suitable to the olive culture as the south of France, which was known for its olive production. He pointed out that in the winter of 1845 the temperature had dipped to a low of 19 degrees Fahrenheit at which time he "could not perceive that a single leaf among 250 olive trees had been touched by the frost." Writing in 1846, he mentioned that it had been twenty-one years since the importation of the trees, and only once during that time—the winter of 1835—had the temperature dropped so low as to hurt the olives. Such observation encouraged Couper and led him to believe that the olive culture could be pursued successfully in his climate. He felt that one devastating year in one hundred years was not sufficient cause for discouraging the culture of so valuable a tree in the United States. Rather, he thought it encouraging, for in France every tree was destroyed to the ground in 1709 and 1788, and they were severely hurt in 1740, 1745, 1748, 1755 and 1768. However, he did doubt whether the tree could be cultivated beyond the influence of the sea air on the coast.[5]

Couper found no difficulty in propagating the olive, for it was readily increased by seed, by cuttings and by grafting. Propagation by cuttings was the easiest and most practical. In using this procedure, limbs 1-1 1/2 inches in diameter were cut in lengths of from 12-15 inches. Trenches 5 feet apart and 6-8 inches deep were prepared. The cuttings were placed in them about eighteen inches apart in an oblique position, so that when the earth was filled in, from one to two inches of the cutting would remain above the ground. On the exposed end a little gardener's cement was smeared and some Spanish moss or loose sand placed on top of it. This was done to diminish evaporation from the stalk. In dry weather the cuttings were watered occasionally until they had taken root. From this time until the third year nothing more was required in cultivation except an occasional hoeing and trimming the plants to a single stem. When the young trees were three years old they were removed to the field and planted at distances of approximately 30-48 feet. The holes were made large and deep. The distance at which the olive trees were planted was regulated by circumstances, however. Approximately twenty-five trees were planted to the acre, when the land was also cropped. But when the land was devoted exclusively to the olive, fifty trees were set to the acre. Subsequent cultivation consisted of removing the suckers, trimming out the dead wood, manuring moderately once every three or four years, and plowing the whole field once a year.

As soon as the olives were ripe, which was indicated by their becoming a dark color and soft, they were spread out over floors to a depth of several inches. In this situation they remained three days, being turned daily and the decayed berries carefully picked out.

On the Couper plantation the ripe olives were processed into pickled olives and oil. Couper pointed out that the quality of the oil was determined by the size of the tree, the soil, and the fruitfulness of the season. These same factors greatly affected yield as well. The average product of a moderate-sized tree in France was ten pounds of fruit, yielding 1 1/2 gallons of oil. In Italy, on the other hand, the average amount was 15 pounds of fruit or two gallons of oil. However, in both countries single trees in a productive season had been known to yield 300 pounds of fruit or 41 gallons of oil. But this was highly unusual. Couper stated that the yield in Georgia was somewhat less. On Cannon's Point his yield from a tree in full bearing was 1 gallon of oil. If the land were cropped also, this would amount to twenty-five gallons per acre. If the land were devoted exclusively to the olive, fifty gallons would be the yield per acre. Estimating the oil at the moderate price of $.75 per gallon, Couper calculated the return to the planter from oil at $18.75 per acre in the former case, and $37.50 in the latter. Couper always recommended the first option of planting only twenty-five trees to the acre and cropping it in some staple such as corn. For, in this situation the planter received a two-fold return from his land. From experience, Couper recorded that the crop planted with olives was diminished only by one-fifth.

Although Couper pickled olives, his main concern was in extracting the oil and bottling it for sale. The manufacture of this oil was quite simple and required no very complicated or expensive machinery. The latter consisted of a mortar and pestle or some other contrivance for separating the pulp from the seed and rendering it into a paste. A revolving stone, like one for a grist mill, was necessary for crushing the stones or seed and a lever or screw press for the pressing of the oil from the pulp and stones. Also necessary were bags of coarse cloth to contain the pulp and wooden or earthenware vessels for receiving the oil from the presses and for separating it from the mucilage. In the actual process of extracting the oil the olives were placed in the mortar and pounded moderately until the pulp was reduced to paste and detached from the stones. The stones were then removed and the pulp was put into strong, coarse bags and placed under the press for extraction of the oil. After this process the oil mixed with mucilage was run into wooden vessels, half filled with water. After standing from twelve to twenty-four hours, to give time for the mucilage to separate from the oil, the oil was decanted into other vessels where it remained for about twenty days. It was then ready to be decanted again and put into barrels. It could be shipped in this condition or put into bottles of various sizes. Couper found that this expression was of first quality. Still, there was a second squeezing. The pulp or cake that remained in the bags from the first pressing, was taken from the bags, broken up, and moistened with warm water. This mixture was then returned to the bags and pressed for a second time. The quality of the oil from this expression was nearly equal to the first and could be mixed with it.

Couper also obtained oil from the stones or seeds. After having been separated from the pulp in the mortar by use of a screen, they were placed under a revolving grinding stone that crushed them. The contents were then put into bags and pressed in the same manner as the pulp. The yield was an inferior oil of harsh taste but salable nonetheless. The waste material of this manufacture, including the refuse from the pulp expressions, made a valuable fertilizer.[6]

The only other Georgia planter to experiment with the olive culture in Georgia besides the Coupers was Thomas Spalding. He secured his trees from Leghorn in Italy and by 1827, had five bearing trees and from forty to fifty trees which would soon be bearing. Although Spalding felt that the olive was a useful addition to all coastal orchards in his area, he never cultivated the tree to the extent that Couper did. He observed, though, that his trees had "grown with the vigor of our native oak...and for their age, are nearly as large as oaks would have been." But the winter of 1835, killed all his trees and this setback stifled his interest in the culture.[7]

After years of experimentation, James Hamilton Couper concluded that the olive could be grown successfully on the sea islands of Georgia. Not only were the soils of the region conducive to the culture, but the climate also. Moreover, crop land utilization could be kept at a maximum, for other crops could be grown on the same acreage in conjunction with olives. In addition, the manufacture of the crop's product into oil or pickled olives was relatively easy and inexpensive, to say nothing of the added benefit its cultivation gave to crop diversification. Of additional value also was the use of the refuse from the manufacture of the oil as a good fertilizer. In 1875, James Hamilton Couper's olive grove was still producing oil commercially, and, as late as 1895, pickled olives from his orchards were sent to the International Cotton Exposition in Atlanta.[8]

Besides his interest in crop diversification, Couper was keenly interested in soil agronomy. He felt that it was of utmost importance that a plantation maintain its soil fertility and that the planter get the maximum benefit from his soil. It was particularly imperative in his case, because all three of his major staples had to be grown in restricted areas, and he could not move to more virgin areas in the interior of the state when his lands were exhausted. Therefore, Couper sought to preserve the fertility of the lands he possessed by means of deep plowing, the proper use of fertilizers and crop rotation.

Couper believed in deep subsoil plowing, whereby the soil could be properly mixed with the clays lying further down. He believed that the depth of tillage was almost as important as the quality of the soil. Pointing out that manure spread over a field would not sink by its own volition and must be mixed well into the soil, he wrote, "just so deep as you plough, so deep will your manure sink, and consequently so deep will your soil be." In preparing a field for the planting of any crop, manure should first be spread and the soil should be sufficiently plowed to depth of twelve inches. Another plowing was needed to set the rows for reception of the seed. Subsequent shallow plowings were also needed to eradicate the weeds. If the initial plowing were not at least to a depth of twelve inches, the roots would find the lower depths of the row too hard and compact to penetrate, and the growth of the plant would be stunted. Yet, with deep plowing the roots would extend sufficiently deep to utilize the nutrients, and the result would be a more luxuriant growth. Also, this would place the roots beyond the reach of drought. Couper maintained that fields not fertilized should be plowed to the same depth.

In his records Couper related the practices of two eminent British agriculturists, Arbuthnot and Ducket, both of whom advocated deep plowing. Arbuthnot invented a swing plow with wheels to be pulled by two horses. This was used for gaining a depth of 12-18 inches. He considered one well-timed deep plowing to a proper depth as more important than the repeated shallow plowings so common elsewhere. Ducket also found that deep plowing greatly increased the yield of his fields.

Couper suggested six conditions a soil needed to meet before it could return its highest possible yield. The first was richness. This was maintained by manuring with vegetable and animal remains. Second was depth. This was necessary for full development of the plant and gave the roots a firmer hold in the ground. Third was friability. Unless the soil were loose, it was impossible for the roots to extend in search of food. Also, excess moisture could not penetrate it and the roots would be small, confined to the surface, and exposed to every vicissitude of season. Fourth was fineness of tilth. A soil might be friable and yet not be of fine tilth. Unless a soil was pulverized into very small particles it was difficult for it to absorb moisture and for the roots to secure their nutrients. The fifth condition was ample drainage. If a field were not properly drained the roots of the plants would remain close to the surface and would not penetrate to the desired depths. Consequently, they would be subject to extremes of climate—drowned by rains and parched by drought. Sixth was openness of the surface. Crops should not be planted so close together in the row nor should the rows be situated so close that the plants interlocked, thus preventing the soil from "breathing properly," for Couper believed that atmospheric influences on the soil were also important. He counseled against drawing up earth to growing plants. He felt it placed the roots at an unnatural depth, compelling the plant to throw out a new root system. Couper believed that if a soil were sufficiently deep, dry, and friable the roots would assume a sufficient and natural depth for the purposes of nourishment and support.[9]

Couper had no great faith in commercial fertilizers concocted by some chemist. Man had not been fair with nature; otherwise the operation would not be necessary. Still, he did believe in adding extraneous animal and vegetable matter to his fields to aid in restoring or preserving fertility. For this purpose, he used cane leaves, the expressed cane stalk pulp, and rice straw. The straw collection was placed 1 1/2-3 feet deep in the sheep, hog, or cattle pens. When this compost matured, it was spread on the rice fields and mixed well with the soil before spring planting. A particular preparation of sea-weed and marsh mud was used on the sugar cane and cotton fields. Just before planting, if and when it was available, Couper would lightly dress some of his fields with refuse from his olive oil manufacture. All the same, he did fall prey to the "guano craze" of the 1850s, for his records show that in 1854, he purchased fourteen tons of "salts and guano" for $36.00 a ton and one ton of pure Peruvian guano for $46.00.[10]

It is true that most planters fertilized their fields and that James Hamilton Couper was not unique in his advocacy of deep plowing. But his third practice for restoring and maintaining soil fertility was little used in the rice belt, save for a few other enlightened agriculturists. This was the practice of crop rotation.

Couper believed that crop rotation was the first great principle of agriculture, which nature itself suggested to man. Nature had provided many plants, but certain groups were not to be grown to the exclusion of others. Planters should rotate their crops, for rotation was nature's great fertilizer. Nature had divided the plant world into two great families which complimented each other. When the soil was tired of one type it was ready for another which did not require the same soil elements. One of these groups was ameliorative and tended to enrich the soil; the other was exhaustive and depleted the soil. The first group, having large succulent leaves and much open and tender bark, absorbed most of their nourishment from the atmosphere. On the other hand, the second group, those with firm and narrow leaves, and close and hard bark, derived their food chiefly from the soil. The root systems of the former went deep into the ground gathering nutrients as well as moisture from a great depth; they were tap or tuberous root systems. The roots of the latter extended near the surface and were called fibrous. The broad leafed plants of the first group were less debilitating, and, if a part of their remains were plowed under after maturing, they returned more nutrients to the soil than they took from it. On the contrary, narrow-leafed crops were highly exhausting even if some of their remains were plowed under. The first group was leguminous; the second culmiferous (jointed), made up of grain or grass plants. It was in the skillful arrangement of the two families of plants that all agricultural improvements must be directed. This was the philosophy underlying crop rotation, and Couper believed that by adhering to it land could be made to maintain its fertility. In addition, exhausted land could be redeemed by planting more ameliorating than exhausting crops.

Couper developed two distinct rotations that worked best for him at Hopeton. One was for highlands, the other for tidal swamplands. On the former he recommended the following sequence for a period of sixteen years:

1st year	sweet potatoes, manured, 1/3 roots, and 2/3 in vines preceded by cowpeas ploughed in, or cut green for forage.
2nd year	cotton
3rd year	corn, with a dressing of cottonseed, and a secondary crop of cowpeas, planted along side of the rows.
4th year	cotton
5th year	cane, manured with well rotted manure; spread broad-cast and well buried.
6th year	cotton
7th year	corn, with a dressing of cottonseed, and after crop cowpeas.
8th year	cotton
9th year	cowpeas, cut green for forage and followed by turnips, manured.
10th year	cane
11th year	cotton
12th year	corn with a dressing of cottonseed, and a mixed crop of pumpkins.
13th year	cotton
14th year	cane, manured.
15th year	cotton
16th year	corn, with an after crop of peas.[11]

Couper believed that this rotation fulfilled as nearly as any the principles he espoused on crop rotation. For example, the most valuable plants adapted to the soil and climate were used. Cotton, sweet potatoes, peas, turnips, and pumpkins which had broad leaves were alternated with cane and corn, which were narrow-leafed. The broad-leaved plants which ameliorating recurred more frequently, occupying the soil nine years as primary, and part of six years as secondary crops, while the narrow-leafed species occurred only seven times. Moreover, the fibrous rooted plants, cane and corn, were alternated with cotton and peas which were tap rooted, and sweet potatoes and turnips which were tuberous. The cultivation of the same crops on the same land year after year was avoided. Also, manure was applied at regular intervals, derived from the crops planted in the rotation and given only to the crops most benefited by it. The soil was kept constantly in a state of production, yielding crops valuable for sale, provision, forage, or the formation of manure. At no time was the land idle; therefore, there was no loss of interest on the capital invested in it.

The other cycle of rotation employed by the innovative Couper was on tide lands adapted to the culture of cane, cotton, and rice. This cycle extended over a period of nine years and was as follows:

1st year	cowpeas, land ploughed or deeply turned up early in the fall, and half-bedded—ploughed and harrowed in the spring, and sowed broadcast with peas, 1 1/2 to 2 bushels per acre.
2nd year	cane, manured with well-rotted trash and pea vines ploughed in.
3rd year	cotton, on cane trash listed in.
4th year	rice
5th year	cotton
6th year	cane, manured.
7th year	rice

If it be desirable to increase the quantity of rice, then after the third year, the rotation may be,

4th year	rice
5th year	rice
6th year	cotton
7th year	cane
8th year	rice
9th year	rice

The land should every year, after a rice crop be ploughed in ridges, immediately after the harvest and be kept dry during the winter. And the ridges to be reversed or leveled before planting in the spring.[12]

As in the previous rotation, the advantages of this cycle were that the land was continuously cropped with valuable staples, with the restorative and debilitating plants carefully balanced to maintain fertility. Unlike the first rotation, however, more exhausting crops were planted and fewer ameliorative ones. This was because the debilitative character of rice was reduced by silt deposits from the river during the various floodings of the crop.[13]

Couper often used a third rotation by which he cultivated both cotton and corn in a mixed state on the same land. In some years he would plant a particular field predominately in cotton with every third row in corn. In succeeding years he would switch the rows, and in some years every other row would be planted in corn. The corn, he believed, tended to keep the cotton from growing into leaves and stalk and made it; produce more fibre. In addition, by squeezing the rows closer together and applying extra manure, it was possible to achieve nearly as great a yield from each crop as if they had been planted separately.[14]

James Hamilton Couper kept copious accounts of his agricultural pursuits. In his records he constructed maps showing crops planted at Hopeton from 1820 to 1841, and wrote remarks concerning the success of or failure of his crops.

Upon examining Couper's field-by-field account of his crop land use during the period on record, it is obvious that he used a crop rotation system. In most cases his sequence of cropping sufficiently balanced crops of a leguminous character with those of a culmiferous. Particularly noteworthy are the rotations practiced on field Number Two South and West Old Field. For periods of thirteen years in the former case and twelve years in the latter, Couper carefully arranged plants that would maintain or even increase the fertility of these fields. On field Number Two cotton, which is ameliorative, was planted in 1819. Then for the next seven years a combination of cotton mixed with peas and corn was planted. The only crop in this series to be exhaustive was corn, and the three crops were rotated by rows each year. Some years corn and peas were planted every third row; in other years every other row. This series was broken in 1827, when rice (culmiferous) was planted for the next three years. This was followed by cotton and rice splitting the acreage in 1830, and cane and corn occupying the same position in 1831. This was a very ameliorative rotation and was most likely applied to this field because of poor soils. Similarly, on West Old Field an ingenious rotation was devised whereby the less exhausting or restorative crops, cotton, rape,[15] sweet potatoes, and pumpkins, were grown in mixed cultivation with the debilitating crops, cane and corn.

It is clear from studying Couper's extant crop records that he carefully analyzed the soil composition of his fields and tried to arrange for a rotation to fit them. If a field were of low fertility, less exhausting crops were planted; if it were fertile, more exhausting crops and of longer duration could be sustained.[16] However, questions now present themselves as to how beneficial crop rotation was, not only to Couper but to the few other enlightened planters who engaged in it. Furthermore, if crop rotation was as beneficial to the agricultural system as Couper and other scientific agriculturists maintained, why was it not adopted by the majority of planters?

J. D. Legare, editor of the *Southern Agriculturist*, made extensive tours of the major rice plantations along the rice coast of South Carolina and Georgia. After a visit to Hopeton in 1832, Legare commented that nowhere in the area was crop rotation practiced as systematically as on the Couper plantations. Furthermore, he stated that crop rotation was not practiced on most of the estates he visited. Couper explained to Legare why he felt crop rotation was so important. For example, he asserted that his system of rotating various staples with rice was very favorable to the increased production of each. It was particularly so with the rice crop, which yielded 60-70 bushels per acre when planted after a dissimilar crop. But, if rice were planted on the same field for a succession of years, the yield would fall to 45-50 bushels per acre. Couper's average yield for the fourteen-year period on record ending with 1840 was 53.5 bushels per acre. This yield was certainly above both the Georgia average of 50 bushels per acre and the South Carolina average of 40 bushels per acre. However, on individual fields Couper had yields as high as 85 bushels per acre.

Allston of South Carolina and Spalding of Georgia were among the few rice planters who practiced crop rotation. Both testified to its benefit. Spalding credited his unusually high average yields of 60 bushels per acre to crop rotation, and Allston commented that he had made "prize rice" as a result of the practice. The reason other planters of the rice coast did not follow the lead of Couper, Spalding and Allston was that it interfered with their specialization in the rice industry. Rice was such a valuable money crop that few dared to plant another just to rejuvenate the soil.[17]

In further defense of a rotation system, Couper pointed out that the continued cultivation of land did not necessarily mean that it would lose fertility; indeed, with proper management fertility could be maintained without excessive use of fertilizer. This idea was proven on Couper's own lands. His records show that during the period of management of Hopeton and his other plantations there was no decline in yields after continuous years of cropping. In fact, several fields showed their heaviest yields toward the end of the period on record and their lowest yields at the beginning of their cultivation. Evidence points to the fact that there was little soil exhaustion at Hopeton.[18]

Couper's advice was sound, and by 1834, his reputation as a scientific agriculturist had been established. It was in that year that J. D. Legare resigned his position as editor of the *Southern Agriculturist*. In a farewell address to his readers, he recommended to all young farmers that they familiarize themselves with James Hamilton Couper's pronouncements on crop rotation and follow his example as a model planter.[19]

In 1818, James Hamilton Couper began his career as a neophyte planter but by 1860, he had established himself as a planter worthy of emulation. His agricultural career spanned four decades of the antebellum era and saw a multiple farm transformed into one which produced predominately rice. Through the years he became known for his superior knowledge of diking and water control—a knowledge he had gleaned from the Dutch themselves. As a scientific agriculturist, he believed in crop diversification, well understanding the folly of too much dependence on one crop. In this attempt he introduced new and valuable crops into his area and suggested new uses for old ones. So successful was he with the olive culture that planters along the Atlantic coast, as well as editors of such progressive agricultural journals of the day as the *Southern Agriculturist* and *De Bow's Review*, sought his opinions. He was also greatly concerned with soil conservation. By corresponding with leading agriculturists abroad and subscribing to a collection of foreign agricultural publications, he kept abreast of the newest and most effective methods. In his efforts to conserve the soil he utilized deep plowing effectively and experimented with the proper use of fertilizers—taking soil samples to ascertain exactly what additives his fields needed. He worked out a detailed system of crop rotation which matched his soils with crops for the most advantageous results.

He was, without doubt, a first-rate agriculturist. At one time the cargo of a Couper schooner bound for market would contain cotton, sugar, rice, and olive oil. James Hamilton Couper was a pragmatic farmer whose contribution lay in showing others how farming could be accomplished successfully.

Notes

[1]James Hamilton Couper Plantation Records, 4 vols., 4:4, Southern Historical Collection, University of North Carolina, Chapel Hill; Merton E. Coulter, *Thomas Spalding of Sapelo* (Baton Rouge: Louisiana State Univeristy Press, 1960) 87-89.

[2]J. D. Legare, "Account of an Agricultural Excursion Made into the South of Georgia in the Winter of 1832," *Southern Argiculturalist and Register of Rural Affairs* 6 (May-November 1833): 360-61; Allen Johnson and Dumas Malone, eds., *Dictionary of American Biography* 20 vols. (New York NY: Charles Scribner's Sons, 1930) 4:468; Coulter, *Thomas Spalding*, 100; Julia Floyd Smith, *Slavery & Rice Culture in Low Country Georgia, 1750-1860* (Knoxville: University of Tennessee Press, 1985) 225-26.

[3]Margaret Davis Cate and Orrin Sage Wrightman, *Early Days of Coastal Georgia* (St. Simons GA: Fort Frederica Association, 1955) 55; Legare, "Account of Agricultural Excursion," 250-52; James Hamilton Couper to Mitchell King, 1846, Mackay Stiles Papers, Southern Historical Collection, University of North Carolina, Chapel Hill. Portions of a letter reprinted in George M. White, *Statistics of the State of Georgia* (Savannah GA: W. Throne Williams, 1849) 276-82.

[4]"Cultivation of the Olive in the Southern States," *De Bow's Review* 3 (March 1847): 265-66; Thomas Jefferson to M. Cathalan, fils, 22 March 1804, Mackay Stiles Papers, Southern Historical Collection; James Hamilton Couper to Mitchell King, 1846, Mackay Stiles Papers, Southern Historical Collection; John Couper, "Remarks on the Culture of the Olive Tree," *Southern Agriculturist and Register of Rural Affairs* 1 (July 1828): 303; John Couper, "General Observations on the Olive, Orange, and Date Trees Growing in Georgia; and the Method of Cultivating the Ruta Baga Turnip as a Second Crop after Corn," *Southern Agriculturist and Register of Rural Affairs* 8 (July 1835): 350; John Couper, "Account of an Attempt to Cultivate the Olive," *Southern Agriculturist and Register of Rural Affairs* 3 (May 1830): 234.

[5]James Hamilton Couper to Mitchell King, 1846, Mackay Stiles Papers, Southern Historical Collection.

[6]Ibid.

[7]Coulter, *Thomas Spalding*, 95; Thomas Spalding, "Brief Notes on the Cultivation of Cotton, Rice, Sugar Cane, the Grape Vine, Silkworms, and Olives," *Southern Agriculturist and Register of Rural Affairs* 1 (March 1828): 108-109.

[8]*Savannah* (GA) *Morning News,* Magazine section, 16 May 1965, 6.

[9]James Hamilton Couper Plantation Records, 4:3-6, Southern Historical Collection.

[10]Legare, "Account of Agricultural Excursion," 366; James Hamilton Couper Plantation Records, 2:493; 4:9, 11, 14-15, Southern Historical Collection; James Hamilton Couper to Mitchell King, 1846, Mackay Stiles Papers, Southern Historical Collection. Because of the leguminous nature of cotton it took less fertilizer than either rice or sugar cane; indeed, planters with naturally fertile lands did not need to fertilize their cotton fields on a regular basis.

[11]James Hamilton Couper, "Essay on Rotation of Crops," *Southern Agriculturist and Register of Rural Affairs* 4 (February 1833): 58-59.

[12]Ibid., 61-62.

[13]Couper, "Essay on Rotation of Crops," 58-64; James Hamilton Couper Plantation Records, 3:1-54, Southern Historical Collection.

[14]James Hamilton Couper Plantation Records, 3:26, 30, 34, 38, Southern Historical Collection; William Allister Noble, "Sequent Occupance of Hopeton-Altama, 1816-1956" (Master's thesis, University of Georgia, 1956) 69.

[15]Rape is an herb of the mustard family often grown as forage for livestock and for its seeds.

[16]James Hamilton Couper Plantation Records, 3:1-54, Southern Historical Collection.

[17]Ibid., vols. 2, 4; Legare, "Account of Agricultural Excursion," 410-13; Noble, "Sequent Occupance of Hopeton-Altama," 53; Coulter, *Thomas Spalding*, 79; J. H. Easterby, ed., *The South Carolina Rice Plantation as Revealed in the Papers of Robert F.W. Allston* (Chicago: University of Chicago Press, 1945) 265-66; Lewis Cecil Gray, *History of Agriculture in the Southern United States to 1860* 2 vols. (Washington DC: Carnegie Institution, 1933) 2:726-27; Albert Virgil House Jr., ed., *Planter Management and Capitalism in Ante-Bellum Georgia: The Journal of Hugh Fraser Grant, Rice Grower* (New York NY: Columbia University Press, 1954) 47.

[18]James Hamilton Couper, "Essay on Rotation of Crops," *Southern Agriculturist and Register of Rural Affairs* 4 (January-February 1834): 59; Noble, "Sequent Occupance of Hopeton-Altama," 76; James Hamilton Couper Plantation Records, 3:1-54, Southern Historical Collection.

[19]J. D. Legare, "Farewell Address of the Editor," *Southern Agriculturist and Register of Rural Affairs*, VII (December, 1834), 661.

CHAPTER IX

Slavery and Plantation Management

James Hamilton Couper was one of the largest slaveowners in the South, and his success at plantation management won him the acclaim of his peers. Considered the epitome of the benevolent master, his expertise in the handling of slaves was well known to planters of the rice coast. It was his reputation in this area that attracted both American and foreign visitors to his door. He particularly interested reformers, who were intrigued with his methods of slave management and his opinions on the institution itself.

What were Couper's attitudes toward the Negro and the institution of slavery? To be sure, he accepted black bondage as the necessary foundation upon which his world rested and strove to protect it from detractors in the North and in England. In a letter of March 1856, he denounced the dismissal of the Honorable Amelia Murray, Lady-in-Waiting to queen Victoria, for her pro-slavery views. Miss Murray had visited Hopeton the year before and, following her return to England, had insisted upon printing her views on Southern slavery. Her account was so complimentary to the institution that it horrified British public opinion, resulting in her curt dismissal from court.

In his support of Miss Murray, Couper called her book "an unaffected, unprejudiced and sensible view of the country." He praised her insight into the real condition of slavery in America and felt that she had seized upon the "true and strong points of the case." He asserted that the world was indebted to her for a clearer understanding of Southern slavery and that her opinion on the subject was the best that had ever "emanated from Northern or European mind." He concluded that her persecution was another example of the truism that the world loved "not truth, but a subservient concurrence of opinion."[1]

On another occasion, Couper told the Swedish novelist Fredrika Bremer, who visited Hopeton in 1851, that the tropical races could never attain the development and intelligence of native whites in the temperate zones. He considered the former deficient in the powers of abstract thought, systematization, and reasoning. The Negro race, according to Couper, typified the highest state of the life of feeling, and their primitive life conditions imprisoned them. Religion, however, was a means of elevating them. They were receptive to culture, he felt, and might, during their subjection to a more developed race, evolve a very respectable capacity for thought and artistic appreciation. They might arrive at a somewhat higher degree of semi-civilization. Couper regarded slavery in America as a school for the children of Africa in which they could be educated for eventual self-government in their native land. He viewed slavery as a benefit to them. However, the master of Hopeton realized that the winds of change were blowing against the institution as world opinion shifted steadily against it. Consequently, he did not envision slavery as a permanent fixture on the American scene, and to avoid a race problem in the future, the best idea was the eventual recolonization of all blacks in Africa.[2]

James Hamilton Couper had an ample laboratory in which to develop and execute his ideas on slave and plantation management. There were four principal plantations under his care. First, there was Hopeton, the plantation along the Altamaha River on which he lived. To the south on St. Simons Island were the two plantations of Cannon's Point located on the northeast end of the island, and Hamilton on the southeast end. Added to these was Barrett's Island plantation, lying south of and adjacent to Hopeton in the Altamaha delta. Hopeton and Barrett's Island plantations were chiefly devoted to rice, while Hamilton and Cannon's Point were mainly given to the culture of long staple cotton. In 1853, Couper merged Barrett's Island plantation with the Hopeton property, and the Hopeton agricultural unit reached the mammoth size of 7773 acres. A slave force of approximately 1500 blacks worked under Couper's direction on these various plantations.[3]

Much has been made of Couper's reputation as a benign paternalist who looked upon his slaves as "his people" and belonging to "his family." If a theme could be extracted from Couper's dealings with his bonded humanity, this would be it. Some indication of his charitableness can be gained from reading the travel accounts of those who visited Hopeton. One observation came from Mrs. Basil Hall, who, along with her husband, a captain in the British Royal Navy, and their little daughter Eliza, came to the Georgia coast on the invitation of Couper. They arrived in March 1828, and on Tuesday, 17 March, she wrote a friend from Hopeton:

> …We have been with a man of a very different stamp from those we are in the habit of meeting. I mean our host, Mr. James

Hamilton Couper of Hopeton.... It does you good to meet such man, not to reconcile you to slavery on principle, but to show how much the evil which appears to be irremediable at present may be softened by proper management.[4]

In 1830, Hopeton was in the ecclesiastical parish of a Northern-born Episcopal priest, the Reverend George F. Clarke, who wrote that his parish contained "white families and 1000 slaves." He apparently lived at or near Hopeton, for he periodically referred to his host as "Mr. Couper." He commented that he saw no cruelty at Hopeton and observed that the servants did not work as hard as the wives of Northern farmers. He added, "I wonder how many wealthy men of his day, would rise from their dinner tables to shake the hand of an aged servant, a sight I once witnessed at Hopeton."[5]

In January 1846, Sir Charles Lyell, president of the Geologic Society of London, with his wife, Lady Lyell, came to spend two weeks at Hopeton. They were keenly interested in plantation life and especially the treatment of the Negroes. Lyell found Couper to be a benevolent slave-owner and discerned an hereditary regard and attachment between master and slave. Hopeton reminded him of a medieval manor; there were about 500 slaves on the plantation at that time.[6]

Fredrika Bremer was also highly interested in Couper's treatment of his slaves. He had been mentioned to her "as a reformer, who had introduced trial by jury among his slaves, with many educational institutions, to prepare them for a future of liberty." This had created in her a desire to see him and to examine his paternalism at close range. However, she did not find him the reformer she had imagined, but "merely a disciplinarian, with great practical tact, and also some benevolence in the treatment of the Negroes."[7]

Of all the visitors to Hopeton probably none was more convinced of Couper's benevolence than Amelia Murray. As this was her first visit to a slave plantation, she did not know what to expect, for she had been told since childhood that American slavery was most brutal. However, after her stay, she freely admitted that those long-held views were completely erroneous. She visited the various establishments at Hopeton and commented that the slaves were better dressed than the English peasantry and looked happier. She was so impressed with slave management at Hopeton that, before leaving, she had become an ardent supporter of the system.

Her conversion seems to have been genuine, and she wondered if there were any parts of Africa, the West Indies, or South America in which the natives were as well cared for and as happy.[8]

The English lady marveled at the affection displayed by the slaves at Hopeton toward their master. She recounted that, when hurricanes threatened the rice fields, the slaves worked freely eighteen out of twenty-four hours to save the crop. Upon leaving, she commented: "We have been blindly endeavoring to counteract this intention (slavery), believing ourselves more religious, virtuous and benevolent than these slaveholders... I must tell of my honest convictions, and the truth..."[9] These and other visitors to Hopeton testified that James Hamilton Couper was charitable in the treatment of his slaves.

The ultimate objective of slave management was the creation of a highly disciplined, highly specialized and well-coordinated labor force. Specialization and interdependence were most important. James Hamilton Couper believed in efficiency, and his slaves were as rigidly organized as workers in a factory. To secure the most profitable work from his wards, he placed them in "hand" categories. This grouping according to ability, age and sex indicated what level of work each slave was capable of and expected to do. An accurate check on their performance was made each day.

Field hands were divided into work groups according to sex. There were four efficiency ratings for both sexes. The first category was that of full hands. Prime young men and women who were expected to carry a full work load were placed here. Those who could not carry such a load were put into one of the three remaining efficiency categories—the three-quarter, one-half or one-quarter units. Those not able to do any work at all were classed as non-hands. They consisted of the ill, the very old and the very young. When a slave's ability to perform changed, his classification changed. For example, a young man of seventeen might be shifted from a three-quarter hand to a full hand, while a fifty-five year old man, because of increasing age, might be dropped from a full hand to a three-quarter hand.[10]

Couper used three work division methods—the gang system, the task system and the jobber system. In the gang system each gang worked under a separate driver whose authority was limited to his own gang. This driver was subject to a head driver who supervised all the gangs. Above the head driver in the chain of command was the overseer, and, of course, ultimate authority rested with Couper. The character of the gang was appropriate to the type of work it was assigned to do. For example, in ditching only prime full hands were used. For moting and assorting cotton, where numbers and not strength were required, women of one-half hand category were used. In the harvesting of cane, number one women cut the cane, number two women stripped the blades and number three women bound and carried the cane. However, the method most frequently used by Couper was the task system. Sub-drivers and head drivers also supervised this mode of work. Each slave was given a precise assignment; when he finished, he was off for the day. In addition to the field hands, there were a number of jobbers. They too were put into classes, with one individual in each class having charge of it and reporting at the end of each day the work done. The principal classes were carpenters, coopers, blacksmiths, masons, carters, stockminders, hospital attendants, nursery supervisors, gardeners and grounds-keepers.[11]

Couper meticulously supervised the labor of all plantation personnel. At the end of each work day the drivers, head drivers and chief artisans made their reports of the work done that day to the overseer in the presence of Couper. The reports were rendered in great detail, giving the size of work force, job or task involved, and the specific field or area in which the work was done. These reports were jotted down by Couper on slate tablets and then copied in his "Journal of Plantation Work," which was a copious account of the work accomplished on the plantation each day by the various slave divisions. After the reports were received, the work for the following day was arranged and the head driver was given his directions. He distributed the orders to the sub-drivers and heads of classes, and they, in turn, transmitted them to the hands under their charge. The quantity of land in each field was known precisely to Couper, and he made daily checks on each field to ascertain the validity of the reports and to make sure all operations were performed properly.[12]

The slave's work day began promptly at 6:00 A.M. At 9:00 A.M., work was stopped for the slaves to have breakfast and rest, and at 10:00 P.M. the work was resumed. Many of the slaves finished their tasks by 2:00 P.M., and all regular field work stopped an hour later.[13] The number of hours slaves worked in the rice fields of the Georgia and South Carolina low country was certainly less than that required on the short staple cotton plantations of middle Georgia or the sugar plantations of

Louisiana or the West Indies, all of which practiced the "sun-up to sun-down" rule. On those plantations slaves worked at least twelve hours a day and sometimes more. Indeed, the task system employed by Couper was extraordinarily benevolent. Some overseers even complained that the slaves had too much leisure time, a factor which encouraged idleness. Following his visit with Couper, Sir Charles Lyell commented that the Hopeton slaves, "when disposed to exert themselves, could finish the day's task in five hours." On the plantations of the rice coast the work day did not usually exceed ten hours and was oftentimes less, sometimes not exceeding five or six hours. Hence, Couper, with his general requirement of a seven to eight-hour work day and the possibility of some slaves finishing in five hours, was certainly lenient when compared with both planters outside the rice coast and with other planters of the low country in setting a work regimen for their slaves.[14]

However, during the cane harvest much more was required of the Hopeton slaves, for when the crop became "ready," it had to be gathered as quickly as possible or irreparable damage could be done the staple. During this time the workers were on a tight schedule and labored as much as sixteen hours a day. According to the planter, instead of harming the bondsmen, the excitement and importance of harvest time seemed to exhilarate the slaves. Couper wrote, "During that period the hands are cheerful, and at its termination they have improved in general appearance. At no period of the year is there so little sickness, or disposition to avoid work."[15]

Their are other issues besides work load in examining slave treatment. The average weekly allowance of food given by planters in general to their slaves was 3 1/2 pounds of bacon or salted sidemeat and a peck of cornmeal for every adult hand. The daily ration amounted to about 2 pounds of meal and 1/2 pound of pork per adult. This ration provided the core of the slave diet. Many planters supplemented these staples with molasses, and slaves were generally allowed a garden and poultry, which added to the variety of their diet.[16] Unfortunately, there is little available evidence concerning the exact weekly or daily issue of food to Couper's slaves. The only inkling comes from Basil Hall, who wrote that the slaves at Cannon's Point over fourteen years of age received 9 quarts of corn-meal per week and the children 5-8 quarts. He further observed that adult slaves were allowed a quart of salt per month, plus salt fish and occasionally salt beef. He observed that, on occasion, a "heaped-up bushel" of sweet potatoes or two pecks of rice were substituted for the cornmeal allotment. Sir Charles Lyell was of the opinion, after his two-week stay at Hopeton, that the slave diet there was more than adequate. He wrote in his account that "their weekly rations are more than they can eat and they either return part of it to the overseer who makes them an allowance of money for it at the end of the week, or they keep it to feed their fowls."[17] Fredrika Bremer reported simply that the slaves were well fed.[18]

The Hopeton slaves were allowed the standard staples of cornmeal and pork, together with rice, milk and soup. On occasion, the diet was supplemented with beef and mutton, which were produced on the plantation. In addition, the slaves supplemented this diet with vegetables from their gardens and poultry and eggs from their yards. In the late afternoons fishing, snaring and trapping were favorite sports, providing fish, terrapin, rabbit, raccoon, and opossum for slave tables as well as amusement. Also, since Couper was one of the largest sugar growers in Georgia—producing 21,930 gallons of molasses in 1832 alone—it is highly probable that molasses was included in the diet of the slaves. Despite the monotony of the slave diet, its nutritional value was high. Notably it was a diet shared by most of the white small farmers of Georgia.[19]

A properly-clad labor force was as important as a well-fed one. The usual yearly issue for adult males on most plantations consisted of four cotton shirts and four pairs of pants, two cotton and two wool. They also received two hats, one of straw to shield them from the summer sun and one of wool for winter wear. Also, for the winter months the men received a jacket and sometimes an overcoat. The women were provided with four dresses, or enough material to make them, and headkerchiefs. Blankets were issued every two or three years, and all adult slaves generally received about two pairs of shoes a year. The issue of socks and underwear was irregular. Clothing for children generally consisted of a one-piece cotton garment resembling a night shirt.[20]

Again no records substantiates the exact amount of clothing issued at Hopeton. But visitors to the plantation noted that the Hopeton Negroes were well dressed.[21] Certainly, regular issues of clothing were made at Hopeton, and the records show that Couper spent over $1000 each year on these articles. It appears that plantation seamstresses were employed to produce much of the finished clothing. In 1828, $321.89 was expended for shoes, $1,203.25 was spent for domestic plain cloth and blankets. On 5 December of the same year, 246 blankets were purchased for $612.12.[22] Slaves also supplemented their clothing allowance with purchases from town. When Mrs. Couper made her periodic visits to Savannah or Charleston, she always took with her a long list of slave orders for material to be used in making clothes. Significantly, Mrs. Couper made detailed notes of each woman's preferences as to the precise color and shade of cloth to be purchased.[23]

Another of the necessities of slave life was adequate housing. On some model plantations slaves were settled in comfortable, commodious cottages, while on others the slaves lived in hovels with dirt floors. Typical cabins, however, measured 18 feet by 20 feet and consisted of one or two rooms with a loft. The windows had no glass but were closed with wooden shutters. Such cabins generally had no back door but had floors of plank raised off the ground. The chimneys were usually of stone or brick.[24]

Sir Charles Lyell characterized the Hopeton slave quarters, located north of the plantation mansion, as "neat and comfortable cottages."[25] They formed two long columns of houses separated by a wide street; at the farther end was the overseer's cabin. Great live oaks lined the street of the quarters from the Hopeton mansion to the overseer's house. The slave cottages were neat and whitewashed, and all were floored with boards raised from the ground. Each cabin had a hall, fireplace, two sleeping rooms and a loft for children. All were single family units with both front and back doors. Furnishings for the cabins were made on the plantation. On the door of the sleeping compartment the slaves kept a large wooden padlock to guard their valuables from their neighbors when they were at work in the fields, for there was much pilfering among them. Behind each cabin was a yard, where the slaves kept their fowls, hogs and gardens. Almost every slave family kept a dog for their amusement. At first the slave cabins were made of wood, but later additions were constructed of tabby, which added much to the neatness of appearance and to the comfort of the inhabitants.[26]

Another important area of slave welfare besides food, clothing and shelter was medical care. Most planters considered the adequate health maintenance of their slaves a chief objective. To achieve this end, facilities for the treatment of the sick were established on most plantations. Such treatment centers, of course, varied with the size of the plantation. On

126

larger plantations sizable hospitals were maintained, but on smaller units only a single cabin might be used to treat the sick. Occasionally, a planter would set aside several rooms in his own house for such purposes, these health centers were staffed with slave nurses. Rarely was a plantation large enough to employ a resident doctor. Symptoms were treated and, in the case of serious illness, doctors were summoned. Usually, the slaves were attended by the same doctor who treated the master's family. Physicians made regular visits to the plantations. Some planters paid doctors flat yearly fees, the price depending on the size of the slave force.[27]

Again, in this area as in others, Hopeton plantation can be held up as a model. Kenneth Stampp has gone so far as to assert that in Couper's Hopeton hospital, "ailing slaves received the best medical attention the South could provide."[28] James Hamilton Couper kept a well-staffed hospital and nursery for the sick and infants on the plantation. It was located north of the Hopeton mansion and surrounded by live oaks and a large yard of neatly cut grass. A large rectangular building of tabby construction, it was airy in summer and warm in winter, heated with steam supplied by two copper boilers which kept the temperature more constant than fireplaces. The hospital portion of the building consisted of an area measuring 80 feet by 24 feet. It contained four wards, an entrance room, an examining room, a medicine room, a kitchen, and a bathing room. One ward was for "lying-in-women," another for sick women, and two others for men. An interesting observation made by Couper was that although pregnant women received much better care in the hospital, where they could "gossip with their friends without restraint," they usually contrived to be taken by surprise at home. After childbirth, a woman was allowed a month's rest from regular work.[29]

Each patient in the hospital was accommodated with a cot, a straw mattress and pillow, a pillow case, two blankets and a bedspread. The beds were refilled with clean straw once a month, and the pillow cases, blankets and bedspreads were washed at specified intervals. The wards were swept clean every day and washed out once a week. The whole building was white-washed twice a year. The sick were allowed okra, coffee, molasses, gruel and other nourishment when required. A daily account was kept of the names of the sick, their diseases and the treatment given. A head nurse with attendants supervised the operation. A physician apparently was not in residence at Hopeton, but Couper contracted with such an individual to make regular visits to the plantation to see the slaves. In cases of emergency or severe illness, the doctor was summoned immediately. Sir Charles Lyell observed that Mrs. Couper often sat up all night with a sick slave, and it was not uncommon for ailing slaves to refuse to take any medicine except that given to them by their master or mistress. It is possible that her actions resulted from a feeling of responsibility and duty, and that the slaves responded out of respect and confidence.[30]

The nursery was in the same building and adjacent to the regular hospital area. All children under the age of twelve stayed in the nursery. They were placed under the charge of "a careful old woman" as nurse, and had a half-hand to cook for them. Each morning about sun-up the children from the different settlements were brought by their mothers to the nursery. The old nurse in charge saw them "washed and combed." At 8:00 A.M., a breakfast of hominy and molasses was issued to them. At 2:00 P.M., "a dinner of soup made of salt pork, and either Irish potatoes okra, peas or turnips, together with corn dumplings or sweet potatoes" was served. At sunset the children were returned home, and during Sundays they remained there. "Suckling women" were allowed to work near the settlement and came to the nursery to suckle their infants, who were never carried into the fields. To enable these women to be near their infants, one-quarter work was deducted from their tasks. The nursery room, like the hospital, was heated by steam and well ventilated. Attached to it was a spacious porch that faced a large grass-covered yard with plenty of shade trees.[31]

Another area of slave welfare that was important on Hopeton plantation was religious instruction. James Hamilton Couper felt very strongly about this provision and confided to Fredrika Bremer that religion was one way to elevate the slaves' minds which he felt were imprisoned by "natural life."[32] Consequently, many of the Hopeton Negroes were taught to read and write, although the practice was illegal in Georgia, and religious instruction was given regularly. The slaves learned much at Sunday School. Though the Coupers were Episcopalians, Methodist and Baptist ministers were allowed to address the Hopeton Negroes. However, when Stephen Elliott, a good friend of the Couper's became Bishop of Georgia in 1841, the Episcopalians became extremely active and dominated religious activity at Hopeton. The Episcopal priests found that the Negroes had little faith in baptism unless they were immersed. The slaves believed that being totally immersed washed away their sins, and they enjoyed going into the Altamaha River dressed in white gowns with shoes trimmed in silver for the baptismal rite. Couper paid a clergyman $50.00 a year to minister to the religious needs of his slaves.[33]

Foreign visitors to Hopeton were surprised at the religious instruction given the slaves. Before coming to Hopeton, Mrs. Basil Hall thought that planters in the Southern states made very little provision for the religious needs of their chattels. However, before she left, her opinion had been somewhat altered. On Sunday, 17 March 1828, she wrote that the weather was too bad to travel to the church five miles away, but, since the minister lived with the Coupers, church services were conducted in the drawing room at Hopeton. According to her account, "all the Negroes about the house" were gathered in the adjoining hall with two entrances to the drawing room left open, thereby making a large congregation.[34]

In the important area of discipline, Couper also exhibited unusual benevolence, but he realized that correct discipline was necessary for the maintenance of order on his plantations, that the extremes of indulgence and severity were equally fatal to the happiness and good conduct of slaves. Couper's rules and regulations were simple—obedience, attention, honesty and orderly behavior were insisted upon. Every departure from correct conduct was promptly but moderately punished. Couper made his slaves aware, as he did to his own children, that crime or misconduct would be followed by punishment—and "justice was meted out with an even hand to all." Once this policy was established and adhered to, Couper had very little trouble with discipline.[35]

Whipping was accepted as the standard mode of punishment in the antebellum era. Planters generally set limits beyond which their drivers and overseers could not go in disciplining the slaves. The average number of lashes given for an ordinary offense was twenty, and thirty-nine was common for more serious ones.[36] James Hamilton Couper, however, set unusually low limits. No ordinary driver was allowed to give more than six lashes for any offense; the head driver was limited to twelve, and the overseer to twenty-four.[37]

Compared to the practices of other planters in his area and of other plantations the size of Hopeton with its 500 or more Negroes, this policy showed remarkable leniency. For example, neighboring proprietor Pierce Butler allowed each driver to "administer twelve lashes, the head driver thirty-six, and the overseer fifty." Similarly, James H. Hammond of South Carolina, who considered himself to be a relatively benevolent slaveholder, set his highest limit at 100 lashes in a single day.[38] The type of whip used was as significant as the number of lashes. The whip employed on the Couper plantations was a strip of leather "half an inch wide and a quarter of an inch thick." Sometimes a slave would not respond to the lash. In this event Couper sold the slave. He also sold slaves for attempting to run away.[39]

Basil Hall, who was particularly interested in the institution of slavery, came to America with decided opinion against it. But from Cannon's Point he wrote:

> It is a mistake to suppose, that slaves labour sulkily, and under the perpetual threat of the lash. On the contrary, from constant habit, they do, in point of fact, go about their work with cheerfulness; and, as their tasks are limited to what can be readily performed, it is in the power of every slave who chooses, to escape punishment for any length of time...
>
> I do not say that undue severity is nowhere exercised; but the discipline, taken upon the average, as far as I could learn, is not more strict than is necessary for the maintenance of a proper degree of authority without which, the whole framework of society in that quarter would be blown to atoms.[40]

Sir Charles Lyell commented in 1846, that he had come to see Couper on scientific matters but was struck by his host's success in handling his slaves. Upon observing the institution as practiced at Hopeton, he pronounced the discipline lenient but firm and commented that the lash was rarely used there, and on a well-run plantation like Hopeton, "the whip did not crack often or excessively; the threat of its use, in combination with other incentives and threats, preserved order." But the threat was sufficient to have a profound psychological impact on the slaves.[41]

James Hamilton Couper also employed a host of non-punitive incentives which were integrated into the whole fabric of slave management at Hopeton. These incentives affected the institution of slavery as practiced at Hopeton, for the slaves were cognizant of the fact that their master was firm but kindly disposed toward them. It was this realization on the part of the Hopeton Negroes that made for their superior attitude, which manifested itself in improved productivity, efficiency, and general well-being of the plantation.

Slavery and Plantation Management

To begin with, there was the short work day at Hopeton with the most industrious slaves finishing in five hours. This incentive affected work performance, for when their work was finished, they could spend time in personal endeavors. With this in mind, slaves tended to work faster and more efficiently. Hasty and careless work was avoided by a thorough inspection by the driver of a slave's finished task. The slaves could utilize their free time in a variety of ways, such as working in their gardens. In the summer months the slave women busied themselves preserving fruits and vegetables for the winter.

The money incentive was also apparent among the slaves, for, besides selling their extra garden produce they enjoyed snaring of game or fishing in the late afternoons and sold their bounty for profit. Since Couper and his family were fond of boating, some slaves engaged themselves in making canoes, which they sold to their master for $4.00 per canoe. Moreover, they all kept a variety of fowls which they sold, along with the eggs, for profit. Basil Hall commented that Couper paid his slaves 12 1/2 cents for a dozen eggs, a like amount for a frying-size chicken, and 20-25 cents for grown chickens. Ducks, dressed, brought 50 cents each. But, as Hall observed, "they are left at liberty to carry their poultry to a better market if they can find one." Similarly, the slaves collected money by selling back to the overseer food issued in excess of their actual need.[42]

Another incentive Couper employed was allowing slaves to cultivate their own crops to be sold at market prices. Couper rewarded good conduct by allowing male slaves who showed sufficient industry and good character to engage in this practice. For this purpose, Couper set aside a large acreage at the northwestern end of his plantation, called "Pineland," which was designated for slave use. The two main crops planted were corn and potatoes, with corn being the principal crop. On one occasion Couper deviated from his standard practice of one man to the plot and tried a type of collective enterprise with his slaves. He carefully picked twenty-one men and assigned them a fifty-acre plot for three consecutive years. In addition to their normal free time, he gave them half their Saturday labor to till it. The first year, under Couper's direction, they produced $1,500 in crops, for which Couper paid them in silver, hoping to excite their industry. The money was divided equally among them. But the next year, left under their own direction, the crop lessened by one-half, and the third season they let the land go to waste. Couper did not renew the relationship and considered his "collective venture" a failure.

131

He resumed his policy of individual plots, which he found the slaves liked better than holding land in common.[43] With money secured from these various enterprises, the slaves were fond of making purchases from town, usually assisted by Mrs. Couper. Attended by a group of slaves, she made periodic trips to Darien, Savannah or Charleston to secure the desired commodities. Clothing, tobacco and trinkets of various sorts were articles most often bought.[44]

Another item which the slaves were allowed to buy was their freedom. This incentive stimulated initiative, industry and thrift. Amelia Murray recorded a particular dilemma facing Couper when she visited in February 1855. It seems that, years before, Couper had contracted with one of his slaves for manumission as soon as the slave secured enough money from his various enterprises to effect the sale. As Miss Murray recounted, the Negro had judiciously saved his money with the intention of buying his freedom, but upon collecting the desired amount, he changed his mind and earnestly entreated his master not to sell him his freedom.[45]

Another type of benevolence exhibited by planters toward their slaves was the observance of certain holidays during which time the slaves were allowed a respite from their labors. The most common ones were Christmas, Good Friday, Independence Day, and mid-summer when the crop was "laid by." Of these the most extended holiday period was Christmas. Even the severest masters gave their slaves Christmas Day to celebrate. Most planters allowed from three to seven days during the season. James Hammond of South Carolina, for example, allowed his slaves three to four days off. Couper gave his slaves the full week, as did many other planters of large plantations who felt that it was good for morale. On the Couper plantations Christmas week was turned into what Lyell called a "kind of saturnalia," and for three days the slaves were allowed beef and whiskey. It was during one such Christmas at Hopeton, Lyell recounts, that more than thirty violins were silenced because of the objection of a company of traveling Methodist ministers. Hammond wrote in his plantation journal that on Christmas Day he allowed his people barbecued pork, beef, and mutton with "coffee and bread being bountifully provided."

In addition, Couper allowed other holidays which usually had some religious significance. For example, on the Monday following Easter, no work was required of the slaves. Also, on 11 August and 15 November holidays were declared. This was a holy period on the church calendar which marked the beginning and end of the harvest. Couper, as well as other planters, allowed certain holidays for special reasons, such as weddings and the planting and gathering of slave crops in the spring and fall. A North Carolina planter reminded his overseer, "As soon as you have laid by the crop, give the people two days, but…they must work their own crops." Another planter allowed his slaves "a holiday to plant their potatoes," and another a "holiday to gather their potatoes."[46]

In addition to the liberties allowed during holidays, there was a certain amount of social and occupational mobility at Hopeton. Slaves with unusual industry and ability could earn promotion to the top. It was possible for field hands to become drivers or artisans, and drivers could aspire to positions as head driver. Increased responsibility was often accompanied by prestige, power, more free time, better food, clothing, housing and sometimes cash bonuses.[47] Examples of this were noticed at Hopeton. Sir Charles Lyell was surprised to see the respect shown black mechanics at the Hopeton plantation. He observed a group of carpenters putting up sluices and a lock in a canal. The black foreman was following a plan which Couper had observed in Holland during his European tour. Lyell also saw a steam engine of fifteen horsepower made in England and used for threshing rice; the engine had been managed by a Negro for more than twelve years without an accident. When these mechanics came to consult Couper on business, "they spoke to him as independently as English artisans to their employers."[48]

Other examples of slave mobility at Hopeton were afforded by the cases of "Old Tom" and "Abraham-Fire-All," both of whom Couper recognized as having superior ability. "Old Tom" was one of the most interesting bondsmen at Hopeton. He was just under the overseer in authority and considered to be the head driver. A man of superior intelligence, he was the son of a prince of the Foulah tribe in Africa and had been taken a prisoner near Timbuktu at the age of fourteen. He had remained a strict Mohammedan. During the War of 1812, when the British were off the Georgia coast with their fleet, they made an offer of freedom with safe conduct to Canada to all slaves belonging to John Couper. Nearly all would have gone had not "Old Tom," to whom they looked with great respect, declined the offer. Tom told them he had known what slavery was in the West Indies and had made up his mind that the English were worse masters than the Americans. However, about half of John Couper's slaves left with the British only to find their lives shortened in Canada by the severe climate.[49]

"Abraham-Fire-All" was the master cook at Hopeton when Lyell visited. By reputation, Cupidion, the cook of the Marquis de Montalet of Sapelo Island, was the acknowledged master chef of the Georgia coast. Couper, recognizing Abraham's abilities, sent him to *Le Chatelet* to be tutored by the famous Cupidion. After a specified apprenticeship, "Abraham-Fire-All" returned to Hopeton and assumed charge of the culinary arts in the Couper kitchen. One of his favorite recipes was boned turkey, a dish he received from Sans Foix, whereby the bird resumed its original shape. Also, from Cupidion he learned a special French meal, which was enjoyed at Hopeton. This consisted of a puree of artichokes, onions, garlic and cream, served hot. Then came prawn served with a special sauce. This was followed by a *poularde* which was fried in olive oil and covered with whipped cream.[50]

Besides a certain degree of mobility inside the slave hierarchy, the slaves at Hopeton, according to Basil Hall, had some recourse if they felt they were being overworked. Couper made sure that every slave knew his rating on the plantation work scale—that of full, three-quarter, half or quarter hand. The slaves also knew how much work was required of them under the task system. Consequently, if they felt "imposed upon by the driver, they could appeal at once to the master." In addition, a slave might petition his master for a change of classification in the work rating system. Applications were received by Couper each year from slaves who felt that, for one reason or another, their work load should be modified. The proprietor carefully investigated each petition and adjusted those he felt warranted it.[51]

Of all the major crop-producing areas in the South, the rice coast of South Carolina and Georgia was most celebrated for its competent overseers.[52] In this area the overseers seemed to be of better mettle, garnered better salaries and enjoyed longer tenure than elsewhere in the slave South. To avoid incompetency, Couper, before hiring a prospective manager, would check the applicant's credentials, carefully reviewing his record on previous plantations. Because of this meticulous investigation of would-be employees, James Hamilton Couper enjoyed unusual success with his overseers.[53]

The salaries and tenure enjoyed by the Couper overseers were noteworthy. They compared favorably with those received by managers of other plantations on the rice coast and were impressive when contrasted to the other planting areas of the South. The Couper overseers were men who had to be familiar with the cultivation of three of the South's principal crops—rice, sugar cane and cotton. On Hopeton plantation the average tenure of Couper's nine overseers between the years 1827, and 1854, was 3.3 years. Three of these men—Daniel McDonald, Thomas Oden and Baillie Forrester—were employed for terms of eight, seven, and six years, respectively. The average annual salary of Couper's overseers during this period was $765. The highest salary was $1,000; the lowest $200. The wages tended to be low in the 1820s, but fluctuated between $700 and $1,000 after 1830. The tendency on the Couper plantations was for the salary to rise each year of an overseer's tenure. For example, Thomas Oden's salary rose from $600 in 1831, to $1,000 in 1836. At Hamilton, Couper's plantation on St. Simons Island, the average tenure of the seven overseers from 1829 to 1854, was 4.3 years. Two overseers— Jonathan Bowers and William Audley Couper, a younger brother of James Hamilton Couper—enjoyed terms of eight and fourteen years respectively. The average yearly salary for the Hamilton managers for the period under study was $755. The highest salary was $1,000; the lowest $300.[54]

That James Hamilton Couper was a remarkable example of an enlightened, benevolent and progressive slave proprietor there can be no doubt. He was a gracious host to all who visited his plantation and was more than willing to answer their queries about plantation life and management. A methodical man, he was an effective organizer of time and people and had every hour of the day planned for himself and his wards. Moreover, the slave's lot was not particularly onerous on the Couper holdings, and there were numerous examples of benevolence by the proprietor. The slave diet was quite adequate for those times, and the hospital care, housing, and clothing issue compared favorably to any plantation in the region. The slaves' work schedule was certainly lenient if it were possible, as Lyell said, to be finished in five hours. Likewise, in the area of discipline, Couper showed his benevolence by setting unusually low limits for the lash. Concerning religion, Couper paid a clergyman to minister to the needs of the slaves. Mrs. Basil Hall was led to conclude that the slaves religious needs were more than met on the plantation.

Similarly, slave incentives were abundant at Hopeton. The possibility of free time spurred activity in the field. Slaves used their daily respite in various activities, but mostly for making money. From their gardens and yards they sold vegetables, poultry and eggs. They returned the extra food issued them to the overseer for a fee, and the more skilled among them made canoes for sale to the master's family. But perhaps the most jealously guarded prerogative of Hopeton slaves was their right to cultivate their own crops for sale, chiefly corn. And with this money the slaves were allowed to purchase a variety of items, even their freedom. Moreover, from all accounts, Couper treated his slaves with respect and humaneness, even allowing them to appeal over the heads of drivers to the master if they felt imposed upon or mistreated.

Additionally, Couper's manifold abilities aided him in the procurement of good overseers. In the main, they were men of ability who executed their responsibilities with vigor, effectiveness, and competency. In return, they received better wages and enjoyed longer tenure than their counterparts on many other plantations in the South. It is no wonder that Hopeton plantation under the sage management of James Hamilton Couper became known as a model plantation of the Atlantic seaboard. It is fitting that Clement Eaten should remark that "Hopeton plantation, indeed, was a splendid example of paternalism."[55]

Notes

[1]James Hamilton Couper to a friend, March 1856; *Interstate Sugar Cane Growers Association Report, 1908*, 65, Mackay Stiles Papers, Southern Historical Collection, University of North Carolina, Chapel Hill.

[2]Fredrika Bremer, *The Homes of the New World; Impressions of America* 2 vols.(New York NY: Harper and Brothers, 1853) 2:488-89; Mills B. Lane ed., *Neither More Nor Less Than Men: Slavery in Georgia* (Savannah GA: The Beehive Press, 1993) 61.

[3]Frances Anne Kemble, *Journal of a Residence on a Georgia Plantation in 1838-1839* (New York NY: Alfred A. Knopf, 1961) 57; "Altama Plantation, of 6,200 acres, Near Brunswick, Sold to Alfred W. Jones," *Brunswick Advertiser*, n.d; Allen Johnson and Dumas Malone eds., *Dictionary of American Biography* 20 vols. (New York NY: Charles Scribner's Sons, 1930) 4:468; Bureau of the Census, *Seventh Census of the United States, 1850. Agriculture.*, prepared by Robert Armstrong (Washington DC: Government Printing Office, 1853). Couper served as a sort of planter-steward for these four plantations. By 1856 he owned Cannon's Point plantation as an inheritance from his father. He owned Hamilton plantation and the Barrett's Island property exclusively, plus one-half interest in Hopeton. Hence he owned three plantations outright, plus one-half interest in another.

Slavery and Plantation Management

[4]Una Pope-Hennessy, ed., *The Aristocratic Journe: Mrs. Basil Hall's Account During the Sojourn in America 1827-1828* (New York NY: G.P. Putnam's Sons, 1831) 231-32; see also Captain Basil Hall, *Travels in North America, 1827-1828* 3 vols. (Edinburgh, Scotland; Cadell and Company, 1829) 3:215-18.

[5]Caroline Couper Lovell, *The Golden Isles of Georgia* (Atlanta GA: Cherokee Publishing Company, 1970) 217-18.

[6]Sir Charles Lyell, *A Second Visit to North America* 2 vols. (New York NY: Harper and Brothers, 1849) 2:261-63.

[7]Bremer, *Homes of the New World*, 2:488-89.

[8]Amelia Murray, *Letters from the United States, Cuba, and Canada* (New York NY: G.P. Putnam and Co., 1856) 217-23; see also Lovell, *Golden Isles*, 226-29.

[9]Amelia Murray, *Letters from the United States, Cuba, and Canada* (New York NY: G.P. Putnam and Co., 1856) 217-23; see also Lovell, *Golden Isles*, 226-29.

[10]Robert William Fogel and Stanley L. Engerman, *Time on the Cross* 2 vols. (Boston MA: Little, Brown and Co., 1974) 1:203; William Allister Noble, "Sequent Occupance of Hopeton-Altama, 1816-1956" (Master thesis, University of Georgia, 1956) 32-34; *Wills and Appraisements Book D*, Glynn County Courthouse, Brunswick GA, 180-82; Bureau of the Census, *Fifth Census of the United States, 1830. Slave Schedule.*, prepared by Gales and Seaton (Washington, DC: Government Printing Office, 1833).

[11]J. D. Legare, "Account of an Agricultural Excursion Made into the South of Georgia in the Winter of 1832," *Southern Agriculturalist and Register of Rural Affairs* 4 (May-November 1833): 572-76.

[12]Ibid.

[13]Lyell, *Second Visit to North America*, 2:263-65.

[14]Ibid.; Eugene D. Genovese, *Roll, Jordan, Roll: The World the Slaves Made* (New York: Pantheon Books, 1974) 61.

[15]Legare, "Acount of Agricultural Excursion," 527, 529.

[16]Robert William Fogel and Stanley L. Engerman, *Time on the Cross*, 1:110-11; Genovese, *Roll, Jordan, Roll* 62-63; Ulrich Bonnell Phillips, *American Negro Slavery* (New York NY: Grosset and Dunlap, 1929) 279.

[17]Hall, *Travels in North America*, 3:224; Lyell, *Second Visit to North America*, 2:264-265.

[18]Bremer, *Homes of the New World*, 2:491.

[19]Lyell, *Second Visit to North America*, 2:264-65; Noble, "Sequent Occupance of Hopeton-Altama," 37; "A Tribute to James Hamilton Couper," Interstate Sugar Cane Growers Association, 1908, 72-73 Mackay Stiles Papers, Southern Historical Collection; Fogel and Engerman, *Time on the Cross*, 1:109-15; "Puzzle of the Oyster Shell Rings," *Atlanta Journal and Constitution Magazine*, 18 August 1974, 43.

[20]Fogel and Engerman, *Time on the Cross*, 1:116-17; Genovese, *Roll, Jordan, Roll*, 551; Phillips, *American Negro Slavery*, 64, 266.

[21]Murray, *Letters*, 217-23; Lovell, *Golden Isles of Georgia*, 226-28.

[22]James Hamilton Couper Plantation Records, 4 vols., 1:26, Southern Historical Collection, University of North Carolina, Chapel Hill.

[23]Fogel and Engerman, *Time on the Cross*, 1:117.

[24]Kenneth H. Stampp, *The Peculiar Institution: Slavery in the Ante-Bellum South* (New York NY: Alfred A. Knopf, 1956) 292-95; Genovese, *Roll, Jordan, Roll*, 224-35; Fogel and Engerman, *Time on the Cross*, I:115-16.

[25]Clement Eaton, *A History of the Old South*, 2nd ed. (New York NY: Macmillan Co., 1966) 220; Lyell, *A Second Visit to North America*, 2:264-65; Genovese, *Roll, Jordan, Roll*, 526.

[26]Lyell, *Second Visit to North America*, 2:263-64; "James Maxwell Couper Defends Planters of the Ante-Bellum South," *Atlanta Journal*, n.d.; James Hamilton Couper Plantation Records, 3:34, Southern Historical Collection; Legare, "Account of Agricultural Excursion," 167; Hall, *Travels in North America*, 3:224.

[27]Stampp, *The Peculiar Institution*, 311-13; Fogel and Engerman, *Time on the Cross*, 1:117-23.

[28]Stampp, *The Peculiar Institution*, 313.

[29]Ibid.; Lyell, *Second Visit to North America*, 2:264; Legare, "Account of Agricultural Excursion," 573-74; Ralph Betts Flanders, *Plantation Slavery in Georgia* (Chapel Hill: University of North Carolina Press, 1933) 101-102.

[30]Lyell, *Second Visit to North America*, 2:264; Legare, "Account of Agricultural Excursion," 573-74.

[31]Legare, "Account of Agricultural Excursion," 573-74; Lyell, *Second Visit to North America*, 262-63.

[32]Bremer, *Homes of the New World*, 2:488.

[33]Lyell, *Second Visit to North America*, 2:269; James Hamilton Couper Plantation Records, 2:172, 264, Southern Historical Collection.

[34]Hennessy, *Letters to Mrs. Basil Hall*, 231-32.

[35]Lyell, *Second Visit to North America*, 2:265-66; Legare, "Account of Agricultural Excursion," 576.

[36]Genovese, *Roll, Jordan, Roll*, 65.

[37]Lyell, *Second Visit to North America*, 2:265-66; Legare, "Account of Agricultural Excursion," 576.

[38]Stampp, *The Peculiar Institution*, 175; Phillips, *American Negro Slavery*, 271.

[39]Lyell, *Second Visit to North America*, 2:266; James Hamilton Couper Plantation Records, 2:415, Southern Historical Collection.

[40]Hall, *Travels in North America*, 3:226, 228.

[41]Lyell, *Second Visit to North America*, 2:265; Eaton, *History of the Old South*, 220; Fogel and Engerman, *Time on the Cross*, 1:65.

[42]Lyell, *Second Visit to North America*, 2:263, 265; Hall, *Travels in North America*, 3:225.

[43]James Hamilton Couper Plantation Records, 3:30-44, Southern Historical Collection; Noble, "Sequent Occupance of Hopeton-Altama," 78-79; Hall, *Travels in North America*, 3:224; Murray, *Letters*, 219; Lyell, *Second Visit to North America*, 2:268. Though evidence is inconclusive, it is thought that the tract "Pineland," was approximately 1000 acres. A portion of this was set aside for slave crops.

[44]Lyell, *Second Visit to North America*, 2:263.

[45]Murray, *Letters*, 218.

[46]Hall, *Travels in North America*, 3:224; Lyell, *Second Visit to North America*, 2:263; "Slave Life at Hopeton" (typescript), Margaret Davis Cate Collection, Georgia Historical Collection, Savannah GA; Phillips, *American Negro Slavery*, 207, 232, 313-14; Stampp, *The Peculiar Institution*, 79, 365-66, 168-70, 172.

[47]Fogel and Engerman, *Time on the Cross*, 1:149.

[48]Lyell, *Second Visit to North America*, 2:266-67.

[49]Ibid.

[50]Lovell, The *Golden Isles of Georgia*, 111-15; Burnette Lightle Vanstory, *Georgia's Land of the Golden Isles* (Athens: University of Georgia Press, 1956) 138; "Abraham-Fire-All-Cook of Hopeton" (typescript), Mackay Stiles Papers, Southern Historical Collection.

[51]Hall, *Travels in North America*, 3:223.

[52]William Kauffman Scarborough, *The Overseer: Plantation Management in the Old South* (Baton Rouge: Louisiana State University Press, 1966) 201; see also Genovese, *Roll, Jordan, Roll*, 12-22.

[53]Scarborough, *The Overseer*, 29; Legare, "Account of Agricultural Excursion," 574-575; James Hamilton Couper Plantation Records, 1:8-10, 43-47; 2:22, 302, 330. It is difficult to compute an average salary for overseers in general. As William Kauffman Scarborough observed, salaries generally "ranged from between $100 to $2000 per year, exclusive of fringe benefits." More precisely, however, he found that the average salary for overseers in the tobacco and grain regions of the upper South was between $200 and $250. In the short staple cotton belt it was about $450. But the highest salaries were paid overseers in the sugar regions of Louisiana and on the rice coast. By the 1850s the scale of pay in the sugar regions was $500 to $700 on small plantations and $1,000 on "moderate sized units." On the eve of the Civil War some overseers on the largest rice and sugar plantations received from $1,500 to $2,000 per year.

[54]Above data on Couper overseers was compiled by William K. Scarborough from James Hamilton Couper Plantation Records, volumes 1 and 2, Southern Historical Collection, and generously made available to this writer.

[55]Scarborough, *The Overseer.*, 201; Eaton, *History of the Old South*, 220.

CHAPTER X

Pleasures of the Coast

James Hamilton Couper was a cultivated man, with diverse and expanded interests far transcending his agricultural realm. He was a complex individual, a man of many talents, a superbly educated man who had the reading knowledge of five languages, three of which he spoke fluently. Moreover, he kept abreast of world affairs. As traveler and correspondent, he kept in touch with men of importance in Europe and the Mediterranean world. Thus, it is not surprising that such a man would have versatile interests, pleasures and pursuits that carried him in thought and action far from the fields of Hopeton.

One of Couper's most pleasurable diversions from his demanding plantation regimen was the time spent in his library. Here he could forget momentary problems of the present, escaping into his world of books. These were quiet hours of thought and reflection—a time he needed each day. He loved his books avidly and for over forty years he followed the practice of spending three specific periods of the day in his library. He arose at 6:00 A.M. and spent two hours in his study before breakfast. At 2:00 P.M. he retired to his library alone, reading until 4:00 P.M. Fifteen minutes later, he received guests in the drawing room and cocktails were served. Dinner was served at 4:35 P.M. and at 5:30 P.M. Couper again retired to his library for a period of study.[1]

This library in which Couper spent so much time was reported by contemporaries to have been one of the finest in the South. Bookshelves, straight, high and long lined the walls from floor to ceiling and portraits of ancestors hung between the shelves.[2] James Hamilton Couper loved his books with such devotion that he collected monographs on almost every discipline. His selections eventually totaled over 5000 volumes. In those days when books were hard to come by, such a collection was rare indeed. There were all the standard histories and classics, Gelpin's work in ten volumes, a translation of Cicero's works in twenty-two volumes, all the famous old diaries, Boydells' Shakespeare in six volumes, complete editions of the standard English, American and French novels, a full set of the Delphinic Classics, four volumes of Virgil in vellum, English and French poets, the English and American magazines—almost everything, in fact, that a student and lover of good books could desire.[3]

Of special interest were rare books about Egypt and Audubon's *Birds*. The Egyptian books were written by French scholars at about the time Napoleon Bonaparte invaded Egypt. It was during this expedition (1797) that the famous Rosetta stone was discovered which unlocked the secrets of ancient civilizations. These rare volumes were purchased by Couper in 1825, when he visited Europe and the Mediterranean area. In like manner, the rare Audubons were of equal interest and value. At one time the Couper library held a series of Audubon's *Birds of America*, one of the eighty original folio editions printed.[4] The Hopeton library was collected over a period of forty years and represented the encyclopedic tastes and interests of its owner.

Another non-agricultural activity that occupied a good deal of Couper's thinking was his avid interest in the natural history of coastal Georgia. He became one of the foremost authorities on the geology of the coast, and his pronouncements on the subject were sought by renowned scientists in America and abroad. He corresponded with eminent American geologist, William Cooper of New York, and the distinguished British naturalist, Sir Charles Lyell, both of whom visited Couper at Hopeton. Particularly enjoyable to Lyell was the usual canoe ride up the Altamaha River where the master of Hopeton could point out numerous species of rare birds, various forms of marine life and vegetation indigenous to the region.[5] He wrote of one such visit and of his conversation with Couper:

> Mr. Couper told me that, in the summer of 1845, he saw a shoal of porpoises coming up to that part of the Altamaha where the fresh and salt water meet, a space of about a mile in length, the favorite fishing ground of the alligators, where there is brackish water, which shifts its place according to the varying strength of the river and the tide. Here were seen about fifty alligators, each with head and neck raised above the water, looking down the stream at their enemies, before whom they had fled, terror stricken, and expecting an attack. The porpoises no more than a dozen in number, moved on in two ranks, and were evidently complete masters of the field. So powerful indeed are they, that they have been known to chase a large alligator to the bank, and putting their snouts under his belly, toss him ashore.[6]

In 1849, the Reverend George M. White wrote his *Statistics of the State of Georgia*. The work included a great fold-out map describing in detail the major geological regions of the state—a first of its kind. The initial chapter of the volume was devoted entirely to a lengthy discussion of the geology of the state. In his acknowledgments, White mentioned James Hamilton Couper, as indeed he should have, for the map concerning the geology of Georgia was Couper's and the information concerning the states geology was picked from the mind of Couper.[7]

Couper was associated with many scientific societies both in America and abroad. He was a member of the Academy of Natural Sciences of Philadelphia and corresponded frequently with the Geologic Society of London. In a paper read before the latter society on 1 February 1845, Couper enlightened its members on the salient geological features of his coastal homeland. This subject was particularly fascinating to Couper, and he made a study of it in great detail. In his paper he elaborated on the chain of sea islands and marshes, extending along the Atlantic shore, which characterized the Georgia coast. He commented on the area known as the pine barrens, a rather infertile area beginning about twenty miles inland from the coast and stretching northwestward for about fifty miles. He then alluded to the more fertile clay and loam soils of the coastal plain which predominated for about two hundred miles until the flat terrain gradually extended into the rolling hills of the piedmont, which in turn eventually meshed with the region known as the Appalachian Mountain chain. He explained that this peculiar feature marked the Atlantic coast of the United States from the Chesapeake Bay to the mouth of the Mississippi River.[8] But Couper's special interest was the paleontology of coastal Georgia. According to Couper, the whole district consisted of a Newer Pliocene formation overlaid in part, in its shallow valleys, by a clay alluvium of three distinct formations including the salt marsh, the tide swamp, and the inland swamp.[9]

Cognizant of Couper's knowledge of and interest in the geological formations of the Georgia coast, the state of Georgia commissioned him to salvage its unsuccessful canal construction program. In 1826, canal fever was running high, and the Brunswick Canal and Railroad Company was organized to construct a canal which would connect Brunswick with the Altamaha River. The company, however, ran into difficulties and soon abandoned the project. When a new charter was granted in 1834, Couper was among those put in charge of constructing the canal.[10]

He was not in favor of constructing an elaborate canal system to solve the state's transportation needs, but he felt short-distance canals could be useful and agreed to help in the venture. The canal was to be 12 miles long, 54 feet wide and 6 feet deep. It would tap the Altamaha river trade and bring it to Brunswick.[11]

Five hundred Negroes plus a number of Irish workers provided labor for the venture. The canal was finally dug the entire distance but was never opened to traffic. It was as Couper feared; the soil along the Georgia coast was too porous for canals of even limited length.[12]

However, if the canal was a practical failure, it also proved to be a scientific bonanza because Couper found the remains of many prehistoric animals, the most important of which was the Megatherium or giant sloth.[13] In October 1842, he read a paper before the Academy of Natural Sciences of Philadelphia concerning his discovery of these fossil remains.[14] As a result of this discovery, Couper received his widest acclaim in scientific circles. The Megatherium was a giant sloth with tusks, each weighing about 56 pounds, with which the Megatherium used to uproot whole trees for its consumption. Its body was 12 feet long and 8 feet high. "Its haunches were more than five feet wide; its feet were a yard in length, and terminated by terrific claws."[15]

There had been earlier discoveries of the animal in Spain. But the only other finds were made in Georgia. Dr. Samuel L. Mitchell in 1823 on Skidaway Island near Savannah was the first to find remains of this animal. A few years later, Dr. Habersham discovered similar remains in the Skidaway Island deposits. These specimens, however valuable, were limited because only a few parts of the animal, teeth and scattered bones, were found.[16]

In addition to the relics of the Megatherium, numerous other discoveries were made during the digging of the canal. Many marine fossil shells were found at intervals scattered along the whole length of the canal. Many of these shells were found grouped together and were so perfect as to retain their epidermis, which indicated that they originally grew on or near the spot where the findings occurred. The rib and two vertebrae of a whale and shell and leg bones of ancient turtles were also found imbedded in the sandy substratum at the northern end of the canal. In the same substratum but at the opposite end of the canal, fragments of the shell and sternum of two small species of the marsh turtle were discovered.[17]

Couper found that the bones of the different species of mammals occurred together, in groups, and in some cases the greater part of the bones of the same skeleton were found "in immediate juxta-position." They were generally unbroken, when first uncovered, but being soft and tender, fell to pieces if roughly handled. Many of the specimens Couper found to be quite perfect and beautifully fossilized, and in no instance was there any abrasion on the surface or encrustation of marine shells. According to Couper, these circumstances rendered it "highly probable that the carcasses of the various animals were floated, or fell, into the then lake or stream, and sinking to the sandy bottom, were gradually covered to their present depth" by the alluvial deposit from the water.[18]

Couper examined every fossil, identifying each, and giving it its proper scientific name. Examples of relics Couper found were specimens of the Megatherium, the *Elephas premegenius*, *Mastodon giganteum*, hippopotamus, horse, *Bos*, and the hog. He also found specimens of the whale, turtle, and twenty-nine different species of mollusca shells.[19]

Couper made fossil contributions to the London Geologic Society, but his most important collection, the fossil remains of the terrestrial mammals, including the Megatherium, he gave to the Academy of Natural Sciences of Philadelphia. The gifts were made in 1842.[20] Thereafter, Couper made other, though less dramatic discoveries, of fossil remains along the Georgia coast which he presented to the society. For example, in April 1844, Couper sent to Philadelphia a specimen of the rare bird, *Grus Canadensis*, and in February 1851, he sent the society "four species of Fossil Echini."[21]

By 1861, he had collected a large cabinet of very valuable relics which he presented to the Museum of Natural History of the College of Charleston, South Carolina.[22] This gift included a claw of the huge Megalonyx, an animal which lived in the Post-Pleiocene period. This claw was a perfect specimen and the largest ever discovered. The bones of the Megalonyx, or "Great Claw Beast," were rarely found. The largest claw heretofore discovered was much smaller than the one presented by Couper. A complete skeleton of the animal has never been found.[23]

Couper also gave the college a complete suit of the mollusc *Uniospinosa* which included one hundred specimens. He had recovered them from the Altamaha River. This remarkable mollusc was the pride of every cabinet in Europe and North America that was fortunate enough to have a perfect suit. Francis S. Holmes, professor of geology and curator of the Museum of Natural History of the College of Charleston, commented on the gift by Couper:

> To report in detail so large and valuable a donation would occupy many pages and require more time than I can conveniently command at present. Suffice it to say many months of hard labor must be expended in arranging and labeling the specimens. The extent of the collection may be estimated by this fact—that one entire room in the museum has been appropriated to the recent shells alone, and two thirds of this collection is from Mr. Couper. The cases contain several thousand specimens.[24]

James Hamilton Couper loved the coast of Georgia. He enjoyed studying its plants and animals, its land formation and rock deposits. He enjoyed collecting the relics of past ages, which he gave freely to learned societies. A practical man, he was a gentleman amateur at a time when the study of science was a labor of love.

Another interesting diversion Couper allowed himself was architectural design. Being endowed with a natural ability to draw, and, after having read many books on the subject, he began to practice his hobby. Despite his lack of professional training, he was quite successful. He designed three plantation houses, one church and Hopeton's famous sugar mill. Only the church and one of the houses exist today but they are ever-present reminders of one of James Hamilton Couper's many talents.[25]

Of the three plantation houses Couper designed, the first were his own homes of Hopeton and Altama; he then designed his daughter's and son-in-law's home, Malbone. Hopeton was built in 1828, and was patterned after a villa Couper saw while visiting Italy in 1825. It was three stories high with large steps leading to the second floor. The windows were rounded and the outer construction made of tabby. It was a spacious building with twenty-three rooms and formal gardens. Altama, a smaller house, was built in 1856, when most of the children were grown and had left home. This new two-storied edifice was built along the same style as Hopeton with the Italian motif and tabby construction. Then in 1859, when Maggie married Robert Stiles, the son of the United States ambassador to Austria, Couper consented to design their new home. Malbone, as it was called—named after one of Ambassador Stiles's relatives in

Austria, was a large two story red brick dwelling with inset columns. Although the plans for house were prepared by Couper in 1860, the construction was delayed because of the nearness of war. The house was finally completed in 1867, the year after Couper's death.[26]

Perhaps, the most lasting monument to Couper's skill as an architect is Christ Church, Savannah. The parish itself was formally organized in 1733, with a lot being designated for the construction of a church. But construction was delayed due to insufficient funds and the scarcity of qualified builders in the frontier colony. In 1736, the Reverend John Wesley came to Savannah to lead the parish and plans for a church building were revived. Until a suitable structure could be raised, however, the congregation met for a while in an open tent and later in the court house. Finally, Savannah's first church was completed in 1750.[27] By 1837, however, fire and hurricane damage suffered over the course of years proved too much for the structure, and the vestry turned to Couper for a new design. [28]

After long hours of consultation with the vestry as to exactly the type of edifice the congregation wanted, Couper began to visualize the completed church in his mind. As he pictured it, the building would resemble the famous Roman temple at Nimes, France, the Maison Carre he had seen on his European tour in 1825. This was the same building which had so captivated Thomas Jefferson, also an amateur architect. Jefferson had ordered a miniature wooden replica of it as a model for the state capitol building at Richmond. Couper traveled to Virginia to see the wooden model, drew up the plans and placed them before the vestry on 14 July 1837. These gentlemen had some choice, however, for Couper presented them with no less than three separate designs for the church, all similar, but each having different distinguishing characteristics.[29]

The design chosen by the church leaders was one of simple elegance. The building, completed in 1840, was of Greek Revival style. The outside presented a noble front facade of white columns forming a spacious portico. The entire outer covering of the building was of stucco finish and painted white. Beautiful windows of plain style adorned the sides and marble steps led upward to the front portico. The inside of the church was equally impressive and was of the style of Christopher Wren. The marble communion table, the rich appearance of the chancel, the baptismal font; all enclosed within the altar, presented a striking appearance. The ceiling was magnificent with all lines converging into a massive dome of unusual elegance. The dome was cast from the molds of Wren designed for St. Paul's Cathedral in London.[30]

In addition to designing his plantation houses, sugar mill and Christ Church there is strong evidence to suggest that Couper designed yet another—the Lodge and that it still may be standing. The Lodge was built between 1825-1830, and was located on a 369 acre tract in Wayne County near Waynesville, Georgia. Couper acquired the tract in 1825, and sold the property along with the house in 1844. The Lodge was used in the summer months to escape the dreaded "miasma" of the coast. Located in the pine barrens, the house made a perfect refuge. The dwelling was spacious in design. A large front porch and double front doors led into a first floor of four large rooms and hall. A stairway led to a second floor of four like rooms.

Until recently it was thought that the Lodge had been destroyed long ago. However, in 1978, Nell and Dewey Paulk purchased a 38-acre tract near Waynesville in Brantley County which contained an old home that needed extensive repairs However, perhaps due to the extensive renovation necessary, the Paulks sold the home to the Bernard family. The Bernards in turn sold the home to Gordon and Gena Rogers who are in the process of restoring it. Tradition in the area has it that this house was the Lodge.[31]

One more recreation Couper enjoyed was boat racing. In this sport he could see his designing talents, coupled with his own ability to succeed, tested to an extraordinary degree. The scene for this testing was the Georgia coast, for this area with its many islands, rivers and coves was an inviting field for such activity.

In the 1830s and 1840s, boating clubs sprang up in almost every coastal city. Regattas were held at St. Marys, Frederica, Darien, Brunswick and Savannah. At every regatta there was much betting and excitement over which boat would come in first and which owner would walk away with first prize, usually a substantial purse. The boats involved were not sailboats but rowboats. The planters, avid racing fans, liked the manly exercise offered in the event. Special slave crews were picked to be oarsmen, and there was much rivalry among planters as to who possessed the most able and highly-trained crew. A few planters designed racing boats themselves and entered them in the regattas. Therefore, winning for them was a double pleasure. Among those designers was James Hamilton Couper, and three of his most famous boats were the *Walkaway*, the *King*

Cotton and the *Becky Sharp*.[32]

On 17 November 1852, the prestigious Charleston Regatta was held in Charleston harbor, and James Hamilton Couper had entered his smartly designed dugout, the *Becky Sharp*, in the competition. The entries were not limited to South Carolina and Georgia, for some came from as far away as New York. The day was bright and clear, and the bay was alive with boats of every description adorned in gaudy colors. The Battery was a mass of human beings, and the balconies and porches of the surrounding houses were filled to capacity with spectators. People lined the wharves. The crowd numbered in the thousands.[33]

At noon the racing boats cruised by the cheering crowd to cast lots for positions. The members of each crew wore brightly tailored rowing uniforms of white, red, blue and yellow, some with turbans. The Charleston *Mercury* gave this account of the race:

> A flash! A breathing spell, and then another flash. Hurrah, they're started! Here they come. You can almost see the briny drops as they fall from the oars, and hear their merry music. On, on with winged speed. A shout! *Becky Sharp's* ahead, leading the van with easy grace. A few more strokes, and the game is up. The others vie in quiet pursuit. *Becky Sharp* still holds her own. Another cheer, and then one wild, united chorus breaks forth as far, far ahead, she wins the day.[34]

Couper, of course, was elated over his victory and lost no time writing his son Hamilton about it:

> I telegraphed you at 5 o'clock on the 17th Inst. mentioning the victory of the Becky Sharp; and sent you the Charleston *Mercury* containing an account of the race. The Becky Sharp was 'the admired of all admirers' and her fame is spread far and wide. —And she deserves her reputation. There was a heavy swell, a strong wind, and a current of two miles against her and yet she made the distance of a mile less 120 yards, in 6 minutes, without pressing the crew. She road the waves like a duck, skimming from wave to wave, with a continuous gliding motion.[35]

This letter to Hamilton shows a man at play, happy with the achievements of his hobby. And this feeling of satisfaction was true with his other diversions as well. Whether it was the quiet pleasure he derived from perusing the books in his library, or the satisfaction he gained from an architectural design he felt was his best effort; whether it was the exhilaration from finding a fossilized relic of a past age, or the tingling sensation felt when his boat won the regatta, here was the picture of a man happy with himself in his world. This happiness lasted as long as the world he knew remained intact.

Notes

[1] Caroline Couper Lovell, The *Golden Isles of Georgia* (Atlanta GA: Cherokee Publishing Company, 1970) 232-33; Mary Traylor Theisen (great granddaughter of James Hamilton Couper), interview with author, Atlanta GA, 6 May 1972.

[2] *Atlanta* (GA) *Constitution*, 13 April 1923.

[3] *Atlanta Constitution*, 24 June 1888; Mary Traylor Theisen, telephone conversation with author, 4 September 1978.

[4] *Atlanta Constitution*, 15 April 1923.

[5] William B. Hodgson, *Memoir on the Megatherium and Other Extinct Gigantic Quadrupeds of the Coast of Georgia with Observations on Its Geologic Features* (New York NY: Barlett and Welford, 1846) iv-vi, 9-17; see also Bessie Lewis, *Patriarchal Plantations of St. Simons Island* (Brunswick GA: self published, 1974) 8; Sir Charles Lyell, *A Second Visit to North America* 2 vols. (New York NY: Harper and Brothers, 1849) 1:261; Fredrika Bremer, *The Homes of the New World; Impressions of America* 2 vols. (New York NY: Harper and Brothers, 1853) 2:488-89.

[6] Lyell, *Second Visit to North America*, 2:252; see also Lewis, *Patriarchal Plantations*, 8.

[7] N. A. Pratt, "The Story of the Geological Surveys of Georgia," 10 August 1897, 1-28, William Audley Couper Papers, Southern Historical Collection, University of North Carolina, Chapel Hill; George M. White, *Statistics of the State of Georgia* (Savannah GA: W. Throne Williams, 1849) 2.

[8] Hodgson, *Memoir on the Megatherium*, 13; see also *Proceedings of the Academy of Natural Sciences of Philadelphia* 10 vols. (Philadelphia PA: Merrihew and Thompson, 1840-1860) 1:216.

[9] Hodgson, *Memoir on the Megatherium*, 31-37; White, *Statistics of Georgia*, 16-17; Lyell, *Second Visit to North America*, 1:240-56. (Newer Pliocene refers to the Upper Pliocene—about 1,500,000 to about 5,000,000 years ago.)

[10] Margaret Davis Cate, *Our Todays and Yesterdays: A Story of Brunswick and the Coastal Islands* (St. Simons Island GA: Fort Federica Association, 1955) 208-210; James Hamilton Couper Plantation Records, 4:54, Southern Historical Collection, University of North Carolina, Chapel Hill.

[11]Cate, *Our Todays and Yesterdays,* 208-210; James Silk Buckingham, *The Slave States of America* 2 vols. (London: Fisher, Son and Co., 1842) 1:137; Edward J. Harden, *Life of George M. Troup* (Savannah GA: E. J. Purse, 1859) 180-81.

[12]Harden, *Life of George M. Troup,* 180-81; Frances Anne Kemble, *Journal of a Residence on a Georgia Plantation in 1838-1839* (New York NY: Alfred A. Knopf, 1961) 104-105.

[13]Hodgson, *Memoir on the Megatherium,* 13; Lyell, *Second Visit to North America,* 1:257-58.

[14]*Proceedings,* 1:216-17.

[15]James Hamilton Couper to William B. Hodgson, 12 March 1844; 18 November 1846, William B. Hodgson Papers, Perkins Library, Duke University, Durham NC; Hodgson, *Memoir on the Megatherium,* 12, 23-24.

[16]Hodgson, *Memoir on the Megatherium,* 9-17, 40-43.

[17]Hodgson, *Memoir on the Megatherium,* 39; White, *Statistics of Georgia,* 18, 24; Alfred W. Jones, *Altama. Then and Now* (Sea Island GA: self published, 1970) 5; Lyell, *Second Visit to North America,* 1:259.

[18]Hodgson, *Memoir on the Megatherium,* 39-40; White; *Statistics of Georgia,* 17; Lyell, *Second Visit to North America,* 1:258.

[19]Hodgson, *Memoir on the Megatherium,* 44-47; White, *Statistics of Georgia,* 18; Jones, *Altama,* 1, 5; Lyell, *Second Visit to North America,* 1:259. *Elephas premegenius* pertains to the fossil remains of an elephant. *Mastodon gigantium* is the name of a large woolly elephant of prehistoric time. *Bos* is the generic name of prehistoric cow or bison.

[20]Hodgson, *Memoir on the Megatherium,* 44.

[21]*Proceedings,* 2:23-24; 5:159.

[22]Extracts from the Minutes of the Board of Trustees of the College of Charleston, South Carolina, 22 November 1861, John Couper Papers, Georgia Historical Society, Savannah GA; Jones, *Altama,* 5.

[23]Extracts from the Minutes of the Board of Trustees of the College of Charleston, 22 November 1861, John Couper Papers, Georgia Historical Society.

[24]Ibid.

[25]"Malbone, The Home of the Stiles Family, Described in Magazine," *Atlanta Constitution,* 1914; Mary Traylor Theisen, telephone conversation with author, 5 September 1978.

[26]Medora Field Perkerson, *White Columns of Georgia* (New York NY: Bonanza Books, 1955) 118; "Malbone"; Mary Traylor Theisen, telephone conversation with author, 4 September 1978. Malbone, the friend of Stiles' for whom the house was named, was reputed to be, at that time, the world's greatest miniature painting artist.

[27]*A Short History of Christ Church*. Brochure on file at the Georgia Historical Society, Savannah GA.

[28]Christ Church Vestry Minutes, 1837-1840, Georgia Historical Society, Savannah GA; Cornerstone of present Christ Church, laid 23 February 1838, Savannah GA.

[29]F. Bland Tucker, "Architectural History of Christ Church," Christ Church newsletter, 31 December 1972, Christ Church file, Georgia Historical Society, Savannah GA; James Hamilton Couper to W. Thorne Williams, 14 July 1837, Christ Church File, Georgia Historical Society, Savannah GA.

[30]James Hamilton Couper to W. Thorne Williams, 14 July 1837, Christ Church file; Tucker, "Architectural History of Christ Church," Christ Church file; *Savannah Daily Georgian*, 23 March 1840. On file in the Georgia Historical Society and at the Georgia State Department of Archives and History, Atlanta.

[31]Brunswick News, 11 May 1979; Gena Rogers, telephone interview with author, 16 June 1997.

[32]Typescript concerning Couper's interest in boating, Mackay-Stiles Papers, Southen Historical Collection, University of North Carolina, Chapel Hill; E. Merton Coulter, "Boating as a Sport in the Old South," *Georgia Historical Quarterly* 28 (September 1943): 231-47.

[33]*Charleston* (SC) *Mercury*, 18 November 1852.

[34]Ibid.

[35]James Hamilton Couper to Hamilton Couper, 20 November 1852, Mackay-Stiles Papers, Southern Historical Collection.

CHAPTER XI

College, Politics and War, 1846-1866

James Hamilton and Caroline Couper had six sons and two daughters. The children were schooled at home by tutors from Northern universities who instructed the sons, and governesses who taught the daughters their social graces. The children were James Hamilton Jr. (called "Hamilton"), Margaret Wylly ("Maggie" or "Meg"), Alexander ("Alick"), Robert ("Bob"), John Lord ("Lord"), Rebecca, James Maxwell and William.

In the fall of 1846, the Couper's oldest son, Hamilton, left home for college. At the age of seventeen he enrolled at Yale, where his father had studied. Upon arriving, he took a series of competency exams and performed so well that he was allowed to skip the freshman class. His roommate was Lord King, son of Thomas Butler King of Retreat Plantation on St. Simons Island.[1]

Hamilton enjoyed college. He became active in campus life and joined the Calliopian Society because of its Southern character. Had he joined either the Brothius or Linouian societies he would have been the only Southern member. But in the Calliopian Society one half were from the South. Hamilton became an avid debater, taking delight in matching wits with the other students. At first he had to prove himself, for he was younger than the others. But after his first speech class, in which he was able to out-debate a senior, he never felt the need to prove himself again.[2]

During the semester break of January 1847, he spent his time with the John Lords of New York and was treated like a son. While at the Lords he saw Washington Irving who was then visiting the family. It was at this time that he wrote to his mother of the latest men's clothing styles. He quipped, "Tell father he is out of fashion unless he wears his collars standing and hair is cut shorter." In the same letter he asked his mother for $200 to last him until spring.[3]

When the spring break came in the middle of June, Hamilton and a friend from Tennessee took a trip through the country. They went to Springfield, Massachusetts, by rail car and passed through the Connecticut countryside, which he described as beautiful but not as nice as the "wild woods and open country of the South." They went through towns such as Westminister and Macon, New Hampshire, and walked from Amherst to Worcester, Massachusetts. In all, they traveled more than 130 miles in six days before returning to New Haven. It cost him and his friend $10 a piece.[4]

On his tour Hamilton visited the cotton mills at Springfield. He discussed agriculture with the farmers of Massachusetts, where he found the farms small with poor soil. He did not particularly like the hilly country, preferring the flatlands of the Georgia coast. There was much amusement on the trip. As they went around on foot the people thought they were peddlers with notions in their knapsacks for sale. On one occasion, Hamilton's friend, a "great stout fellow," was threatened with a whipping by "a little sneak of an Irishman not one-third his size." The little man was upset because they had trespassed on his land. The Irishman said that he had killed a man six weeks before with one blow of his fist.[5] After the trip Hamilton wrote to his brother Alick about hunting wild pigeons and complained that there was not nearly so much game as there was in Georgia. However, he had flushed a grouse, which he described as a "seven pound chicken which flew over like a partridge." He also went fox hunting and spent the remainder of the break with the Lords.[6]

Hamilton was an eager student. He wrote home that he was reading Dryden, Pope, Locke, Milton, and Shakespeare. In Greek class he read Plato's *Georgis* and in Latin class Tacitus' *Germania*. Moreover, his mother periodically sent him current issues of a French newspaper which he used in practicing his French. He wrote in 1848, that he had taken and was fluent in four foreign languages—Latin, Greek, German, and French. He was so satisfied with his academic progress that he sought permission from his father to skip the senior year at Yale because he felt it to be a waste of time. According to Hamilton, study in the senior year was minimal, and all the students did was frolic. He wanted to spend that time in some lawyer's office preparing himself for the profession of law. His father, however, felt differently and persuaded him to remain in New Haven and finish his studies.[7]

By 1850, Hamilton had graduated from Yale and was enrolled in the Harvard School of Law. During the summer of that year James Hamilton Couper went north on business. He stopped to see Hamilton at Cambridge and both spent time together at Saratoga Springs, a popular resort in New York. Here the elder Couper saw his friend Stephen Duncan of Natchez, Mississippi. After leaving the Springs, Hamilton and his father went on a tour into Canada. Following this excursion James Hamilton Couper returned to Georgia and Hamilton returned to Cambridge, Massachusetts, to resume his studies.[8]

When the fall term opened in Cambridge, the main social event was a vocal performance by Jenny Lind, the famous visiting Swedish singer. The best seats were $9.00 but Hamilton took a medium quality for $5.50. Of her performance he wrote: "There is a liquid flow and flute-like sweetness in her voice, which I had no conception of, while she executes a peculiar trill perfectly birdlike in character. I never expect to hear such from another singer again." She had sung earlier in Boston, where the people had "bored her to death." Since then, she had refused to see any visitors. However, at Cambridge she had a better rapport with the inhabitants.[9]

In the same letter to his mother describing Jenny Lind's visit, Hamilton wrote of politics. He had a regular subscription to the *Savannah Republican*, and from that paper had inferred that there was much secession fervor in Georgia at this time. The Compromise of 1850 had just been passed by the federal Congress, and many states of the South, including Georgia, were unsure whether to accept the compromise and remain in the Union or reject it and secede. Mirroring the Whig sentiments of his father, Hamilton wrote:

> I trust that Georgia will stand firmly by the Union and not suffer herself to be led by the Carolina politicians into a course of conduct as absurd and unjust as anything that I can conceive of—direct violation of the Constitution which she pledged herself to maintain. To assent that there is at this time any danger from Northern agression is to show a perfect ignorance of the state of feeling, in this part of the country at any rate.[10]

What Hamilton had surmised from the Georgia newspaper was true. His home state was undecided as to what course of action to take. Since its introduction into the United States Senate by Henry Clay in early spring, the provisions of the so-called Compromise of 1850 had been anathema to the South. The compromise had to do with lands recently acquired by the United States in her war with Mexico. The question was whether this territory should be slave or free, and the controversy over the problem was endangering the constancy of the Union. Moderate leaders from both sections had worked out a compromise, but many Southerners felt it to be unfair to the South.

In April 1850, Georgia held elections for delegates to attend the Southern Rights Convention to be held in Nashville, Tennessee, in June. The convention would consider the alternative of secession for the whole South. The people of Georgia were hesitant to make a decision at this time, and there was a very poor turnout in the April elections. Many people felt that because of the poor voter participation the state should not even send a delegation to Nashville, and many of the elected delegates resigned.[11]

The problem of securing delegates was illustrated in the case of the first district. W. J. Lawton was elected as a Democratic delegate but declined the honor. Then he was replaced by former Governor George M. Troup, who eventually declined for reasons of health. The Whig candidate elected from that coastal region was James Hamilton Couper. Couper was opposed to secession, and when time came to attend the convention, he too refused to go. Therefore, the first district (Lower Georgia) was left unrepresented.[12]

The state, however, did send to Nashville in June a delegation which consisted of eleven members—eight Southern-rights Democrats and three Whigs. The delegation was led by the fiery secessionists Charles J. McDonald and Henry L. Benning.[13] Proceedings began on 3 June 1850, but little was agreed upon except to endorse the Missouri Compromise and extend its line of 36 degrees 30 minutes to the Pacific coast. The convention adjourned on 12 June with the understanding that the delegates would meet again in November. But the latter meeting achieved fewer results than the one in June since the delegates could not agree on a course of action and consequently broke up on 18 November 1850, amid confusion.[14]

The issue, however, was still unresolved. Finally, it was decided by the several Southern states to hold conventions separately to decide whether or not to stay in the Union. And as destiny would have it, Georgia had hers first.

As far back as 8 February 1850, the Georgia legislature had taken precautions against what it considered a brutal assault on the South's institution of slavery. It had foreseen some sort of settlement such as the Compromise of 1850 and had enacted this law:

That should the Congress of the United States pass any law prohibiting slavery or involuntary servitude in any territory of the United States, or any law abolishing slavery in the District of Columbia, or any law prohibiting the slave trade between the states where slavery may exist, or admit into the United States as a State of this Confederacy the sparsely peopled Territory of California or New Mexico, or should the Governor of this State receive at any time satisfactory evidence that any slave or slaves having escaped from this State to a non-slaveholding State, and that such slave or slaves is or are refused to be given up to the proper owner, by the authorities of the States in which such fugitive or fugitives may be found, then or in either of the foregoing events, it shall be and it is hereby made the duty of the Governor of this State, within sixty days thereafter, to issue his proclamation, ordering an election to be held in each and every county to a Convention of the people of this State, to convene at the Seat of Government within twenty days after said election.[15]

Consequently, when the second meeting of the Nashville Convention offered no solution, the governor of the state, George W. Towns, was advised to invoke the act of February 1850, which had been violated by the admission of California as a free state, and the suspension of the slave trade in the District of Columbia. Therefore, the order was given for the selection of delegates to meet in Milledgeville, the capital, in December. The convention would represent the will of the people and would decide the fate of the state and possibly the entire South. Since the Georgia convention met first, all eyes were on her. She was situated in the heartland of the South between South Carolina and Alabama, and if she refused to secede, the secession movement would be lost. On the other hand, if she voted to secede, perhaps her sister states would follow. Certainly South Carolina had been ready to secede for several years.

The battle for delegates was intense as they fought each other on platforms of whether to stay in the Union. When the election was over, the convention met in Milledgeville on Tuesday, 10 December 1850. On the first day, the 259 members elected from all over the state presented their credentials and took their seats. Governor Towns welcomed them and reminded them of their solemn duty. James Hamilton Couper and Francis M. Scarlett represented Glynn County. Couper was a Whig and was elected on a unionist platform. He made no secret of his opinion that for Georgia to secede at this time would be a grievous error. Francis Scarlett, however, was of the other persuasion.

On the second day, Wednesday, 11 December, the convention organized itself for work. Thomas Spalding, delegate from McIntosh County was chosen president of the convention. The next order of business was to select a special committee to chart the course of the convention. The president was authorized to appoint three members from each of the eleven judicial districts to the committee. The committee was called variously the "Committee of Three" or the "Committee of Thirty-Three." To this committee was delegated the great power of deciding what the state should do concerning secession—to outline an appropriate course of action and present it to the convention. The full convention could then accept, reject, or amend the report brought forth by the committee. Named to the committee from the eastern judicial district were Frances S. Bartow of Chatham County, James Hamilton Couper of Glynn County, and James Monroe Smith of Camden County.

It was moved that the counties should be called in alphabetical order, and as each was called, any member from that county could offer resolutions which would be read and referred without discussion to the "Committee of Thirty-Three." It was also decided that five thousand copies of the proceedings of the convention should be printed by the state and distributed to the counties. Also accepted was a motion of Alexander H. Stephens of Taliaferro County that the "Committee of Thirty-Three" be authorized to have all reports made to the convention printed and given to each member for his use. The convention then adjourned until the next morning.

On Thursday, 12 December, the convention reconvened. Not much was accomplished because the "Committee of Thirty-Three" was hard at work behind closed doors studying the various proposals submitted to it by different members and trying to hammer out a definitive report which it hoped would pass the full convention. The delegates on the floor, however, did adopt a measure authorizing the payment to each member of $100 per day for his services. The convention then adjourned except for the "Committee of Thirty-Three" which worked late into the night.

On Friday, 13 December, the convention again convened. The "Committee of Thirty-Three" presented its report on the state-federal conflict and copies were provided for the members of the convention.

The report was moderate, and since Couper served actively on the committee, it is likely that he was instrumental in its composition. The report traced the conflict between the North and South and pointed out that the South had been grievously offended by the admission of California as a free state and the suppression of the slave trade in the District of Columbia. However, the report counseled Georgia to accept the Compromise of 1850. This would be preferable to breaking up the Union. Four additional provisions of the report maintained: (1) The American Union was secondary to the rights and privileges it was designed to protect; (2) Both sections must agree to compromise in order to save the Union; (3) In this spirit Georgia would accept the Compromise as a permanent adjustment to the problems of sectionalism but cautioned the North against further attacks on the institution of slavery; and, (4) Georgia noted ominously that the longevity of the Union depended on the faithful execution by the North of the Fugitive Slave Law. Georgia would accept the Compromise, but this was the last time she would act in such a conciliatory fashion. Next time, she would secede.

When the reading of the report was completed, Robert Toombs moved that it be accepted without amendment. The motion was tabled, however, to give the delegates time to study the provisions. The convention then adjourned until later that afternoon.

When the afternoon session convened, discussion of the report ensued. W. J. Lawton introduced a motion to discuss and vote on each paragraph separately. The motion failed 83-176, Couper voting with the majority. His colleague from Glynn, Francis Scarlett, voted for the motion. Scarlett seems to have been aligned with the "ultra" or secessionist faction in the convention. On all key issues Couper voted with the moderates, agreeing with delegates like Alexander H. Stephens. Following the defeat of the ultra motion, a vote was taken on Toombs' original motion to accept the committee's report. The vote was 236-23 in overwhelming approval. The convention then adjourned.

On Saturday, 14 December, the convention held its last session. At this time the fireaters made one last attempt to amend the report. They introduced several motions aimed at changing the wording at key points. Couper and the moderates consistently voted against any change, and the attempts failed. The convention then adjourned until 4:00 p.m., and after a brief afternoon meeting, the convention adjourned *sine die*.

159

The report adopted by the Georgia Convention in December 1850 became known as the *Georgia Platform*. It accepted the Compromise of 1850 with all its faults as the last hope of saving the Union, but a stern warning was given the North not to push the South any further, or dire consequences could result. The convention was certainly controlled by the moderates, and the fireaters did not have a chance of persuading the convention to secede from the beginning. The other Southern states held their conventions and followed Georgia's lead in repudiating secession at this time. The South did not like the Compromise of 1850, but she accepted it in preference to severing the bonds of union. Therefore, the Georgia Platform was given the dubious honor of helping to save the Union for ten more years, and, according to the record of the proceedings, the Platform mirrored Couper's views.[16]

The years between 1850 and 1860, were generally good to the Coupers. Hamilton was finishing law school; the other Couper boys were growing up and considering what university they would attend. The girls, Margaret and Rebecca, were thinking of eventual marriage and family. Meanwhile, James Hamilton Couper viewed his children and their aspirations and accomplishments with great satisfaction. But at times a great foreboding would occupy his mind, and one wonders if he did not see the great holocaust that would befall his family and region in the end. John C. Calhoun had put it into words earlier when he said: "The Poor South—What will become of her?"

Hamilton was no longer in Cambridge but had finished his studies there and was in the fall of 1852, employed in the New York law firm of John Lord. His employment there was not surprising since the Coupers of Georgia and the Lords of New York were the best of friends.[17] However, Hamilton did not remain long with Lord and Company, for he missed Georgia and desired to practice law in Savannah. He wanted to be admitted to the Georgia bar and eventually to go into politics. Moreover, Hamilton began to feel the pressure of sectionalism which made him acutely aware that he was a "Southern man." He wrote his father in 1853, "I cannot sacrifice my convictions for expediency." By 1856, he was settled in Savannah in a successful law practice.[18]

If Hamilton felt the pressures of mounting sectionalism, so did his father. As an old-line Whig without a party, James Hamilton Couper began drifting toward the Democratic Party. He wrote Hamilton in 1856, "As a national Party it [the Democratic Party] is the most sound and conservative. At all events I am firmly of the opinion, that the permanence of the union and the maintenance of Southern rights depend on its victory over the Black Republican party. The only position that an old line Whig like myself can take is to join no party, but to give support to the most conservative."[19]

By the mid-1850s James Hamilton Couper's other sons were enrolled in various colleges. Lord Couper was attending the University of Georgia. Bob, Alick, and James Maxwell Couper were at the University of Virginia. Hamilton was pleased with their selection of universities and wrote to his mother, "They won't have to associate with Yankees as I had to do."[20]

In the winter and spring of 1857, tragedy struck. An epidemic of monumental proportions gripped Hopeton. Typhoid fever and pneumonia were raging through the slave population. Forty slaves were in the hospital at one time, many of whom died of the disease. It was a practice at Hopeton that when a slave died, the entire Couper family attended the funeral and an Episcopal priest performed the services. The plague even reached into the Couper household itself, striking the youngest of the Couper children, William aged thirteen. He died of typhoid fever in April 1857.[21]

By 1857, with all the children away except the two daughters, Maggie and Rebecca, James Hamilton Couper moved from Hopeton mansion, which was too large for their diminished family, into a smaller but equally elegant house called "Altama" from Oliver Goldsmith's poem, *The Deserted Village*. Couper designed the house himself as he had Hopeton. It had two stories with an Italian motif. The new residence was surrounded by formal gardens containing virtually every tree and shrub indigenous to the region. After 1857, the huge Hopeton plantation house remained vacant but was kept up by the family and often used on festive occasions.[22]

In the late 1850s, Margaret Couper had developed into a comely Southern belle, and her elder brother Hamilton was always ready to give her advice on courtship and the character of young men. On one occasion he wrote to her:

> Remember my dear the counsel of your brother. Tender words are but uncertain signs of a tender heart. Flirtation is not courtship. All men are villains. Keep very shady as to your own feelings. Always try to draw the enemy out first. Mention

casually that pistol shooting is a gift of your family, and that your four grown up brothers are all crack shots, and single men. If matters come to the worst, and you are formally called upon to surrender, look sweet and tell your fond adorer to 'ask Pa.' If he's the right thing he will extend that courtesy to your parents without hesitation. If he's a sham you'll never hear of him again. Above all never refuse a man until he offers himself, or run away with a sentimental looking young gentleman by moonlight. They are both blunders which you know are worse than crimes.[23]

Maggie paid attention to her brother and by December 1859, she was married to Robert Mackay Stiles, whose father was Ambassador to Austria. Her father gave her $1000 for her trousseau.[24] But Maggie's wedding was one of the last happy events in James Hamilton Couper's life. After that he was in constant depression over the widening gulf between North and South, and a great foreboding consumed his mind. In the summer of 1860, he went to the resort at Saratoga Springs, New York, for a change of scenery and to alleviate his depression.[25]

Couper had ample cause to worry, for his country was being driven irrevocably down the road to war. In November of 1860, the "Black Republican" Abraham Lincoln was elected president, and South Carolina promptly marched out of the Union on 20 December 1860.

The pressure was now on Georgia. Her statesmen had pronounced long and loud that if a Republican were elected president, she would secede. Her citizens felt threatened by the new president and his party and could envision a federal legislature in the future which might be hostile to Southern interests and might well legislate slavery out of existence. In this mood of threatened anxiety the Georgia legislature met and called for the election of delegates to a convention to decide the fate of the state. The convention met in Milledgeville on 16 January 1861. It was reminiscent of the convention that had met in 1850, but there were important differences. This convention was as extreme in sentiment as the other had been moderate. The secessionists from the beginning had the upper hand, and the outcome was a foregone conclusion. Fireaters from outside the state like Robert Barnwell Rhett of South Carolina and William Lowndes Yancey of Alabama had campaigned in the state for secession, and their influence was felt in the convention. Moderates led by

Alexander H. Stephens, Benjamin H. Hill, and Hershel V. Johnson introduced motions to stay the hand of the convention, but they fell before the determined onslaught of the secessionists. Therefore, on 19 January 1861, Eugenius B. Nisbet offered the proposal of secession. It would rescind the ratification of the federal constitution which Georgia had unanimously adopted in 1788, and declare Georgia an independent sovereign nation. As Nisbet read the proposal, he was inundated with cheers. The vote was swift and the count was 208-89 for secession. Thus, Georgia, one of the "Old Thirteen," became the fifth state to sever the bonds of union. On 16 March 1861, the state ratified the Confederate Constitution and became part of the Confederate States of America.[26]

James Hamilton Couper was not a delegate to this convention; he did not offer as a delegate. He was moderate and had always been opposed to secession, but once the die was cast he was as loyal a Southerner as could be found and supported the cause with all he had, particularly with his five sons.[27]

Hamilton, his eldest and the pride of his life, was at this time US district attorney in Savannah with a promising career in law and politics. Hamilton had been moderate in the 1850s, but now he was ultra and determined to do all he could for his state and new nation. He lost no time in joining the Confederate Army and by 2 February 1861, was en route to Fort Pulaski near Savannah with his company—the Oglethorpe Light Infantry. In late January he wrote Governor Joseph Emerson Brown of Georgia suggesting a plan for defending the Georgia coast. He proposed to construct three earthworks on Martello Towers, mounting each with twenty-four or thirty-two pounders—one at the southeast point of St. Simons, one at the southern point of St. Catherines Island, and a third at the northern point of Ossabaw Island. In addition, his plan called for two or three steam tugs, each with a pivot gun. These defenses would require a force of two hundred men in all and would provide, he claimed, all the protection required against marauders.[28]

Governor Brown did fortify the coast, but in December 1861, as federal gunboats plied the area, the inhabitants fled inland. Governor Brown was countermanded by the Confederate Government which felt that all coastal forces should be concentrated to defend Savannah. Thus, by February 1862, all of the coastal islands were held by Union troops. Savannah was secured, however, and did not fall until Sherman's invasion in 1864.[29]

In May 1861, the Oglethorpe Light Infantry was transferred to Virginia. Of their arrival in Richmond, Hamilton wrote to sister Maggie: "The girls smiled and waved their handkerchiefs, the men cheered and threw up their hats, while enthusiastic small, boys and sympathetic little niggers squeaked hooray and flowers and blessings fell thick upon us at every station. Richmond is a beautiful place."[30]

On 21 July 1861, Hamilton took part in the great Southern victory at a little place called Manassas in Virginia. At this time he was Captain of the Oglethorpe Light Infantry of Savannah, Georgia, and attached to the Eighth Georgia Regiment. From the battlefield on 25 July, he wrote to his sister:

...the enemy, with eight regiments, poured into us an inconceivable number of bullets, shell, grape and shot. Perhaps the best way of giving you an idea of the weight of their fire is to tell you that, on visiting the spot after the action, I found no tree without bullet marks, many with several and one sapling about the size of my arm with four mini balls. With the exception of a half-dozen only, all of our injured were hit at that time. We had 240 killed and wounded, out of a little more than 500 men taken in....

All the stuff you hear about the feelings of a man in battle is *bosh*. You are too busy to have much feelings about anything.[31]

The Confederates were still basking in their victory at Manassas in the fall of 1861, when great tragedy struck the Coupers. Hamilton was dying.

In late October S. P. Hamilton, Major of Artillery in General James Longstreet's Corps, rode over to the Eighth Georgia Regiment to see his friend Hamilton Couper. He found Hamilton "lying down in a very drooping condition, and evidently quite ill." Couper told Major Hamilton that he had been ill for about ten days but didn't think it amounted to much. Major Hamilton thought differently and offered to transport Couper to his camp about six miles distant so he could watch him. After examining Hamilton, it was discovered that he was quite sick with typhoid fever. Couper had everything in the way of attention—nursing, stimulants, and nourishment—but it was evident after a week that he would not live. Accordingly, Major Hamilton apprised Hamilton of the doctor's opinion to which Couper replied very coolly, "Well, Hamilton, it may be so, but I do not take so gloomy a view of my case as the doctor does; I hope I will be able to pull through yet."[32]

The next day, Mrs. W. D. Smith of the former Georgia King of Retreat Plantation, came to see Hamilton. After she left, Major Hamilton told Couper that the doctor had said he had only a few more hours to live. Hamilton Couper then replied: "Well, Hamilton, it seems a hard fate for one so young as I am, to be taken off in this way; if I had fallen on the field of Battle, facing the enemies of my country, it would have been something for my relatives and friends to be proud of." Then, pausing for a moment apparently in deep thought, he said, "Yet hard as is my fate I meet it with perfect resignation."[33] On 8 November 1861, Hamilton Couper died.

As soon as word reached Georgia of Hamilton's condition, his sister Maggie had set out for Virginia to bring him home. However, by the time she reached Richmond, her brother was dead.[34] On 12 November 1861, members of the Savannah bar met to eulogize his integrity and his gallantry on the field of battle at Manassas. His death was a substantial loss to them, and they wore mourning bands for thirty days.[35] When James Hamilton Couper learned of his son's death, he went into mourning and entered a deep depression which remained with him for the rest of his life. Hamilton had been his pride and joy.

As 1861, turned into 1862, James Hamilton Couper's depression remained unabated. He was still mourning Hamilton's death when news came of Grant's victories in the West and the fall of New Orleans, which he considered the worst Southern defeat yet.[36] By this time his other sons had entered the war also. James Maxwell Couper was sent to Mississippi to fight in the western theater. Robert, Alexander, and John Lord Couper joined the Chatham Artillery and went to Virginia to fight under Stonewall Jackson.[37]

In September, tragedy struck again. John Lord lay dangerously ill in a Virginia farmhouse. Lord had enlisted despite his mother's misgivings, for he had always been delicate; but he had been determined to do his duty. He had become ill early in August. Suffering from a "bilious fever," he had been sent to a hospital and then removed to a private home. He died soon afterwards of a severe attack of enteric fever. So again back in Georgia the Coupers donned the black garb of mourning, and James Hamilton Couper sank lower into his depression.[38]

In 1863, the Coupers lamented the fall of Vicksburg and Lee's unsuccessful attempt to take a little town in Pennsylvania called Gettysburg. The following year, Alick Couper was wounded in the left arm at the battle of Spotsylvania Courthouse while serving as a private in the Sixty Georgia Regiment. He acted rashly throughout the Wilderness campaign and was wounded while unnecessarily exposing himself.[39]

James Maxwell Couper had a brilliant career in the Confederate Army and came out of it successfully. Graduating from West Point in 1856, with a degree in civil engineering, he enlisted at the outset of the war and became adjutant and later captain of the Twentieth Mississippi Regiment under Colonel Russell. He turned down a commission as major offered him by the governor of Mississippi, preferring to keep his local rank as captain. In the battle of Shiloh, he single-handedly captured the flag of the Fifth Ohio Cavalry. However, his first military experience was at Fort Donelson, Tennessee, in February 1862. His regiment surrendered, but before being taken by the Yankees, Adjutant Couper and Colonel Russell made their escape by wading breast-deep through a broad slough in a snow storm. During the Vicksburg campaign Couper was lauded by his superiors for outstanding service. On 21 June 1863, General John L. Pemberton wrote General Joseph E. Johnston that "Captain Couper understands all my views, and none exposed themselves more fearlessly to danger than Major Lockett and his gallant assistants, Captain Robertson and Couper; it gives me pleasure to name them and ask a recognition of their merit." Couper further distinguished himself at the siege of Vicksburg by floating at night down the river past the federal fleet, to carry dispatches beyond the line.[40] During his stay in Mississippi, James Maxwell Couper fell in love with Eudora Harper of Vicksburg. He was handsome and gallant, and Eudora, beautiful and sentimental. Later they married.[41]

In the fall of 1864, the same year that James Maxwell and Eudora married, General William Tecumseh Sherman let loose his war machine on Georgia. Moving South from Chattanooga in May, he finally occupied Atlanta on 3 September 1864. He was ruthless and was intent on breaking the heart and soul of Georgia. Sherman is supposed to have said: "The Confederacy can stand the fall of Richmond, but not the whole of Georgia." On 15 November he burned Atlanta and immediately set out upon a burning rampage to Savannah. Little mercy was shown to the inhabitants, and the invaders burned and pillaged a swath of land sixty miles wide from Atlanta to Savannah.[42]

The Couper plantations, however, were spared the ravages of Sherman's invasion and were not pillaged. From the outbreak of hostilities until 1862, James Hamilton Couper, his wife Caroline, and their daughter Rebecca Isabelle remained at Hopeton-Altama and tried to continue normal operations. But in 1862, with the threat of Federal gunboats on the Georgia coast, some of the Altamaha plantation families refugeed to their summer homes in Ware County. Since there was a railroad near, and land in the vicinity was plentiful and cheap, Couper moved the entire population of Hopeton-Altama to Ware plantation, an estate he rented or purchased on the outskirts of Tebeauville (Waycross) in Ware County, and suspended, for the time being, all operations at Hopeton-Altama.

In 1863, while at Ware plantation and after several years of declining health, James Hamilton Couper, crushed by the loss of his two sons and the sure knowledge that the South was doomed, suffered a massive paralytic stroke. For the next three years he remained an invalid, requiring the constant attention of his wife and servants.[43] Couper died on Monday, 2 July 1866, and was buried two days later in the graveyard of Christ Episcopal Church on St. Simons Island. On the day of the funeral the three remaining Couper sons, Bob, Alick and James, went down to the island early to be sure everything was ready at the church. A messenger had been sent to the island, and crowds of Negroes from Cannon's Point and the Village were in respectful attendance. Great numbers also came down from Hopeton-Altama.[44]

The funeral procession left Hopeton-Altama and made its way by boat to the island. Many members of the old coastal families were present. Two of those were Fanny Butler and her father Pierce Butler, who were living on Hampton Point plantation. From the pen of Fanny Butler Leigh comes this account of the funeral:

> Mr. James Hamilton Couper died…and was buried at the little church on the island here yesterday. The whole thing was sad in the extreme, and a fit illustration of this people and country. Three years ago he was smitten with paralysis, the result of grief at the loss of his sons, loss of his property, and the ruin of all his hopes and prospects; since which his life has been one of great suffering, until a few days ago, when death released him. Hearing from his son of his death, and the time fixed for his funeral, my father and I drove down in the old mule cart, our only conveyance, nine miles to the church. Here a most terrible scene of desolation met us. The steps of the church were broken

down, so we had to walk up a plank to get in; the roof was fallen in, so that the sun streamed down on our heads; while the seats were cut up and marked with the names of Northern soldiers, who had been quartered there during the war. The graveyard was so overgrown with weeds and bushes, and tangled with cobweb like grey moss, that we had difficulty in making our way through to the freshly dug grave.

In about half an hour the funeral party arrived. The coffin was in a cart drawn by one miserable horse, and was followed by the Couper family on foot, having come this way from the landing two miles off. From the cart to the grave the coffin was carried by four old family Negroes, faithful to the end. Standing there I said to myself, "Someday justice will be done, and the Truth shall be heard above the political din of slander and lies, and the Northern people shall see things as they are, and not through the dark veil of envy, hatred, and malice.[45]

Defeat is always bitter, but a defeat so abject, so searing as that which the South had to endure after 1865 was intolerable to some. James Hamilton Couper was one of those, and it was fortunate that he died when he did. But the living must endure. The Couper children were no exception.

Margaret Couper, or Maggie as she was fondly called by her family, lived with her husband, Robert Mackay Stiles, in Savannah, where they built for themselves a successful life. One of Maggie's favorite hobbies was collecting and preserving family heirlooms and memorabilia. Rebecca, the youngest of the Couper daughters, married her cousin, Charles Spalding Wylly, who in time became a noted historian of the Georgia coast, writing about the glorious days before the calamity.

Robert Couper went to New York, and John Lord, his late father's dear friend, lent him $10,000 to begin planting with, telling him that he need not repay the loan if circumstances prevented it. As it turned out, Couper was not successful, so this amounted to a most generous gift. Robert Couper was very talented, splendidly educated, but very impractical. He painted exquisitely, was an ardent botanist and geologist, a Greek and Latin scholar, a boat designer and an avid reader. His health had been seriously undermined at the prison on Johnston's Island where he was held during the last months of the war. After he failed at planting on the coast, he went to Bartow County, where William Stiles gave him a place at the iron foundry he was running. This venture likewise proved a failure, and after several years as a mining engineer, Robert Couper ended his days at Malbone, the Stiles' home near Cartersville, Georgia, where he lived for many years. He died of heart disease in 1914, and was buried in the little churchyard at Frederica on St. Simons with the other members of the family.

Alexander Couper, who must always have been eccentric and impractical, lived the life of a hermit after the war. Squatting on a small acreage at Altama, he kept a little garden and bees, shot for diversion, took a French newspaper and other magazines, and occasionally walked from Altama to Brunswick to visit his mother who lived to a ripe old age.[46]

The only successful son of James Hamilton Couper was James Maxwell, the captain whose dashing gallantry in the war had earned him honorable mention. James Couper and his wife, Eudora Harper, managed the Couper properties after the war and resumed the planting of rice. Couper employed many of his father's former slaves and those of the Butler estates in the enterprise.[47]

The plantation houses at Cannon's Point and Hopeton-Altama were in bad repair after the war, and the James Maxwell Coupers built a home in Brunswick on Union Street. Eudora Harper Couper was an intensely dramatic person with the soul of a poet, and she befriended Sidney Lanier, the poet, who spent many pleasant hours at her house. In the late afternoons she and Lanier would take long buggy rides along the beautiful shell-paved roads of Brunswick, passing under the moss-laden live oaks and eventually arriving at the marshes. Lanier later said that Eudora Couper, a kindred soul in poetry, inspired his writing of his most famous poem, "The Marshes of Glynn." When the poem was finished, the first public reading of it was at the home of James and Eudora Couper with many invited guests.[48]

In 1881, the Coupers moved to Atlanta and built a handsome three-storied Victorian mansion on Ponce de Leon Avenue. James Maxwell Couper moved his library of over 3,000 volumes, his share of his father's library, from Altama to Atlanta. The splendid library room of the Ponce de Leon residence was a fitting repository for the volumes collected by James Hamilton Couper.[49]

James Maxwell Couper was a staunch defender of the way of life in the South that was now "gone with the wind," and yet, he was a realist when he wrote in 1912:

> Whilst belonging to the class of slave owners, and a Confederate soldier, I say without hesitation, that no greater benefit ever befell any country than the emancipation of the Negroes in the South. The Anglo-Saxon then found that, with his own brain and muscle, he could make the lands of the South the garden spot of the earth.
>
> It is true that a civilized people should have found another solution for the removal of slavery, besides war, but the Fire-Eaters of the South and the Abolitionists of the North, the latter aided by such women as Mrs. Stowe and Fanny Kemble, women of marked talent, are responsible for the misery and suffering incurred in its solution. Slavery was forced upon us by England, and the slaves were brought from Africa and sold to us by New Englanders. Let the world be fair, and it will be seen that all the blame does not rest upon the shoulders of the South.
>
> Thank God, it is over, and I have had the privilege of seeing my people emerge from the dark days of Reconstruction to the present with its glorious promise.[50]

It was with this attitude of understanding and practicality that the descendants of James Hamilton Couper moved into the twentieth century. They had learned well from their more famous ancestor.

Notes

[1] Hamilton Couper to James Hamilton Couper, 8 November 1846, Mackay Stiles Papers, Southern Historical Collection, University of North Carolina, Chapel Hill; Lord King to Thomas Butler King, 27 January 1849, Thomas Butler King Papers, Southern Historical Collection, University of North Carolina, Chapel Hill.

[2] Hamilton Couper to James Hamilton Couper, 17, 29 November 1846; Hamilton Couper to Caroline Couper, 16 January; 24 March 1847, Mackay Stiles Papers, Southern Historical Collection.

[3] Hamilton Couper to Caroline Couper, 16 January 1847, Mackay Stiles Papers, Southern Historical Collection.

[4] Hamilton Couper to Caroline Couper, 19 June; 16, 28 August 1847, Mackay Stiles Papers, Southern Historical Collection.

[5]Hamilton Couper to Caroline Couper, 28 August 1847, Mackay Stiles Papers, Southern Historical Collection.

[6]Hamilton Couper to Alexander Couper, 10 September 1847, Mackay Stiles Papers, Southern Historical Collection.

[7]Hamilton Couper to James Hamilton Couper, 20 January; 14 February 1848; Hamilton Couper to Caroline Couper, 16 June 1848, Mackay Stiles Papers, Southern Historical Collection.

[8]James Hamilton Couper to Caroline Couper, 9, 20 July; 21, 23 September 1850, Mackay Stiles Papers, Southern Historical Collection.

[9]Hamilton Couper to Caroline Couper, 10 October 1850, Mackay Stiles Papers, Southern Historical Collection.

[10]Ibid.

[11]Richard Harrison Shryock, *Georgia and the Union in 1850* (Durham NC: Duke University Press, 1926) 264-65.

[12]Ibid.; Edward J. Harden, *The Life of George M. Troup* (Savannah GA: E. J. Purse, 1859) 528-29; *National Intelligencer*, Washington DC, 19, 21 March; 11 April 1850; *Augusta* (GA) *Chronicle*, 13 June 1850. Newspapers on file at the Georgia Department of Archives and History, Atlanta GA.

[13]*Augusta Chronicle*, 19 June 1850.

[14]*Savannah Daily Georgian*, 4, 6, 7, 8, 15 June; 19, 21 November 1850 (microfilm, Georgia Department of Archives and History, Atlanta GA).

[15]*Acts of the State of Georgia 1850* (Milledgeville GA: Richard M. Orme, 1850) 122-23.

[16]*Proceedings of the Georgia Convention of 1850* (manuscript), n.p., Georgia Department of Archives and History, Atlanta GA.

[17]Hamilton Couper to Caroline Couper, 30 November 1852, Mackay Stiles Papers, Southern Historical Collection.

[18]Hamilton Couper to James Hamilton Couper, 1 February 1853; Hamilton Couper to Caroline Couper, 19 January 1856, Mackay Stiles Papers, Southern Historical Collection.

[19]James Hamilton Couper to Hamilton Couper, 24 June 1856, Mackay Stiles Papers, Southern Historical Collection.

[20]John Lord Couper to Caroline Couper, 30 April 1854; Hamilton Couper to Caroline Couper, June 1857, Mackay Stiles Papers, Southern Historical Collection.

[21]James Hamilton Couper to James Maxwell Couper, 13 April 1857; Hamilton Couper to Caroline Couper, 22 April 1857, Mackay Stiles Papers, Southern Historical Collection.

[22]Mary Traylor Thiesen (great granddaughter of James Hamilton Couper), interview with author, Atlanta GA, 6 May 1972; Caroline Couper Lovell, *The Golden Isles of Georgia* (Atlanta GA: Cherokee Publishing Company, 1970) 230-33.

[23]Hamilton Couper to Margaret Couper, 26 August 1856, Mackay Stiles Papers, Southern Historical Collection.

[24]Ibid.; Hamilton Couper to Margaret Couper, 26 October 1859, Mackay Stiles Papers, Southern Historical Collection; typescript concerning Margaret Couper's wedding, Mackay Stiles Papers, Southern Historical Collection.

[25]Hamilton Couper to Caroline Couper, 21 July 1860, Mackay Stiles Papers, Southern Historical Collection; Mary Traylor Thiesen to James E. Bagwell, 21 November 1975, Mary Traylor Thiesen Private Collection, 1804-1977, Atlanta GA.

[26]E. Merton Coulter, *Georgia A Short History* (Chapel Hill: University of North Carolina Press, 1960) 320-21.

[27]Typescript concerning James Hamilton Couper's views on secession and war, Mackay Stiles Papers, Southern Historical Collection.

[28]Hamilton Couper to John Lord Couper, 2 February 1861, Mackay Stiles Papers, Southern Historical Collection; Charles Spalding Wylly, *The Seed That Was Sown in the Colony of Georgia: The Harvest and Aftermath, 1740-1870* (New York NY: Neale Publishing Company, 1910) 158-63.

[29]George Alexander Heard, "St. Simons During the War Between the States," *Georgia Historical Quarterly* 22 (June 1938): 250-54.

[30]Hamilton Couper to Margaret Couper, 26 May 1861, Mackay Stiles Papers, Southern Historical Collection.

[31]Hamilton Couper to Margaret Couper, 25 July 1861, Thiesen Collection, Atlanta GA

[32]Extract from journal of S. P. Hamilton, Mackay Stiles Papers, Southern Historical Collection; Lord King to Florence B. King (sister), 13 November 1861, Thomas Butler King Papers, Southern Historical Collection, University of North Carolina, Chapel Hill.

[33]Extract from journal of S. P. Hamilton, Mackay Stiles Papers, Southern Historical Collection.

[34]Lord King to Florence B. King, 13 November 1861, Thomas Butler King Papers, Southern Historical Collection.

[35]Eulogy of Hamilton Couper by the Savannah bar, Couper Family Papers, Georgia Historical Society, Savannah GA.

[36]John Lord Couper to James Maxwell Couper, 3 May 1862; Mackay Stiles Papers, Southern Historical Collection.

[37]Ibid.; John Lord Couper to James Hamilton Couper, 11 June 1862; James Maxwell Couper to Robert Couper, 18 July 1864, Mackay Stiles Papers, Southern Historical Collection.

[38]Robert Couper to James Maxwell Couper, September 1862, Mackay Stiles Papers, Southern Historical Collection.

[39]James Maxwell Couper to Robert Couper, 18 July 1864, Mackay Stiles Papers, Southern Historical Collection.

[40]"Military Record of James Maxwell Couper" (typescript), Couper Family Papers, Southern Historical Collection.

[41]James Maxwell Couper to Eudora Harper, 1 June 1861; Caroline Couper to James Couper, 30 May 1862, Thiesen Collection, Atlanta GA.

[42]William T. Sherman, *"War is Hell!" William T. Sherman's Personal Narrative of His March through Georgia*, Mills B. Lane, ed. (Savannah GA: The Beehive Press, 1974) 143-96.

[43]John Lord Couper to James Maxwell Couper, 3 May 1862; Caroline Couper to James Maxwell Couper, 5 April 1863, Mackay Stiles Papers, Southern Historical Collection; Alfred W. Jones, *Altama: Then and Now* (Sea Island GA: self published, 1970) 14.

[44]Georgia King to Sister Florence, 7 July 1866, Thomas Butler King Papers, Southern Historical Collection. Georgia King attended the funeral of James Hamilton Couper.

[45]Frances Butler Leigh, *Ten Years on a Georgian Plantation Since the War* (London: Richard Bentley and Sons, 1883) 45-47.

[46]Typescript concerning the Coupers after the war, Mackay Stiles Papers, Southern Historical Collection Papers; Mary Traylor Thiesen to James E. Bagwell, 21 November 1975, Thiesen Collection, Atlanta GA.

[47]James Maxwell Couper, "James Maxwell Couper Defends Planters of the Ante-Bellum South" (Mackay Stiles Papers, Southern Historical Collection).

[48]James Maxwell Couper Jr., to John B. Mayfield, 22 July 1938; Eudora H. Couper to DeWitt Miller, 15 March 1897, Thiesen Collection, Atlanta GA.

[49]Mary Traylor Thiesen to her children, 7 July 1963, Thiesen Collection, Atlanta GA.

[50]James Maxwell Couper to Caroline C. Lovell, 12 August 1912, Mackay Stiles Papers, Southern Historical Collection.

Bibliography

I. **Primary Sources**
A. Manuscript Sources

Margaret Davis Cate Collection. Georgia Historical Society. Savannah GA. Contains much material on Georgia coastal history. A microfilmed copy with index is located at the State Department of Archives and History, Atlanta. A duplicate copy is located at Fort Frederica National Monument, St. Simons Island, Georgia.

Christ Church File, 1733-1978. Georgia Historical Society. Savannah GA. Miscellaneous file containing materials relative to Christ Church, Savannah, Georgia.

Christ Church Vestry Minutes, 1837-1840. Georgia Historical Society. Savannah GA. Original Church Vestry minutes filed by years.

Corbin, Francis Porteus. Papers, 1762-1885. Perkins Library. Duke University. Material is included on the planting career of James Hamilton Couper and on rice culture at Hopeton and Wright's Island plantations, Altamaha River, Georgia.

James Hamilton Couper Plantation Records, 1818-1854. 4 volumes. Southern Historical Collection. University of North Carolina, Chapel Hill..

John Couper Family Papers, 1827-1923. Georgia Historical Society. Savannah GA. Contains material on the Couper family's Georgia rice and sea-island cotton interests.

Couper, William Audley. Papers, 1817-1900. Southern Historical Collection. University of North Carolina, Chapel Hill. Miscellaneous material concerning the Couper, Page, and King families. William Audley was the younger brother of James Hamilton Couper.

Rice Gold

Fraser-Couper Family Papers, 1810-1884. Letters. Georgia Historical Society. Savannah GA. Personal letters dealing with plantation life on the Georgia rice coast from a female point of view.

Hodgson, William B. Papers, 1830-1870. Perkins Library. Duke University. Contains valuable letters between Hodgson and James Hamilton Couper on the geology of Georgia and scientific excavation.

Houstoun-Wylly Family Papers, 1827-1828. Georgia Historical Society. Savannah GA. Mary Williamson Houstoun's letters describe life on the Georgia rice coast in the 1820s.

King, Thomas Butler. Papers, 1763-1925. Southern Historical Collection. University of North Carolina, Chapel Hill. Contains much correspondence between Couper and King families, especially during the Civil War period.

Mackay Stiles Papers. Southern Historical Collection. University of North Carolina, Chapel Hill. Contains excellent records of the Couper, Wylly, and Maxwell families. It is the single most valuable source concerning the life of James Hamilton Couper.

Proceedings of the Georgia Convention of 1850. Georgia Department of Archives and History. Atlanta, Georgia. Manuscript on unnumbered pages.

Mary Traylor Thiesen Private Collection, 1804-1977. Atlanta GA. This collection which is kept by Couper's great granddaughter is invaluable and contains voluminous memorabilia concerning the Coupers.

B. Government Documents and Legal Records

Acts of the State of Georgia. Milledgeville: Richard M. Orme, State Printer, 1850.

Bureau of the Census. *Fifth Census of the United States, 1830. Slave Schedule.* Prepared by Gales and Seaton. Washington, DC:

176

Government Printing Office, 1833. Filed at Lake Blackshear Regional Library, Americus, Georgia.

———. *Seventh Census of the United States, 1850. Agriculture.* Prepared by Robert Armstrong. Washington, DC: Government Printing Office, 1853.

———. *Eighth Census of United States, 1860. Agriculture.* Prepared by Robert Armstrong, Washington, DC: Government Printing Office, 1864.

———. *Rice Crop of the United States, 1712-1911* Compiled by George K. Holmes. Washington, DC: Government Printing Office, 1912.

Deed Book: 5-A, AA, G, 3-G, 5-G, H, 4-K, N, NN, 5-Q, 4-S, UU, WW. Glynn County Courthouse, GA. Record of Wills—Book G.; Wills and Appraisements Book: D, E, and F. Glynn County Courthouse, Brunswick, GA.

Governors' Letterbook: Official Letters of the Governor of Georgia, 1829-1843. Atlanta: Georgia Department of Archives and History. Microfilm.

Military Record of Georgia, 1829-1841. Atlanta: Georgia Department of Archives and History. Microfilm

C. Newspapers

Augusta (GA) *Chronicle*, 1850. On file at the Georgia Department of Archives and History, Atlanta.

Charleston (SC) *Courier*, 1838. Filed in the South Caroliniana Library, University of South Carolina, Columbia.

Charleston (SC) *Mercury*, 1852. On microfilm at the University of North Carolina Library, Chapel Hill.

National Intelligencer (Washington DC), 1850. On file in the Georgia Southern University Library, Statesboro GA.

Savannah Daily Georgian, 1838, 1840. Filed at the Georgia Department of Archives and History, Atlanta.

Savannah Georgia Gazette, 1793. On file at the Georgia Historical Society, Savannah.

Wilmington Advertiser, 1838. Filed in the James Earl Carter Library, Georgia Southwestern State University, Americus, Georgia.

D. Periodicals

Allston, R. F. W. "Rice." *De Bow's Review* 1(April 1846): 320-57; 4 (December 1847): 502-11.

————. "Sea-Coast Crops of the South." *De Bow's Review* 16 (June 1854): 589-615.

Capers, William Henry. "On the Culture of Sea-Island Cotton." *Southern Agriculturist and Register of Rural Affair s* 8(August 1835): 401-12.

Corbin, Richard. "Letters of a Confederate Officer to his Family in Europe During the Last Year of the War of Secession" *Magazine of History 6* Extra No. 24 (1913): 391-487.

Couper, James Hamilton. "Account of, and Directions for Erecting a Sugar Establishment." *Southern Agriculturist and Register of Rural Affairs* 4 (May 1831): 225-32, 281-88.

————. "Essay on Rotation of Crops." *Southern Agriculturist and Register of Rural Affairs* 6 (February-March 1833): 57-67, 113-20; 7(January-February 1834): 1-9, 57-69.

Couper, John. "Account of an Attempt to Cultivate the Olive." *Southern Agriculturist and Register of Rural Affairs* 3(May 1830): 234-39.

————. "General Observations on the Olive, Orange, and Date Trees Growing in Georgia; and the Method of Cultivating the Ruta Baga

Turnip as a Second Crop after Corn." *Southern Agriculturist and Register of Rural Affairs* 8(July 1835): 350-59.

———. "On the Origin of Sea-Island Cotton." *Southern Agriculturist and Register of Rural Affairs* 4(May 1831): 242-45.

———. "Remarks on the Culture of the Olive Tree." *Southern Agriculturist and Register of Rural Affair s* 1 (July 1828): 303-308.

"Cultivation of the Olive in the Southern States." *De Bow's Review* 3 (March 1847): 265-68.

De Bow, J. B. "Manufacture of Sugar In Louisiana." *De Bow's Review* 3 (May 1847): 376-96.

House, Albert Virgil, Jr. "Charles Manigault's Essay on the Open Planting of Rice." *Agricultural History* 16 (October 1942): 184-93.

King, Roswell, Jr. "On the Management of the Butler Estate and the Cultivation of the Sugar Cane." *Southern Agriculturist and Register of Rural Affairs* 1 (December 1828): 527-35.

Legare, J. D. "Account of an Agricultural Excursion Made into the South of Georgia in the Winter of 1832." *Southern Agriculturist and Register of Rural Affairs* 6 (May-November 1833): 243-48, 297-304, 358-67, 410-16, 460-66, 515-29, 571-77.

———. "Farewell Address of the Editor." *Southern Agriculturist and Register of Rural Affairs* 7 (December 1834): 661-62.

———. "On our Southern Agricultural Concerns." *Southern Agriculturist and Register of Rural Affairs*1 (October 1828): 448-53.

McLeod, Mrs. Hugh (Rebecca Lamar). "The Loss of the Steamer *Pulaski*." *Georgia Historical Quarterly* 3 (March 1919): 63-95.

"Meteorology of Cotton and Cane Fields." *De Bow's Review* 18(January 1855): 45-49.

Spalding, Thomas. "Brief Notes on the Cultivation of Cotton, Rice, Sugar Cane, the Grape Vine, Silkworms and Olives." *Southern Agriculturist Register of Rural Affairs* 1 (March 1828): 106-10.

————. "Cotton—Its Introduction and Progress of Its Culture in the United States." *Southern Agriculturist Register of Rural Affairs* 8 (January 1835): 35-46, 81-87.

————. "On the Cultivation of the Sugar Cane, Erecting of Proper Buildings, and Manufacture of Sugar." *Southern Agriculturist Register of Rural Affairs* 2 (February 1829): 55-65.

————. "On the Introduction of Sea-Island Cotton into Georgia." *Southern Agriculturist Register of Rural Affairs* 4 (March 1831): 131-33.

United States Department of Agriculture. "The Sea Island Cotton of the South, Its History, Characteristics, Cultivation Etc." *De Bow's Review, After the War Series* 3 (January 1867): 84-89.

Wood, Jordan. "An Account of the Process of Cultivating, Harvesting, and Manufacturing of Sugar Cane." *Southern Agriculturist Register of Rural Affairs* 3 (May 1830): 227-37.

Zoega, Blachette. "On the Manufacture of Sugar." *Southern Review* 3 (May 1829): 329-52.

E. Books and Pamphlets

Bremer, Fredrika. *The Homes of the New World; Impressions of America.* Translated by Mary Howitt. 2 volumes. New York: Harper and Brothers, 1853.

Buckingham, James Silk. *The Slave States of America.* 2 volumes. London: Fisher and Son and Co., 1842.

De Bow, J. D. B. *The Industrial Resources of the Southern and Western States.* 3 volumes. New Orleans LA: Office of *De Bow's Review*, 1853.

Bibliography

Easterby, J. H., editor. *The South Carolina Rice Plantation as Revealed in the Papers of Robert F. W. Allston.* Chicago IL: University of Chicago Press, 1945.

Grant, Hugh Fraser. *Planter Management and Capitalism in Ante-Bellum Georgia: The Journal of Hugh Fraser Grant, Rice Grower.* Edited by Albert Virgil House Jr. New York NY: Columbia University Press, 1954.

Hall, Captain Basil. *Travels in North America, 1827-1828.* 3 volumes. Edinburgh, Scotland: Cadell and Company, 1829.

Hodgson, William B. *Memoir on the Megatherium and Other Extinct Gigantic Quadrupeds of the Coast of Georgia with Observations on Its Geological Features.* New York NY: Bartlett and Welford, 1846.

Kemble, Frances Anne. *Journal of a Residence on a Georgia Plantation in 1838-1839.* edited by John A. Scott. New York NY: Alfred A. Knopf, 1961.

Lane, Mills B. editor. *Neither More Nor Less Than Men: Slavery in Georgia.* Savannah GA: The Beehive Press, 1993.

Lyell, Sir Charles. *A Second Visit to North America.* 2 volumes. New York NY: Harper and Brother, 1849.

———. *Travels in North America, in the Years 1841-1842; with Geological Observations on the United States, Canada, and Nova Scotia.* 2 volumes. New York NY: Wiley and Putnam, 1845.

Murray, Amelia M. *Letters from the United States, Cuba and Canada.* New York NY: G. P. Putnam and Co., 1856.

Pope-Hennessy, Una, editor. *The Aristocratic Journey: Mrs. Basil Hall's Account During Her Sojourn in America 1827-1828.* New York NY: G. P. Putnam's Sons, 1831.

Proceedings of the Academy of Natural Sciences of Philadelphia. 10 volumes. Philadelphia PA: Merrihew and Thompson, 1840-1860.

Sherman, William T. *"War is Hell!" William T Sherman's Personal Narrative of his March Through Georgia.* Edited by Mills B. Lane. Savannah GA: The Beehive Press, 1974.

Thompson, Mortimer M. *What Became of the Slaves on a Georgia Plantation? Great Auction Sale of Slaves at Savannah, 2, 3 March 1859.* A Sequel to Mrs. Kemble's Journal. n.p., 1863.

White, George M. *Historical Collection of Georgia.* New York NY: Pudney and Russell, 1855.

————. *Statistics of the State of Georgia.* Savannah GA: W. Thorne Williams, 1849.

II. Secondary Sources
A. Books and Pamphlets

Bonner, James C. *A History of Georgia Agriculture 1732-1860.* Athens: University of Georgia Press, 1964.

————. *The Georgia Story.* Oklahoma City OK: Harlow Publishing Co., 1961.

Candler, Allen D. and Clement A Evans, editors. *Cyclopedia of Georgia.* Atlanta GA: Brown Publishing Company, 1906.

Cate, Margaret Davis. *Our Todays and Yesterdays: A Story of Brunswick and the Coastal Islands.* Brunswick GA: Glover Bros., 1926; Reprint, Spartanburg SC, 1979.

————. *Altama Plantation.* Brunswick GA: n.p., n.d.

———— and Orrin Sage Wrightman, *Early Days of Coastal Georgia.* St. Simons Island GA: Fort Frederica Association, 1955.

Bibliography

Clifton, James E. *Life and Labor on Argyle Island: Letters and Documents of a Savannah River Rice Plantation*. Savannah GA: Beehive Press, 1978.

Coleman, Kenneth. *Georgia History in Outline*. Athens: University of Georgia Press, 1960.

————. *The American Revolution in Georgia. 1763-1789*. Athens: University of Georgia Press, 1958.

Coulter, E. Merton. *Georgia, A Short History*. Chapel Hill: University of North Carolina Press, 1960.

————. *Georgia's Disputed Ruins*. Chapel Hill: University of North Carolina Press, 1937.

————. *Thomas Spalding of Sapelo*. Edited by Wendell Holmes Stephenson and Fred C. Cole. Southern Biography Series. Baton Rouge: Louisiana State University Press, 1940.

————. Wormsloe: *Two Centuries of a Georgia Family*. Athens: University of Georgia Press, 1955.

Easterby, J. H., editor. *The South Carolina Rice Plantation as Revealed in the Papers of Robert F. W. Allston*. Chicago:University of Chicago Press, 1945.

Eaton, Clement. *A History of the Old South*. 2nd edition. New York: Macmillan Co., 1966.

————. *The Growth of Southern Civilization, 1790-1860*. Edited by Henry Steele Commager and Richard B. Morris. The New American Nation Series. New York: Harper and Row, 1961.

Fancher, Betsy. *Georgia's Golden Isles*. Garden City NY: Doubleday and Company, 1971.

Ferguson, T. Reed. *The John Couper Family at Cannon's Point.* Macon GA: Mercer University Press, 1994.

Flanders, Ralph Betts. *Plantation Slavery in Georgia.* Chapel Hill: University of North Carolina Press, 1933.

Fogel, Robert William, and Stanley L. Engerman, *Time on the Cross.* 2 volumes. Boston MA: Little, Brown and Co., 1974.

Garden History of Georgia 1733-1933. Edited by Hattie C. Rainwater from materials complied by Lorraine M. Cooney. Atlanta GA: Peachtree Garden Club, 1933.

Genovese, Eugene D. *Roll, Jordan, Roll: The World the Slaves Made.* New York: Pantheon Books, 1974.

————. *The Political Economy of Slavery: Studies in the Economy and Society of the Slave South.* New York NY: Pantheon Books, 1965.

Granger, Mary, editor. *Savannah River Plantations.* Savannah GA: Georgia Historical Society, 1947.

Gray, Lewis Cecil. *History of Agriculture in the Southern United States to 1860.* 2 volumes. Washington DC: Carnegie Institution, 1933.

Grice, Warren. *Georgia Through Two Centuries.* New York NY: Lewis Historical Publishing Co., 1966.

Harden, Edward J. *The Life of George M. Troup.* Savannah GA: E. J. Purse, 1859.

Hardin, William. *A History of Savannah and South Georgia.* Atlanta GA: Cherokee Publishing Co., 1969.

Heyward, Duncan Clinch. *Seed From Madagascar.* Chapel Hill: University of North Carolina Press, 1937.

Bibliography

Johnson, Allen and Dumas Malone, editors. *Dictionary of American Biography.* 20 volumes. New York NY: Charles Scribner's Sons, 1930.

Jones, Alfred W. *Altama: Then and Now.* Sea Island GA: self published, 1970.

Jones, Charles C. *The Dead Towns of Georgia.* Spartanburg SC: Morning News Steam Printing House, 1878.

Leckie, George C. *Georgia: A Guide to Its Towns and Countryside.* Atlanta GA: Tupper and Love, 1954.

Leigh, Francis Butler. *Ten Years on a Georgian Plantation Since the War.* London: Richard Bentley and Sons, 1883.

Lewis, Bessie. *Patriarchal Plantations of St. Simons Island.* Brunswick GA: self published, 1974.

Lovell, Caroline Couper. *The Golden Isles of Georgia.* Atlanta GA: Cherokee Publishing Company, 1970.

Otto, John Solomon. *Cannon's Point Plantation 1794-1860: Living Conditions and Status Patterns in the Old South.* New York NY: Academic Press, 1984.

Parrish, Lydia. *Slave Songs of the Georgia Sea Islands.* Brunswick GA: Creative Age Press, 1942.

Perkerson, Medora Field. *White Columns in Georgia.* New York NY: Bonanza Books, 1955.

Phillips, Ulrich Bonnell. *American Negro Slavery.* New York NY: D. Appleton and Co., 1918.

———. *Life and Labor in the Old South.* New York: Grosset and Dunlap, 1929.

Postell, William Desite. *The Health of Slaves on Southern Plantations.* Baton Rouge: Louisiana State University Press, 1951.

Purse, D. G., and Stubbs, W. C. *Cultivation of Sugar Cane...Part First. Sugar Cane: A Treatise of Its History, Botany and Agriculture...Part Second. Sugar Cane: Its History in Georgia, Florida, and South Carolina, 1767 to 1900....Recollections of Hopeton Plantation....*2 volumes. Savannah GA: D. G. Purse, 1901.

Sass, Herbert R., and Huger-Smith, Alice. *A Carolina Rice Plantation of the Fifties.* New York NY: William Morrow and Company, 1936.

Scarborough, William Kauffman. *The Overseer: Plantation Management in the Old South.* Baton Rouge: Louisiana State University Press, 1966.

Shryock, Richard Harrison. *Georgia and the Union in 1850.* Durham NC: Duke University Press, 1926.

Sitterson, J. Carlyle. *Sugar Country.* Lexington: University of Kentucky Press, 1953.

Stampp, Kenneth M. *The Peculiar Institution: Slavery in the Ante-Bellum South.* New York NY: Alfred A. Knopf, 1956.

Smith, Julia Floyd. *Slavery and Rice Culture in Low Country Georgia 1750-1860.* Knoxville: University of Tennessee Press, 1985.

Upchurch, John C. editor. *The Southern United States: Essays on the Cultural and Historical Landscape.* 18 volumes. Carrollton: West Georgia College, 1979.

Vanstory, Burnette Lightle. *Georgia's Land of the Golden Isles.* Athens: University of Georgia Press, 1956.

Vocelle, James Thomas. *History of Camden County.* St. Marys GA: self published, 1914.

Bibliography

Waring, Joseph Frederick. *Cerveau's Savannah*. Savannah GA: Georgia Historical Society, 1973.

Wooster, Ralph A. *The Secession Conventions of the South*. Princeton NJ: Princeton University Press, 1962.

Wylly, Charles Spalding. *Annals and Statistics of Glynn County, Georgia*. Brunswick GA: n.p., 1897.

————. *The Seed that was Sown in the Colony of Georgia: The Harvest and Aftermath, 1740-1870*. New York NY: Neale Publishing Company, 1910.

B. Periodicals

Coulter, E. Merton. "Boating as a Sport in the Old South." *Georgia Historical Quarterly* 27(September 1943): 231-47.

————. "Mary Musgrove, 'Queen of the Creeks': A Chapter of Early Georgia Troubles." *Georgia Historical Quarterly* 11 (March 1927): 1-30.

Green, Fletcher M. "Georgia's Board of Public Works. 1817-1826." *Georgia Historical Quarterly* 22 (June 1938): 117-37.

Heard, George Alexander. "St. Simons During the War Between the States." *Georgia Historical Quarterly* 22 (June 1938): 249-72.

House, Albert Virgil. "Labor Management Problems on Georgia Rice Plantations, 1840-1860." *Agricultural History* 28 (October 1954): 149-55.

Nightingale, B. N. "Dungeness." *Georgia Historical Quarterly* 26 (December 1939): 369-83.

Sitterson, J. Carlyle. "Ante-Bellum Sugar Culture in the South Atlantic States." *Journal of Southern History* (May 1937) 175-87.

C. Newspapers

Atlanta (GA) *Constitution*, 1923, 1974. File located on microfilm at the University of Georgia Library, Athens GA.

Brunswick (GA) *Advertiser*, 1879. On file at the Georgia Historical Society, Savannah GA.

Brunswick(GA) *News*, 1979. On file at the office of the *Brunswick News*, Brunswick GA.

Savannah (GA) *Morning News*, 1965. On file at the Georgia Department of Archives and History, Atlanta GA.

D. Personal Interviews

Rogers, Gena. Interview with author. 16 June 1997. Brantley County GA. Author's files.

Thiesen, Mrs. R. J. (great granddaughter of James Hamilton Couper). Interview with author. 6 May 1972. Atlanta, GA. Author's files.

E. Theses and Dissertations

Dudley, Margaret McClung. "James Hamilton Couper." Master's thesis, University of Virginia, 1982.

Noble, Bill. "Ante-Bellum Hopeton and Current Altama Plantations." Dissertation, University of Missouri Library, 1989.

Noble, William Allister. "Sequent Occupance of Hopeton-Altama, 1816-1956." Master's thesis, University of Georgia, 1956.

Stone, James Herbert. "Black Leadership in the Old South: The Slave Drivers of the Rice Kingdom." Ph.D. dissertation, Florida State University, 1976.

Index

Index